POVERTY NARRATIVES AND POWER PARADOXES IN INTERNATIONAL TRADE NEGOTIATIONS AND BEYOND

In this work, Amrita Narlikar argues that, contrary to common assumption, modern-day politics displays a surprising paradox: poverty – and the powerlessness with which it is associated – has emerged as a political tool and a formidable weapon in international negotiation. The success of poverty narratives, however, means that their use has not been limited to the neediest. Focusing on behaviours and outcomes in a particularly polarizing area of bargaining – international trade – and illustrating wider applications of the argument, Narlikar shows how these narratives have been effectively used. Yet, she also sheds light on how indiscriminate overuse and misuse increasingly run the risk of adverse consequences for the system at large and devastating repercussions for the weakest members of society. Narlikar advances a theory of agency and empowerment by focusing on the lifecycles of narratives and concludes by offering policy-relevant insights on how to construct winning and sustainable narratives.

AMRITA NARLIKAR is President of the German Institute for Global and Area Studies (GIGA) and Professor at Hamburg University. Her previous books include *Bargaining with a Rising India* (co-authored, 2014), *The Oxford Handbook on the World Trade Organization* (co-edited, 2012), and *Deadlocks in Multilateral Negotiations* (edited, Cambridge University Press, 2010).

Poverty Narratives and Power Paradoxes in International Trade Negotiations and Beyond

AMRITA NARLIKAR

German Institute for Global and Area Studies (GIGA)

CAMBRIDGE
UNIVERSITY PRESS

University Printing House, Cambridge CB2 8BS, United Kingdom

One Liberty Plaza, 20th Floor, New York, NY 10006, USA

477 Williamstown Road, Port Melbourne, VIC 3207, Australia

314–321, 3rd Floor, Plot 3, Splendor Forum, Jasola District Centre, New Delhi – 110025, India

79 Anson Road, #06–04/06, Singapore 079906

Cambridge University Press is part of the University of Cambridge.

It furthers the University's mission by disseminating knowledge in the pursuit of education, learning, and research at the highest international levels of excellence.

www.cambridge.org
Information on this title: www.cambridge.org/9781108415569
DOI: 10.1017/9781108234191

© Amrita Narlikar 2020

First published 2020

Printed in the United Kingdom by TJ International Ltd, Padstow, Cornwall

A catalogue record for this publication is available from the British Library.

ISBN 978-1-108-41556-9 Hardback
ISBN 978-1-108-40160-9 Paperback

To
Mahadevi Ambabai of Kolhapur

Contents

Acknowledgements

Writing a book is always a delightful intellectual adventure. This book turned out to be a longer adventure than planned. This was in good measure because just a year into the project, Germany made me an offer I could not refuse. I decided to move from Cambridge to Hamburg. Managing between a demanding 'day-job' as president of a rapidly internationalizing German Institute for Global and Area Studies (GIGA) and as professor at Universität Hamburg, plus trying to help build bridges between the worlds of academia and policy, I found that I had somewhat overestimated the number of hours in a day. And while all that we were achieving together in Hamburg was most gratifying, this also meant that my book deadline had to be postponed. This caused me much dismay.

With hindsight, the timing has actually turned out to be not so bad after all, and has made the book all the more worthwhile to complete. The British electorate chose 'leave' in the referendum; Trump came to power. And as the world changed, the real-world relevance of the arguments I was planning to make became even clearer. The 'day-job' and the move to Germany together gave me exposure to many new ideas and experiences that were directly relevant for the project, and access to some wonderfully clever people to brainstorm with. I can safely say that, at least in comparison to the book that I had planned to complete in 2016, this is a richer book. But the delay did generate one huge cost: Willy Brown will not get to see it.

I knew Willy Brown as the Master of Darwin College, and the Montague Burton Chair of Industrial Relations at the University of Cambridge. He was a powerful force for the good. And he was the first person with whom I had the tremendous good fortune to discuss the idea of my project. He shared my excitement for the counter-intuitive argument that I was trying to make, and we debated over examples and counter-examples, drawing on his extensive knowledge and experience in industrial bargaining. His unexpected passing is a profound loss to many of us: I, for my part, cannot imagine Cambridge without him. It saddens me that he will not see this book in its published version. Naturally, neither he nor anyone else I mention in these acknowledgements is responsible for any errors or omissions that might affect this book – I bear that responsibility alone. But I hope that he would have approved of the implementation of the idea that we had brainstormed about with such spirit and delight all those years ago.

Willy's feedback on my preliminary idea, and subsequent suggestions on a concrete research proposal, were crucial in my successful application for a Leverhulme Fellowship. At that time, the project was entitled, 'The Power of the Poor: International Economic Negotiations in a Globalizing World.' The award of a prestigious Leverhulme Research Fellowship for the academic year 2013–2014 brought me the necessary resources and time to focus on the project, and laid the foundations for this book. I am very grateful to the Leverhulme Trust for its support.

In the course of writing this book, I benefited enormously from the feedback of many academic colleagues on different parts of the project. At my two former institutions, Cambridge and Oxford, I was fortunate to receive detailed, helpful, and cross-disciplinary inputs from political scientists, economists, historians, and lawyers. I owe a big debt of gratitude to Martin Daunton, Andrew Hurrell, Markus Gehring, Louise Fawcett, Leo Howe, Charles Jones, Dan Kim, Des King, Brendan Simms, Nigel Brown, and Laurence Whitehead. Away from the dreaming spires of Oxford and the swans that swim around Darwin island in Cambridge, the project was further enriched thanks to stimulating exchanges with Biswajit Dhar, Kathy Hochstetler, Sophie Haspeslagh, Louis Pauly, Samir Saran, Oliver Stuenkel, Diana Tussie, and Brendan Vickers. Daniel Drezner appeared rather miraculously at a time when I needed just the right push for completion, and generously shared helpful suggestions on parts of the manuscript. Fen Osler Hampson and I are working together on an edited book project on narratives for the Processes of International Negotiation (PIN) network, and the inspiring conversations with Fen have been very useful for the refinement of my own thinking on the themes covered in this book. Other distinguished scholars of negotiation, who form a part of the PIN network, also offered valuable comments on several parts of the argument, especially Bill Zartman, Valérie Rosoux, Guy Olivier Faure, Paul Meerts, Moty Cristal, and Mikhail Troitskiy.

In Germany, I am involved in two 'Excellence Clusters' – SCRIPTS in Berlin and CLiCCS in Hamburg. As a Principal Investigator in SCRIPTS, I found my interactions with Tanja Börzel, Mark Hallerberg, Thomas Risse, and Michael Zürn useful for the political economy component of this book.

As a member of CLiCCS, I benefited from exchanges with Anita Engels, Jochem Marotzke, and Detlef Stammer, specifically on the burning topic of climate change. For their practical advice on academic life in Germany and for stimulating conversations, I am thankful especially to Ulrich Mücke, Juergen Rüland, and Jörg Rüpke.

I presented parts of this project in different forums, and received much constructive feedback. These included Freie Universität Berlin, the inaugural Albert Ballin Forum of Hapag Lloyd, the Global Solutions Summit, ECPR General Conference, Brandt Commission Anniversary Conference, Cambridge Conference on Global Food Security, T20/G20 Outreach Process, University of Freiburg, Körber Foundation's Bergedorf Round Tables, several GIGA Forums, the PIN Annual Conference, and the WTO. I also had the opportunity to test some of the ideas presented in this book via the courses that I taught at Universität Hamburg and Cambridge University. I am thankful to my many students for all the invigorating debates that we have had together.

Nascent forms of the material presented in this book were previously published in *Third World Quarterly* (with Shishir Priyadarshi, 2014), *International Negotiation* (with Diana Tussie, 2015), *Current History* (2015), *Foreign Affairs* (2015, 2017, 2018), and *International Affairs* (2017). I am thankful for all the comments that I received towards these publications from the journal editors and referees, which were a big help in honing the argument further.

Rigorous policy-relevant debate is what I had always yearned for, and have seldom found myself wanting in this regard since coming to Germany. I have had many engaging exchanges with colleagues from the German Federal Foreign Office, and received invaluable feedback from them. Here, a special note of thanks goes to Thomas Bagger: I have learnt a great deal from him in the course of bilateral discussions as well as panel debates. Plus he introduced me to the inspiring work of Václav Havel, who wrote about a different kind of 'Power of the Powerless.' My other superb sparring partners in the Foreign Office have included Stephan Steinlein, Sebastian Groth, Katrin aus dem Siepen, Sabine Sparwasser, Katharina Stasch, Marian Schuegraf, Ralf Beste, and Walter Lindner. In the last years, I have also had stimulating exchanges with journalists. Andreas Cichowicz has consistently posed tough but fair questions, and been ready to lend a sympathetic ear and great advice. Other journalists with whom I have had the privilege to work and debate with include Stephan-Andreas Casdorff, Carsten Germis, and Theo Sommer.

Over the previous two decades of my researching international organizations, I have learnt a lot from conversations with diplomats based in Geneva and national capitals, and also officials working for the WTO and other international organizations. Although I ultimately chose to rely on documentary (primary and secondary) sources for this project, these conversations have been very important in shaping my thinking on the subject. I am most thankful for the insights they have shared with me in the last years.

The Hamburg Ministry of Science, Research and Equalities (BWFG) and the Federal Foreign Office are the core funding institutions of the GIGA. The BWFG, along with the Foreign Office, played the leading role in bringing me to Germany. Rolf Greve from the BWFG was instrumental in securing the ideal conditions for me to settle into my new position; on the Foreign Office side, Katrin aus dem Siepen showed incredible personal commitment in the same direction. For the personal interest that they have taken in my research and my wellbeing in Hamburg over the years, I use this opportunity to further thank Olaf Scholz, Dorothee Stapelfeldt, Wolfgang Schmidt, Horst-Michael Pelikahn, Peter Tschentscher, Katharina Fegebank, Eva Gümbel, Corinna Nienstedt, and Rolf Greve.

Much of this book was written at the GIGA. My team within the GIGA has been stellar in its support. For intellectual banter, friendly collegiality, and reliable support, I want to particularly acknowledge the contributions of André Bank, Bert Hoffmann, and Jann Lay, and also Nadia Javanshir, Olaf Kruithoff, Indi-Carola Kryg, Nikolai Röhl, Verena Schweiger, and Maren Wagner. My student assistants, Andrew Crawford and Gilbert Knies, did a fantastic job in helping me with data collection. Nora Kürzdörfer's meticulous and timely work on the index made her help indispensable. Henner Fürtig has been a constant source of wisdom and camaraderie, ever since I arrived at the GIGA. Peter Peetz, Patrick Köllner, and Sonja Bartsch – as my Managing Director, Vice-President, and Research Manager, respectively – are superb allies; we share the responsibility of key tasks, and I appreciate their reliability, collegiality, and commitment. My biggest debt in the institute is to Julia Kramer. Through her loyal support and sound advice, she has helped me in countless ways in the last years, with both her official and unofficial hats on.

Cambridge University Press has been a dream to work with. I have been lucky to have found such a patient and experienced editor in Matt Gallaway, himself an accomplished author. From the proposal stage to the completion of the book, his constructive criticism has been invaluable and his commitment matchless. He has been most tolerant of my missed deadlines, and consistently constructive in his critique and suggestions. My thanks also go to other members of the Cambridge University Press team, including Cameron Daddis, Laura Blake, Neena Maheen, and Liz Steel, for their terrific management of every detail of the production process.

I have been spoilt by the continued support of friends located in different parts of the world. I would like to thank Janet Gibson, Jocelyn Probert, Adrian Kent, Ewan Harrison, and Konrad Banaszek for their interest and camaraderie throughout this process. Asha Katdare has always been a wonderful source of support and optimism, as are Nita Khanna, Arjun Khanna, and Meena Pimplapure – they are a part of the family, and they are also valued friends.

Settling into a new country, learning a new language, and adapting to a new culture is seldom easy. But my task was made easier because of the amazing backing that my family and I received from new friends in Germany. Kerstin and Michael Tschöcke, Paul Tschöke, Heinrich Heyszenau and Verena Kulenkampff, Ram and Mona Bhatt, Pierre Müller and Janny Kopicki, and Madan Lal and Vimla Raigar have formed key parts of our support network here. Gerhard and Graciela Homuth (Uncle Gerhard and Auntie Graciela) have become a part of our adopted German family. I am grateful for the merriment that we have shared, and the readiness of all these beautiful people to step in whenever a need has arisen.

Aruna and Anant Narlikar – my parents – have been with me every step of the way, intellectually and emotionally. It is to Anant that I owe my commitment to research. Plus, he has taught me the magic of stories and what a difference they can make to people's lives, and it is perhaps not surprising that I have now found my way to the study of narratives. Aruna's comments on different versions of this manuscript have given me valuable food for thought, her famous cakes (surpassing even Anatole's of Wodehouse fame) have given me tasty sustenance, and her poetic delights have cheered my soul. Puppy Don is a source of boundless laughter, lightness, and love.

1

Introduction

Poverty Narratives and Power Paradoxes

Poverty has historically been regarded as a burden that individuals, states, and non-state actors must bear. Often equated with powerlessness, it is a disadvantage that needs to be overcome. In this book, I argue that, contrary to common assumption, modern-day politics displays a surprising paradox: powerlessness has emerged as a political tool and a formidable weapon in international negotiation. Effective and persuasive narratives about poverty are bringing about a fundamental transformation of powerlessness itself into a source of power.

This book analyses the sources of the newfound effectiveness of poverty narratives, the mechanisms whereby it is exercised, and the outcomes it has generated. I focus specifically on behaviours and outcomes in a particularly polarizing area of bargaining – international trade – but also illustrate wider applications of the argument in other settings. The empirical cases reveal inspiring examples of agency and empowerment for the hitherto marginalized and excluded. But the wide-ranging and highly effective *use* of arguments of poverty and powerlessness by the genuinely poor and weak constitutes only one aspect of the story; *overuse* and *misuse* comprise the other sides. And while the use of poverty narratives may have emerged as a winning strategy, repeated misapplication risks blunting this weapon. In this book, I trace the origins, workings, and implications of the power of the powerless, and also advance broader theoretical insights on the lifecycles of narratives.

In this introductory chapter, I identify the central puzzle driving this book in Section 1.1. Section 1.2 provides an overview of the theoretical approach and methodology I use. Section 1.3 outlines the structure of the book.

1.1 THE PUZZLE

The central argument of this book derives its inspiration partly from the pioneering work of Mancur Olson. Writing in 1965, Olson noticed a surprising phenomenon within groups (with members of unequal size) striving for collective action: 'the exploitation of the great by the small'.[1] The source of this power lay in the ability of small players to freeride on the efforts of large players, whereas the latter incurred a disproportionate share of the costs of providing public goods.[2] Olson's study was very important in illustrating that apparent smallness could be an advantage, at least as far as costs of burden-sharing were concerned. The empirical and policy implications of this theoretical insight were significant. Olson himself offered numerous applications, ranging from the disproportionately high costs of being the largest firm in a market to being the largest member of an alliance system aimed at collective security provision (such as the North Atlantic Treaty Organization, NATO). But the implications of Olson's astute observation also showed the limitations of the power of smaller or weaker players.

As developing countries learnt the hard way, the apparent tolerance by developed countries to allow them certain degrees of freeriding often came at a cost. Poor countries were relegated to the sidelines in key decision-making processes, and also dramatically constrained in their ability to set the agenda in international organizations.[3] Olson's intervention showed us that the small had some ability to manoeuvre at the margins. But if this was all they had or could have, then the powerless would almost never emerge as global agenda-setters and rule-makers.

---

[1] Olson (1965).

[2] This insight offered potential for understanding asymmetric bargaining in different situations, and bore relevance for future scholars concerned with the distributive impact of globalization. Surprisingly, however, while Olson's research generated many further studies in the area of public choice, its impact on negotiation analysis and globalization studies was limited. Most works usually assumed that, at least as far as exercising agency was concerned, small players had the cards stacked against them (key exceptions included Benwell 2011; Keohane 1971; Odell 2010; Schelling 1957; and Zartman 1985, 1997). Even for James Scott (1985), the 'weapons of the weak' involved the use of a 'hidden transcript' on the part of the weak and 'covert forms of retaliation' (Howe 1998), rather than outright challenge and a reversal of power relations. There were some economists who adopted an important but different focus: they pointed to the gains resulting from globalization for the poor (e.g., Bhagwati 2004). But the main mechanisms for the gains of growth, development, and even possible equity were rooted primarily in the impersonal and systemic forces of markets and complex interdependence. They seldom dealt directly with questions of agency and empowerment.

[3] The negotiation processes of the General Agreement on Tariffs and Trade (GATT) provided a dramatic illustration of this phenomenon. Through several decades, developing countries enjoyed the benefits of belonging to the system due to the 'Principal Supplier Principle' that required only major players to exchange concessions, which were then extended to all the contracting parties. But this also greatly limited their ability to influence the evolving agenda of the GATT, as discussed in detail in Chapter 2.

The decades following the end of the World War largely corroborated this assumption. Developing II countries frequently complained of the disregard that many international organizations showed to their causes and concerns, and also that they were being systematically marginalized from decision-making processes. Although they were not reluctant to still assert their voice and fight battles along North–South lines, any gains they made were few and hard won. More often than not, these gains were of four types, and all of them were limited.

First, developing countries were sometimes able to secure some exemptions and exceptions for themselves, such as Special and Differential Treatment in the General Agreement on Tariffs and Trade (GATT). But these achievements proved to be a double-edged sword. On the one hand, they gave poor countries the breathing space they sought from the rules. But on the other hand, these exemptions also reinforced the marginalization of developing countries from the system.

Second, developing countries were sometimes beneficiaries of aid from rich countries. But aid policies were driven by a mix of strategic imperatives of the Cold War and moral imperatives of charity. And although developing countries could cleverly play off bilateral donors from the East and West against each other, they were fundamentally objects of foreign economic and security policies rather than masters of their own fates.

Third, the international economic system also came to accommodate some of the concerns of developing countries via best endeavour clauses. The United Nations General Assembly, for instance, adopted a resolution in 1970 that proclaimed the launch of the second UN Decade for Development and advanced a corresponding international development strategy. This strategy also set an important goal for Official Development Assistance from developed countries: 'Each economically advanced country will progressively increase its official development assistance to the developing countries and will exert its best efforts to reach a minimum net amount of 0.7 per cent of its gross national product at market prices by the middle of the Decade'.[4] In practice, however, poor countries could not hold their richer counterparts to account with such a best endeavour (and therefore unenforceable) commitment.

Finally, developing countries also attempted to break the vicious cycles of powerlessness and victimhood by bypassing the existing rules of the game and creating new ones. They advanced alternative epistemic theories

[4] UN General Assembly (1970).

(e.g., dependency theory), built alternative institutions (e.g., the creation of the United Nations Conference on Trade and Development in 1964 as an alternative and more development-friendly forum to the GATT), and proposed alternative visions of order (e.g., the New International Economic Order, NIEO). But the most that these strategies usually achieved were short-term stalemates and even greater polarization. In spite of all their efforts, and caught between the increasingly intrusive conditionalities of the International Monetary Fund (IMF) and increasingly intrusive rules of the GATT as negotiated in the Uruguay Round, developing countries found themselves deeply disempowered through the 1980s and the greater part of the 1990s. But then, around the turn of the century, something began to change.

Towards the end of the 1990s, powerlessness – conceptualized as poverty in the international economic context – began to gain increasing recognition as a serious worldwide concern, and the poor began to acquire greater visibility and voice. Different international organizations were compelled to include pro-poor considerations in every step of the negotiations, rather than as a mere afterthought. Examples included declarations such as the UN Millennium Development Goals (launched in 2000), and also other negotiations and programs that went beyond what game theorists refer to as 'cheap talk'. The UN Commission on Human Rights established a new mandate on food security and appointed the first Special Rapporteur on the Right to Food in 2000. The World Trade Organization (WTO) launched the negotiations of the Doha Development Agenda in 2001, and thereby signalled that it was finally placing the long-standing concerns of developing countries at the heart of its agenda. The IMF and World Bank inaugurated their initiative for the Highly Indebted Poor Countries in 2002. This action was, moreover, not limited to international organizations.

The Jubilee 2000 movement arose under the umbrella of the Catholic Church, and demanded that Third World debt be written off. The movement expanded across countries, and celebrities such as Bono and Bob Geldof joined the jamboree to further raise public awareness. In 2005, millions of people wore white bands to express their solidarity with the 'Make Poverty History' campaign, and 225,000 people marched through the streets of Edinburgh in order to persuade the G8 leaders meeting at Gleneagles to take action against global poverty. These movements were not the sole preserve of the middle classes of rich countries. The World Social Forum met for the first time in Porto Alegre in 2001, and then continued to bring together a very diverse group of activists to summits that were held on an annual basis in a developing country. Across countries and across different decision-making forums, poverty had emerged as a political issue that could no longer be brushed under the carpet. From the margins, the poor moved to the centre of international economic negotiations.

Poverty emerged as an essential part of political debate both within, among, and beyond countries, and in international organizations. It acquired the power to drive mass campaigns, to influence policy at the highest levels, and to sell us stuff. Even though there was little new about the phenomenon of poverty per se, around the turn of this century and in the following decade, poverty became a part of the global 'scenery' as never before. How did this change come about, and what are the ramifications of these developments? To understand the transformation of poverty into a form of power, I turn to the study of narratives in negotiations.

1.2 THEORETICAL APPROACH AND METHODOLOGY

1.2.1 *Narratives in Negotiations*

Different forms of powerlessness are facts of social, political, and economic life. But 'facts' themselves are shaped, and acquire meaning and relevance, through narratives.[5] As poverty narratives interact and change, they have the potential to overturn, perpetuate, or exacerbate power asymmetries.

The study of narratives has a rich history in the Humanities. To scholars of history and literature, it has been obvious that stories matter. Moral philosopher Alasdair Macintyre proposed that 'man is in his actions and practice, as well as in his fictions, essentially a story-telling animal'.[6] Drawing partly on Macintyre's work, William Fisher advanced the idea of 'narrative rationality' in communication theory, which he contrasted with 'traditional rationality'.[7] Fisher proposed that traditional rationality was based on 'argumentative competence', which presupposes knowledge of specific issues and modes of reasoning. In this framework, rationality was 'something to be learned, depended on deliberation, and required a high degree of self-consciousness'. In contrast, narrative rationality 'does not make these demands. It is a capacity we all share'. Fisher then went on to show that argumentation was not the only way to sway voters in public debate. In fact, voters were often moved more by 'perceptions and appraisals of discourse and action', which served as stories and narratives.

---

[5] Bruner (1998) writes, facts 'live in context; what holds most human contexts together is a narrative'.

[6] Macintyre (1981).

[7] Fisher (1984).

Intricate and interesting details to his approach aside, one important contribution of Fisher's work was to highlight that we might need to go beyond conventional notions of rationality to understand the drivers for decision-making and actions by individuals and groups. Here, his work complemented the writings of others in the social sciences, some of which had preceded him. Notably, John Maynard Keynes had pointed out in 1936 that under conditions of uncertainty decisions are not 'the outcome of a weighted average of quantitative benefits multiplied by quantitative probabilities'; rather, decisions 'can only be taken as a result of animal spirits'.[8] Herbert Simon had also demonstrated that, contrary to common assumptions in economics and political science, decision-makers were guided by 'bounded rationality' and had to rely on 'satisficing' rather than optimizing behaviour.[9] Daniel Kahneman and Amos Tversky had convincingly challenged traditional expected utility theory, and instead offered 'prospect theory' as an alternative model in the field of behavioural economics.[10] Specifically, the two authors had shown the importance of 'framing' in decision choices; frames adopted by the decision-maker in turn were 'controlled partly by the formulation of the problem and partly by the norms, habits, and personal characteristics of the decision-maker'.[11] Parallel developments had taken place also in political science: for example, Graham Allison on the limitations of rational-actor models in decision-making;[12] Irving Janice on groupthink in foreign policy-making;[13] and Raymond Cohen on the importance of culture in international negotiations.[14] Different schools of thought – ranging from constructivism to sociological institutionalism – focused on the role of norms as a key explanatory variable for international behaviour.[15] All these different insights were valuable in expanding our narrow notions of rationality, and offering sometimes less parsimonious and also potentially more useful explanations of real-world phenomena. But in highlighting the importance of *narratives* – defined broadly as stories – as a major influence on the understanding and interpretation of political 'fact', Fisher had brought something important and new.

---

[8]   Despite Keynes's visionary contributions, standard economic theory did not incorporate these insights. Rather, it assumed 'People act only for economic motives, and they act only rationally' (Akerlof and Shiller 2009).
[9]   Simon (1955, 1972).
[10] Kahneman and Tversky (1979).
[11] Tversky and Kahneman (1981).
[12] Allison (1971).
[13] Janis (1972).
[14] Cohen (1991).
[15] E.g., Finnemore (1996); Acharya (2004).

Unlike the richly researched higher level of ideas, norms, and identities, and also the more tactical level of framing, the realm of stories had remained under-researched, even though its potential applications to the social sciences were many. Finally, the new sub-field of 'narrative economics' began to lead the way.

Robert Shiller, who coined the term 'narrative economics', defines the field as follows:

> By narrative economics, I mean the study of the spread and dynamics of popular narratives, the stories, particularly those of human interest and emotion, and how these change through time, to *understand* economic fluctuations. A recession, for example, is a time when many people have decided to spend less, to make do for now with that old furniture instead of buying new, or to postpone starting a new business, to postpone hiring new help in an existing business, or to express support for fiscally conservative government. They might make any of these decisions in reaction to the recession itself (that's feedback), but to understand why a recession even started, we need more than a theory of feedback. We have to consider the possibility that sometimes the dominant reason why a recession is severe is related to the prevalence and vividness of certain stories, not the purely economic feedback or multipliers that economists love to model.[16]

Shiller thus shares Fisher's definition of a narrative being a story, and hones this idea further. He conceptualizes a narrative as 'a simple story or easily expressed *explanation* of events that many people want to bring up in conversation or on news or social media because it can be used to *stimulate the concerns or emotions* of others, and/or because it appears to advance *self-interest*'.[17] Michael Zürn further points to the use of narratives for legitimation purposes.[18]

Related to narratives are various other concepts – cultures, identities, norms, beliefs, ideas, frames – which have attracted different degrees of attention from different academic disciplines. These concepts have sometimes been used interchangeably or inconsistently, across and even within fields. Narrative economics offers a systematization of some of these concepts, and potentially allows us to move beyond a debate on semantics. Paul Collier develops a framework for analysis, and unpacks some of the terms and

---

[16] Shiller (2017) (emphasis added).
[17] Shiller (2017) (emphasis added).
[18] Zürn (2018).

intuitions associated with the culture variable.[19] Incorporating 'culture' into the study of economics is useful, he argues, because it facilitates a balance into one's analysis 'by accepting that both knowledge and preferences are socially generated and that self-interested rationality is a component of behaviour rather than its exclusive determinant'. Culture is constituted by mental frameworks: beliefs, and social networks. There are three types of beliefs: identities (which 'influence preferences'), narratives (which 'influence how causal relationships are (mis)understood'), and norms (which 'determine self-imposed constraints').[20] Collier argues that actors behave rationally with the goal of utility maximization, while being simultaneously conditioned by their beliefs. These beliefs, in turn, are 'contaminated' by 'endowments of irrationality', that is participation in pre-existing social networks through which actors acquire beliefs in the first place. Previously and 'pre-rationally' acquired beliefs, and path dependent participation in future social networks, together produce dysfunctional cultures. Principals (CEOs in organizations, heads of families, and governments in the case of states) can influence a culture directly by addressing beliefs and indirectly by changing participation in networks.[21]

Naturally, the three types of 'beliefs', as identified by Collier, interact with each other. I focus here primarily on one set of beliefs – narratives, that is causal stories (and resulting solutions) about poverty – to explain how powerlessness is being fundamentally transformed. My motivation for doing so stems partly from the fact that narratives have thus far not received the scholarly attention that they deserve in either political science or political economy. This is in contrast to norms and identities, which have attracted considerably more research at least in political science.[22] But even more so, my interest derives from the fact that, in comparison to relatively deep-rooted

---

[19] Collier (2016).

[20] Collier (2016), p. 14, writes, 'Narratives are importantly different from identities and norms. The latter are entirely generated psychologically: they have no necessary relationship to objective reality. In contrast, a narrative conveys some aspect of objective reality, albeit potentially in a highly distorted form'.

[21] Causation can also work in the reverse direction, where politicians and practitioners tap into pre-existing culture and thereby change narratives and influence new networks (e.g., Narlikar 2017 on how India's Prime Minister Narendra Modi is drawing on Indian traditions to build domestic support for climate change mitigation).

[22] By way of illustration, research on identities and norms in the field of international relations goes back to the 1990s, for example Finnemore (1996); Goldstein and Keohane (1993); Katzenstein (1996); Keck and Sikkink (1998); Klotz (1995); Wendt (1992). In economics, the turn to understanding the 'subjectivity' factors is relatively recent; for a particularly helpful overview and applications, see Akerlof (2007).

norms and identities, narratives are more mutable. Shiller describes them as 'major vectors of rapid change in culture, in zeitgeist, and ultimately in economic behaviour'.[23] In terms of their ability to trigger 'rapid change' by 'going viral', narratives are thus potentially the more responsive and pliable tool for policy intervention and can further contribute to the shaping of identities and norms. It is precisely this intermediate and understudied level – between norms and identities on the one hand, and the more tactical level of framing on the other – that makes the subject of narratives so interesting.

It is worth recalling that, prior to the work done in narrative economics, Goldstein and Keohane had developed a similar categorization of ideas and their influence on foreign policy: world-views, principled beliefs, and causal beliefs.[24] The two schemes have some overlap with each other. Culture and identity would be a rough overlap with the 'world-views' box; norms would be a good fit with the 'principled beliefs' box; narratives would occupy a 'causal beliefs plus' box. Goldstein and Keohane define causal beliefs as 'beliefs about cause-effect relationships which derive authority from the shared consensus of *recognized elites*, whether they be village elders or scientists at elite institutions'. Narratives include such beliefs, but also go beyond them. For example, narratives can – but need not – be based on a shared political or epistemic consensus. Some populist narratives in fact are formed explicitly *against* 'recognized elites'. Narratives can, in fact, originate in an urban myth or historical tradition, be true or false, be the work of individuals with no office or position, and 'go viral' through a variety of mechanisms used by individuals or groups of actors through word-of-mouth or social media – to thereby exercise an influence on foreign policy.[25] They represent understandings of phenomena, usually appeal to both emotion and self-interest, and can serve as mechanisms of legitimation. Box 1.1 represents my interpretation of the degrees of abstraction in the concepts that are commonly used in narrative economics. Narratives and frames are easier to operationalize and change than culture, identity, and norms. Although narratives are my main focus, I also engage with the question of how narratives relate to norms and frames in the course of this book.

---

[23] Shiller (2017), p. 972.

[24] Goldstein and Keohane (1993).

[25] Public intellectuals and thought leaders, as well 'pessimists, partisans, and plutocrats', whom Daniel Drezner (2017) identifies as shaping the 'ideas industry', all can – and often do – have a role to play in the development, dissemination, and dissipation of narratives.

Box 1.1 Concepts commonly used in narrative economics

Culture
|
Identity
|
Norms
= values
|
Narrative
= stories about causation
|
Frame
= perspectives

As norms and identities change – partly in response to narratives, but also other factors (including changes in the balance of power, resource constraints, and the interactions between identities and norms) – they in turn influence and reshape narratives. These feedback loops form a part of my investigation into narratives about poverty. Importantly, however, the mutability of narratives means that changes within them do not depend solely on these feedback loops. In other words, one does not necessarily need a fundamental transformation of norms or identity – or major exogenous shocks – to find a narrative changing. Rather, the process of working a narrative by influential actors – via its use and misuse – can itself be enough to alter its purpose and efficacy. Their fluidity and dynamism make narratives an easier and swifter policy instrument than norms and identities. But this also makes them harder to regulate and steer. This is also why it is all the more crucial to understand how actors shape narratives, how narratives evolve, and the different influences that they exercise on outcomes in different parts of their lifecycles.

It is worth noting that the recent attention to narratives in economics has a somewhat pessimistic entry point – perhaps only suitably so for an academic field that Thomas Carlyle dubbed the 'dismal science'. Traditional approaches in the discipline – so the current thinking goes – have proven inadequate in our understanding of financial crises, unemployment, persistence of poverty traps, and so forth; narratives have the potential to explain why markets do not work as smoothly and seamlessly as standard economic theory suggests.[26] Collier's agenda-setting paper is explicit, even in its title, in emphasizing that the study of cultural variables is key to understanding '*economic*

---

[26] Akerlof and Shiller (2009).

failure' at different levels of human interaction.[27] My book, in contrast, has a different and possibly more hopeful central message. Narratives about poverty have indeed exacerbated the further disempowerment of the already powerless in the past, and risk doing so again in the not-too-distant future. But, very importantly, alternative narratives about the same phenomenon, when put to effective use, can and have transformed weaknesses and marginalization into strength and influence. Through my analysis, I show that culture can be a source of perversity and failure, but also a valuable resource for successful reform.

1.2.2 *Why Poverty Narratives and Why Trade?*

I conduct my investigation into the conversion of powerlessness, weakness, and victimhood into power – via narratives – by focusing specifically on the role that poverty plays in trade negotiations.

My reason for focusing on poverty as an indicator of powerlessness stems from two sources.

First, scholarly and public perceptions usually associate poverty with exclusion, marginalization, and powerlessness. For example, a World Bank report, which conducted over 20,000 interviews of poor people living in twenty-three developing countries and economies in transition, provides one illustration of this link: 'The common theme underlying poor people's experiences is one of powerlessness'.[28] This study is not unusual in assuming that at least as far as exercising agency is concerned – the capacity to act in order to change their own circumstances – the poor have the odds stacked against them. Multiple aid and consumer campaigns – including 'Make Poverty History', 'Jubilee 2000', and the 'Fairtrade' movement – are motivated by the supposed helplessness of the poor and the desire to assist them.[29] Poverty serves as a useful cipher for powerlessness.

---

[27] Collier (2016).

[28] World Bank, http://siteresources.worldbank.org/INTPOVERTY/Resources/335642-1124115102975/1555199-1124115201387/cry1.pdf .

[29] A few scholars depart from this dominant view and point to the gains resulting from globalization for the poor, and the main drivers for these gains are rooted in the forces of complex interdependence. If the poor turn out to be beneficiaries of globalization, it is largely a result of systemic working, rather than as empowered agents and agenda-setters. But even this story of relative optimism was somewhat unsatisfactory for me, akin to Olson's limited promise of the gains of freeriding for the small. Normatively, the poor as passive beneficiaries offered a rather depressing view. But empirically too, from my previous work, I had seen that poor countries could be resourceful, and they could empower themselves (e.g., Narlikar 2003). An important motivation for writing this book was to unpack and systematize the mechanisms of this empowerment, and also explore ways in which these could be strengthened further.

Second, strides in poverty reduction notwithstanding, poverty remains endemic across the world. It is a form of powerlessness that still affects a very large number of people: in 2015, 736 million people lived in extreme poverty, that is on less than $1.90 a day. This constituted 10 per cent of the world's population. In low income countries, 43 per cent of the population was extremely poor. Sub-Saharan Africa has the dubious distinction of being the only region in the world where the number of people living in extreme poverty has increased, and the region is home to one-third of the global poor. But extreme poverty is not an African problem alone, or indeed only a problem of the Least Developed Countries. For the category of lower middle-income countries, the proportion of people living below the international poverty line was 13.9 per cent. If one looks beyond the minimum level of extreme poverty, and does a count of people living under $3.20 a day (defined as the lower middle income class poverty line by the World Bank), the proportion increases to 71.1 per cent in Low Income Countries, 43.7 per cent in lower middle-income countries, and 7.5 per cent in higher-upper middle-income countries.[30] And while absolute and severe poverty affects large sections of the developing world, poverty for many is a relative concept, and national poverty lines in rich and developed countries reveal that a significant proportion of the population here is also 'poor'. For example, using its own definition of poverty, the European Union had 23.5 per cent of its population as being 'at risk of poverty or social exclusion' in 2016.[31] Applying a different criterion, the US Census Bureau classified 12.3 per cent of Americans as poor in 2017.[32] In 2018, the UN Special Rapporteur on extreme poverty and human rights announced a fact-finding mission to the United Kingdom: 'The United Kingdom is one of the richest countries in the world, but millions of people are still living in poverty there'.[33] Given that poverty is pervasive in not only the developing world but also in developed countries, using it as one signifier of powerlessness seemed like a good place to start in order to develop a theory of agency and empowerment.

My focus on trade stems from the fact that even though trade is seen as a positive-sum game in theory – and hence a possible source of empowerment for all, including the poor – in practice, the visibly distributive consequences of trade within countries make its politics especially volatile and polarized. Political economy considerations exacerbate this polarization, with

[30] http://povertydata.worldbank.org/poverty/home, accessed on 28 January 2019.
[31] https://ec.europa.eu/eurostat/statistics-explained/index.php/People_at_risk_of_poverty_or_social_exclusion, accessed on 31 October 2018.
[32] www.census.gov/library/publications/2018/demo/p60-263.html, accessed on 31 October 2018.
[33] www.ohchr.org/EN/NewsEvents/Pages/DisplayNews.aspx?NewsID=23808&LangID=E, accessed on 1 November 2018.

well-organized special interests groups exercising far greater influence on trade policy than the numerically large, but usually less organized, groups of consumers. As such, international trade bargaining presents a 'hard test case'. If we were to see the power of the powerless at work *even* in this challenging political environment – characterized by the difficulties of collective action for consumers, vocal and well-organized protectionist producers, and clearly visible distributive consequences that make special interest groups more entrenched and reluctant to make concessions – then chances are that this paradoxical power might have still greater applicability in other issue areas.

The institutional context of trade negotiations is also interesting. The multilateral organization that governs trade – the WTO, and its predecessor, the General Agreement on Tariffs and Trade (GATT) – has been more egalitarian than many other international organizations (e.g., the International Monetary Fund or the UN Security Council). Its decision-making processes have been based on consensus, and every member (no matter how big or small, rich or poor) enjoys one vote. This institutional context should have served as an equalizer for poor countries. In practice, however, the GATT was referred to as a 'Rich Man's Club', and developing countries frequently complained that their concerns were being systematically marginalized. Many of these problems persisted after the formation of the WTO. Institutional egalitarianism, at least on its own, had not proven to be enough to empower the powerless in the multilateral trade regime. And yet, around the turn of the century, something fundamental changed.

Concerns about poverty began to be taken much more seriously within the WTO, and also outside it. Poor countries were able to hold negotiation processes to ransom. In bilateral and regional trade deals too, which developed countries tried to turn to, the concerns of domestic groups that were poor or vulnerable had to be kept at the forefront – without the blessing of these groups, negotiation processes were almost certain to fail. This happened despite the fact that the main actors pushing for this pro-poor agenda were still largely poor, institutional decision-making processes were still much the same, and the domestic distributive consequences of trade within economies were still polarizing. So how did this change come about? The answer lies in a change in dominant narratives.

1.2.3 *Mechanisms of Change: How Winning Narratives Emerge and Evolve*

Different and sometimes conflicting narratives about the causes, implications, and solutions to poverty have historically existed simultaneously, and also in states of constant flux as they interact with other beliefs and actors. At any one point of time though, a particular narrative can acquire greater legitimacy, acceptability, and followership, and thereby becomes the dominant narrative. We can recognize that it may be a winning narrative if we see an increase in the number of references to it in scholarly publications and policy papers, and if it enters into policy debates and political statements. But 'the proof of the pudding' is to be found in changes in negotiation processes and outcomes; if negotiators align their behaviour to match the causal understandings that a narrative has captured, we know that it is an influential – possible even a dominant or winning – narrative.

Two broad narratives about poverty had wrestled with each other since the post–World War II era, albeit in various permutations and acquiring different nuances over time. One narrative understood poverty primarily as a domestic issue, and thus proposed the welfare state and other domestic policies as a response. The other explained poverty as at least as much a product of external factors as domestic factors, and therefore demanded different forms of redressal, ranging from Special and Differential Treatment (SDT, i.e., exceptions to the rules, which they believed were important to allow them to develop) to a change in the rules of international trade. The first narrative had dominated policy debates for almost half a century after the post-war system was established and had support – roughly speaking – from the global north. Around the turn of the millennium though, the second narrative began to emerge as the winning narrative, creating unprecedented conditions in favour of empowerment of the powerless. This change was mainly a result of four strategies that developing countries (sometimes in conjunction with other actors) successfully used. The first two related to the construction of the narrative itself, while the latter two related to its effective dissemination.

First, in a variety of ways, the Best Alternative to Negotiated Agreement – BATNA – improved for poor countries. Market opening, under the auspices of the WTO and its expanding membership, offered new opportunities for competitive economies from the developing world. Even for the less competitive ones, the rise of the so-called BRICS (Brazil, Russia, India, China, South Africa) offered new sources of aid and investment, as well as greater political clout to back the cause of development. By making them less dependent on the charity of the rich, better BATNAs strengthened the bargaining positions of developing countries. The emerging markets also benefited from this deepened relationship with other developing countries, not least in the form of greater legitimacy for coalitions and the causes they led. In this book, I show how Least Developed Countries (LDCs) as well as middle-income developing countries/emerging markets were able to harness the advantages offered by improved BATNAs.

Second, developing countries and other (traditionally weak) actors developed new ways of framing their specific demands and broader narrative. Framing matters. As Tversky and Kahneman write, 'The psychological principles that govern the perception of decision problems and the evaluation of probabilities and outcomes produce predictable shifts of preference when the same problem is framed in different ways'.[34] Frames are different from narratives. Narratives are *causal explanations* that are adopted as a result of a variety of inputs – ranging from scientific knowledge and cultural tradition to personal experience; they represent different *understandings* of the world. Tversky and Kahneman, in contrast, describe frames as 'alternative perspectives on a visual scene';[35] they represent different ways of *seeing* the world. One can, for example, frame one's narrative with the help of statistical data, or one can use stories of individuals; the prior frame is usually founded on at least a claim to scientific foundations; the latter is founded on emotion and norms. Similarly, narratives can be framed as revolutionary ones, where demands are presented in terms of an overthrow of the system, or they can be presented as working with the system and the norms that it represents. The global south showed greater successes when framing the narrative as not being completely antithetical to the regime.[36] Framing their demands with reference to the damage that particular policies were causing for powerless individuals further bolstered their negotiation success.[37]

Third, the formation of effective inter-state bargaining coalitions was a major step towards increasing the influence of developing countries in the WTO. While bargaining through coalitions was not a new development, the improved effectiveness of these coalitions was. In the book, I discuss the successes of these coalitions in terms of their new structures and strategies.

Fourth, transnational social movements began to play a bigger role in trade politics. Developing countries now showed greater willingness to work with civil society actors in both the global south and north. This was in stark contrast to their previously defensive stance, when they had vacillated mainly between wariness and animosity towards attempts by non-state actors to exercise a voice in multilateral trade negotiations. Additionally, outside of the institutional context of the WTO too, there were other powerful voices that included non-governmental organizations (NGOs) and went beyond them,

---

[34] Tversky and Kahneman (1981), p. 453.
[35] Ibid., p. 453.
[36] Odell and Sell (2006) make this argument specifically with respect to the TRIPS and public health coalition; this book offers further evidence to support their hypothesis.
[37] Keck and Sikkink (1998) make this argument

for instance celebrity ambassadors.[38] The campaigns led by these different players successfully brought the plight of the poor to television screens as well as social media of millions of people around the world, and demanded redress.

Working together in coalitions, transnational social movements, and networks, the poor could no longer be ignored, and the powerless could no longer be marginalized. Add to this the increasing connectivity afforded by digital communication – and especially social media platforms – which served as a further leveller of power differentials. This meant that poor countries could appeal to a much wider audience. They could connect with key nodes (other countries, NGOs, celebrities) to spread their message across networks, and they could do so at relatively low costs. Even under-represented countries in Geneva now had the possibility of gaining greater access to the system. Countries and peoples who had long been marginalized from key decision-making processes harnessed these technologies effectively, and acquired a voice that was disproportionately bigger than what their economic size would normally suggest.

Together, these factors allowed a previously sidelined narrative to gain dominance. This was still a poverty narrative that had competed with the dominant one. It recognized external factors as a source of the problem of poverty in developing countries, and further insisted on creating better opportunities for the poor to ensure their equal participation. In this sense, the narrative did not change. But for it to acquire the greater prominence that it did, several other things did change. Actors backing the narrative discovered new BATNAs and harnessed them effectively; the tactics that they used to frame the narrative changed; the coalitions and transnational social movements that they used for dissemination changed, and their methods of mobilizing support expanded with the use of social media platforms.

Most immediately, the emergence of this narrative as the winning one ensured unprecedented agency for developing countries, the poor within these countries, and also the poor in developed countries. But all four mechanisms, which had facilitated the emergence of this narrative and thereby ensured agency for the marginalized, were also liable to overuse and misuse. Through the course of this book, I trace the multiple uses to which poverty narratives have been put, and also the roles that different actors played in shaping, harnessing, and reshaping them.

1.2.4 *Actors and the Stories behind Their Negotiation Landmarks*

The starting point of this book is the story of the empowerment of the powerless. As such, the book is most immediately concerned with states that

---

[38] Cooper (2009).

are poor in aggregate or per capita terms. But, as is increasingly recognized in public debate, poverty is not a phenomenon that is restricted to the global south. Relative and absolute poverty are matters of concern also for developed countries, and these concerns have only been rising since the financial crisis of 2008. This book is thus just as interested in how developed countries draw on poverty narratives in international trade bargaining – be it poverty in their own countries, or poverty in the global south, or both. Three sets of actors play a key role in this study:

(a) The LDCs, defined by the UN as countries that have low incomes, are highly vulnerable to economic and environmental shocks, and have low levels of human assets. These three criteria reflect serious structural impediments to sustainable development.[39]

(b) The middle-income economies, particularly Brazil, China, India, and South Africa whose low GDPs per capita tell quite a different story in comparison to the iconic status that is ascribed to them as 'BRICS' growth markets: in 2017, China ranked 79th, Brazil 81st, South Africa 89th, and India 122nd out of 187 countries.[40]

(c) The developed countries, particularly the United States and European Union member countries, which have experienced relative decline amidst the changing balance of power, and which cannot ignore the discontent of their domestic constituencies that have faced stagnating or declining incomes.[41]

All three sets of actors appeal to their varied experiences with poverty as they negotiate international agreements, and are also answerable to the constituencies of the poor in whose name they adopt certain negotiating positions. In different ways, all three groups have played meaningful roles in harnessing and shaping the different poverty narratives, and thereby transforming the politics of powerlessness. Importantly, while these state actors (and the poor within them) form my central point of reference, the book also engages with the agendas espoused by non-state actors that claim to speak on behalf of the poor, try to correct state actions that they disagree with, and attempt to influence global trade rules.

---

[39] www.un.org/development/desa/dpad/least-developed-country-category/ldc-criteria.html.

[40] GDP per capita calculated at purchasing power parity in www.imf.org/external/datamapper/ PPPPC@WEO/THA. Russia is not a central focus of the study because of its late entry into the WTO in 2012.

[41] Poorer than their Parents? Flat or declining incomes in advanced economies, Report by McKinsey Global Institute, www.mckinsey.de/files/mgi-income-inequality-july-2016.pdf, accessed on 13 December 2017.

In each chapter, I focus on four negotiation landmarks involving the different sets of actors. I rely on four types of primary sources to trace the process whereby poverty considerations have entered the debate and influenced outcomes: submitted proposals and statements by the key actors, trade policy review reports, minutes of specific committees, and ministerial declarations. The results are further substantiated via an overview of the secondary literature and various policy reports/commentaries on the particular subjects covered.

It is worth mentioning at this point that, while trade bargaining forms the central focus of this book, the power of the powerless is limited neither to this field, nor indeed to the area of international politics. Rather, we see a similar use of poverty narratives, and their evolution, across many forums of global governance as well as across different issue areas of our daily lives. I develop my argument on the use and misuse of poverty narratives by using the detailed case of trading bargaining, and thereby make the case for the emergence, plateauing, and potential decline of the power of the powerless. But, towards the end of each chapter, I also draw on a range of examples from other areas such as climate change mitigation, ethical consumerism, migration, and G20 negotiations. This broad sweep helps illustrate the extent to which poverty narratives have been used, and also gives us some comparative leverage to explore whether differences in issue-area and governance institutions have produced differences in practice of the power of the powerless.

1.3 BOOK OUTLINE

The book proceeds in five chapters. Following this introductory chapter outlining the central puzzle, plus theoretical and methodological approach, Chapters 2–4 conduct detailed case studies of key landmarks in trade negotiations. The chapter division is based on the relatively ineffective presence, then successful use, and finally increasing overuse and misuse of the power of powerlessness. An important contribution of this book is to trace the lifecycles of narratives: how narratives emerge, acquire dominance, change, and possibly die. The chapter division also reflects this lifecycle and is roughly chronological, even though we see some overlaps in the different ways in which the narratives are being used and misused. In each chapter, I cover three negotiation landmarks in the multilateral trade regime, plus also have a fourth case where I investigate decision-making processes and how they have reflected poverty narratives.

The main contribution of this book lies in the fields of Global Political Economy and International Relations, but the phenomenon of the power of the powerless goes considerably beyond the detailed case studies that this book offers of the WTO. This is why I also investigate the development of poverty and powerlessness narratives in other issue-areas and institutions in a fifth section of each chapter. I also show that there are several areas of domestic public policy too, where powerlessness has become a major source of motivation and justification. And just as the benefits of using the poverty advantage in international politics are mixed, so is the case when parallel manifestations of powerlessness are used in the politics of the everyday.

1.3.1 *Chapter 2: The Disempowered Many*

In Chapter 2, I trace the negotiating history of the post-war multilateral trading system, from the 1940s to 1995 (i.e., the creation of the WTO), through the lens of poverty narratives. I show how the two main narratives emerged, and how they interacted with each other. I further explain why the narrative that 'won' and achieved dominance for the next several decades was largely unsympathetic to the cause of poverty alleviation, especially when mitigation strategies were discussed in the context of the developing world. I conduct this analysis via three negotiation landmarks, plus a fourth case of decision-making processes.

First, I trace the creation of the GATT in light of the institutional features and provisions of the 'stillborn' ITO. There were multiple reasons for the failure of the ITO. But, very importantly from our perspective, the emergence of the much more limited GATT as the key forum for multilateral trade negotiations also marked the emergence of a dominant narrative that did not place the cause of development or poverty concerns at its core. Even as developing countries were beginning to emerge from colonial bondage, the narrative that emerged with the failure of the ITO did not place much emphasis on external factors as a cause for their impoverishment. I investigate how and why this narrative came to prevail as the key underlying narrative for the system, despite the existence and near-win of a competing narrative that would have established the ITO.

The second turning point came via changes in the GATT to better accommodate the needs of developing countries into the system. This was the result of multiple efforts of activism by developing countries within the GATT system, as well as through parallel initiatives in other relevant forums. Three steps were particularly important: first, the establishment of an escape clause for developing countries via Article 18B; second, the inclusion of Part IV on Development, which was added to the GATT in 1965; and, third, the inclusion of the Enabling Clause that allowed systematic derogations from the principle of Most-Favoured Nation treatment for developing countries. On the one hand, the three steps together represented an important success for the poor in getting their concerns included in the GATT. On the other hand, they also clearly illustrated that the concerns of development and poverty were – at best – to be treated as an addendum, an afterthought, rather than fully integrated into the system of rules. And along with the promise of SDT came the expectation of 'graduation' into reciprocity, which further limited the apparent victory of the global south.

The third important landmark was the completion of the Uruguay Round of trade negotiations in 1994 – the most comprehensive trade round in the history of the GATT, which also culminated in the establishment of the WTO in 1995. Through much of the round, developing countries found themselves on the defensive. In the competing narratives on causes of underdevelopment and ways out of poverty traps, the call for SDT began to get short shrift. The principle of reciprocity underpinned the new narrative, which flourished in the early years of the WTO.

The fourth illustration of the limitations of the power of the poor, even in an institutionalized and apparently egalitarian context, came from decision-making processes in the GATT. Despite its one-member-one-vote system, and consensus-based decision-making that at least theoretically allowed even the smallest and weakest country to exercise a veto, the GATT was regarded as a 'Rich Man's Club' where developing countries complained bitterly of their marginalization. I trace how this decision-making system emerged and thrived.

The four empirical examples show two striking phenomena. First, developing countries – some even when they were negotiating from positions of extreme weakness (such as India, which was a British colony when the ITO negotiations began) – did not shy away from exercising a voice in the negotiation process. Second, on process and outcomes, developing countries often found themselves on a defensive footing, despite all their attempts – alone and in coalitions, within the system and outside – to shape and change the agenda. Their demands were usually greeted with scepticism. The battle to insert development concerns and equal rights into the regime was uphill and steep. The Uruguay Round and the creation of the WTO, in some ways, took the system even further back as far as the demands of developing countries were concerned.

Together, the four cases show that developed countries adapted the winning narrative somewhat, as a result of persistent pressure from developing countries, for instance via SDT provisions. But the putative causal explanation offered by even the adapted and updated narrative remained largely unchanged: the causes of poverty were rooted fundamentally in the corrupt polities and inefficient economies of developing countries themselves; the international playing field did not need levelling.

1.3.2 *Chapter 3: Winning against the Odds*

Around the turn of the century, a change got underway. Poverty came to acquire a new importance in debates on trade, and began to shape the agenda within the new organization in unprecedented – and indeed unanticipated – ways. And, against all odds, and increasingly as the rule rather than the exception, David started winning against Goliath.

These developments were all the more surprising given that the provisions of the newly-created WTO had, in fact, reduced the development-oriented exceptionalism and flexibilities of the GATT. The central way in which this came about was because stories about the causes of poverty, which gave more credence to exogenous variables and recognized the need for changes in the international rules of the game (rather than only governance patterns within developing countries), entered the mainstream. Chapter 3 traces the remarkable ways in which a new empowerment of the poor emerged in the organization, despite the toughness of the new institutional context. Three landmark WTO negotiations (each of which centred on a ministerial conference) plus the decision-making processes of the organization offer useful comparative insights into the role of a south-led poverty narrative in shaping this change.

First, just how path-breaking a change was in the offing came to light in the dramatic failure of the Seattle Ministerial to launch a new round of trade negotiations in 1999. The round-that-never-was would have been called the Millennium Round, and was supposed to focus on sustainable development. But developing countries successfully joined forces and launched an unprecedented and successful attack against both the proposed negotiating goals of the ministerial conference as well as the processes that were being used to reach these goals. While the breakdown in negotiations occurred within the official WTO setting of its ministerial conference, the external context – marked by demonstrations and riots by activists of diverse political persuasions – was also very important. Above all, it reinforced the necessity of conducting trade negotiations with greater attention to the needs and demands of the poor – as conceptualized by the poor themselves rather than by others claiming to either speak on their behalf or one-size-fits all universalism.

The Doha Ministerial Conference in 2001 marked the second important landmark in the empowerment of the powerless. While there were several

reasons for member countries of the WTO to avoid a breakdown in negotiations this time, particularly interesting was the shape that the breakthrough
took and the process whereby it was achieved. An organization, which had
historically steered clear of addressing development as its central goal, now
whole-heartedly embraced its cause by launching the Doha *Development*
Agenda. Nor was this commitment to development in name only. The TRIPS
and Public Health Declaration provides one example of the concrete successes that developing countries achieved in 2001. I examine how and why
some of the poorest countries were able to secure these victories, tracing their
new networking strategies, improved BATNAs, and new forms of framing that
helped insert their preferred narrative onto centre stage.

The third case study in Chapter 3 focuses on the Cancun Ministerial
Conference of 2003. The ministerial ended in a bitterly polarized deadlock.
This particular deadlock stemmed partly from poor signalling mechanisms on
the part of the different parties. Developed countries had anticipated that the
discontent that developing countries were expressing at the conference was
little more than 'cheap talk'; at crunch time, they would cave in to bilateral
and group pressure. In fact, Cancun represented a wake-up call to all parties
that protests about poverty would no longer stay on the outside of international
organizations. The poor were serious about getting redress. And if this did not
happen, they had effective strategies in place to bring international negotiations to a grinding halt.

Finally, for the fourth case, I investigate how decision-making within the
WTO, even without a formal process of reform, adapted and changed to
accommodate the voices of the poor. These *de facto* changes were unforeseen,
not least because the working processes of the WTO were deeply entrenched
in the practices of the GATT, and the power imbalances that underpinned
them. And yet, the WTO changed from being the quintessential 'Rich Man's
Club' to one of the most equitable organizations, which not only made room
for the rising powers of Brazil, India, and China at its high table, but also gave
more voice to the LDCs.

The cases of empowerment of the poor in the WTO are interesting and
uplifting in their own right, especially against the backdrop of the resistance
that similar pro-poor narratives had encountered in the GATT. Chapter 3 also
takes the external context into account. Actors and activists operating within
the WTO were able to create positive feedback loops with developments
outside, especially across the transnational NGO community. They were
aided by supportive transnational movements such as 'Make Poverty History',
and also the unenforceable but normatively promising UN initiative of the
Millennium Development Goals. They became more effective in instituting

collective action through coalitions, and developed framing tactics that were more effective in the institutional context. They exploited their improved BATNAs. In the aftermath of the financial crisis in 2008, both legitimacy and power balances swung even further away from the rich and powerful, and towards the poor and weak, for instance via movements like 'Occupy Wall Street' and 'We are the 99%'. Harnessing these synergies, unlikely groups of actors came together, and transformed poor empowerment from a narrow and technocratic concern to something that came to embody the spirt of the times.

Climate change negotiations – an arena where developing countries had long complained of being patronized, and to being held hostage to the double standards of the west – provided an illustration of the general trend that was underway. At the Conference of the Parties in Copenhagen (COP 15) in 2009, developing countries emerged as successful veto-players, and managed to block the final agreement. In Paris (COP 21), it was clear that the clout of developing countries had expanded even further from veto-players to agenda-setters:[42] agreement was reached this time, but on terms that acknowledged the constraints that poorer countries faced. The emergence of the G20 as a parallel, and sometimes even alternative, forum to the G7 in the aftermath of the financial crisis in 2008 was another indication of the growing centrality of the hitherto marginalized in international economic negotiations; the expansion of the G20 over the years to include guests from smaller economies reinforced this trend.

Admittedly, the emergence of this *Zeitgeist* did not take place simultaneously across all international organizations or issue-areas. There were time-lags and institutional differences. But the WTO deserves credit for following closely behind the UN's initiative on the MDG, and then overtaking the UN on both process and content. The ability of the WTO to pioneer progress on this front may have derived at least partly from its relatively high level of institutionalization and the potential enforceability of its decisions. But the fact that we saw similar moves towards the empowerment of the hitherto marginalized occur in other areas of politics and everyday life too suggests something more than an institution-specific explanation. Hitherto powerless individuals reclaimed past marginalization and victimhood, and developed narratives of empowerment, for example via #MeToo and *Fridays for Future*. But as the power of the powerless and its uses evolved, some serious problems emerged down the road.

---

[42] Tsebelis (1995) is to be credited with the concept and terminology of 'veto-players' and 'agenda-setters'. He develops these concepts with reference to domestic political systems: presidential, parliamentary, multicameral, and multiparty. I applied some of these intuitions to the international level in Narlikar (2007).

1.3.3 Chapter 4: When Fair Is Foul and Foul Is Fair

The growing dominance of a narrative led by the global south, which emphasized the rights of the powerless, effectively resulted in the creation of a new normal in power relations. For example, through the first decade of the twenty-first century, when developing countries pointed to their lower per capita incomes and refused to accept the burden of providing certain global public goods (e.g., on trade or climate change mitigation), developed countries had few rebuttals. After decades of hard graft, the concerns of the poor were finally accepted into the mainstream and came to occupy the heart of international negotiations in trade and also other areas. This was surely a good thing. But this successful exercise of power on behalf of the poor and the powerless majority of the global south also resulted in two adverse consequences: overuse and misuse of the narrative. Together these adverse consequences risk undoing many of the recent gains achieved. Chances are, if the recent trends continue, all parties – the rich and the poor – will be left worse-off, and the poor and the weak will be worse affected than the rich and strong.

The first case that I investigate in Chapter 4 is from the Doha negotiations in the agricultural sector. India is an important example here, both domestic-ally and internationally. Looking at the domestic side, the agricultural sector in India has underperformed for decades, and has also been amongst the most impermeable to reform, even as India's status as a rising power and emerging market has risen. High levels of corruption have meant that the gains from agricultural subsidies and tax exemptions have accrued to rich businessmen and middlemen, while the intended beneficiaries of such measures have continued to suffer in abject poverty, undernutrition, and starvation. Related to the ossification in India's agrarian politics are the limitations of the indus-trial sector, which render transitioning from agriculture to manufacturing difficult for many people. Resistance to reform derives at least partly from both uses and misuses of the poverty narrative within the country, which then also translates to the international level. Acting in the name of its poor farmers and in support of the same policies though, India has repeatedly – and sometimes single-handedly – held up any deal on agriculture in the Doha negotiations.[43] In Chapter 4, I illustrate the costs that India's use of the poverty

---

[43] It is important to note at this point that India's stance on agriculture is certainly not the sole cause for the long series of deadlocks that afflicted the DDA for over fifteen years. The European Union and the United States, as well as China and others, bear their own shares of responsibility at different points in time in the negotiations. Chapter 4 will take some of their negotiating

narrative has generated: for its poorest farmers, other sectors, trading partners, and the credibility of the WTO as a whole. I argue that some limited use of the poverty narrative could have generated better outcomes for all parties involved, rather than its blanket overuse in this case.

My second case-study in Chapter 4 analyses the use of a similar poverty narrative, but this time by developed countries justifying their actions in the name of the LDCs through the DDA negotiations. It is true that a successful delinking of any package for the LDCs from the Doha outcome in its entirety has protected the world's poorest countries from at least some of the costs of delay and deadlock. Perhaps it was no coincidence that this limited success for the LDCs was strategically useful for the middle-income and rich countries too: they could, for example, claim that they were doing their bit for the cause of development, without making the wide-ranging and far-reaching concessions that the DDA expected of them. But, even here, developed countries kept their concessions limited and unenforceable. Interestingly, they justified this apparent stinginess by arguing that any concessions granted to the category of LDCs as a whole would be unfair to the few within this group with which the rich countries already had preferential trade arrangements. By claiming to act in the name of a subset of the poor, the rich countries thus managed to avoid making meaningful concessions even towards the small group of LDCs. This second case is an example of how the power of the powerless can and has been instrumentalized and used against the poor and the weak.

In the third case, I show how developed countries have effectively utilized the poverty narrative to act in the interests of the poor within their own jurisdictions. Worryingly, some of these anti-poverty initiatives take the form of a backlash against the original purpose of empowering some of the world's poorest people, and target the poor of the developing world. In this context, I focus specifically on President Trump's trade politics, from his declaration on Twitter that 'trade wars are good and easy to win' and his tirades against the WTO, to his actual imposition of tariffs on trading partners.

Trump's attacks on the multilateral trading system have certainly not helped its credibility or sustainability. But to blame Trump for all the miseries of multilateral trade today is to confuse the symptom with the cause. There is a significant portion of the American electorate that believes that the gains of globalization have passed them by. This group attributes the increasing

positions into account. But India is especially relevant here because of its long-standing and almost consistent use (even as a rising power) of the poverty narrative as a justification to refuse to make concessions, and hence the focus on it in this case-study.

inequality in their society, and the job losses and declining wages that people personally face, to the costs of international trade. Usually, the pernicious hardships that these groups endure have several causes, which range from technological change to inadequate national welfare mechanisms that can allow a better distribution of the gains of globalization. The Trump administration is not the first in recent times to be taking protectionist measures in the name of the poor in the United States. But the current US administration has indeed harnessed the prevalent discontent very effectively, and fanned it further by building a narrative that links domestic inequalities and poverty *within* the United States to global trade governance. And while few trading partners have escaped his ire, this narrative is particularly scathing on the supposed misuses of the system by the rising powers, especially China, and argues that prosperity elsewhere has come at the expense of impoverishment of America and Americans.

Finally, in terms of WTO decision-making too, the empowerment of the powerless has not proven to be an unmitigated good. More voices at the high table have increased the legitimacy of the decision-making process, but have also undermined its efficiency. Recurrent deadlocks have heightened polarization. The fact that this polarization has occurred in the context of a negotiating round dedicated to development has ended up pitting the developed and developing countries even more strongly against each other. The turn to regional agreements was an example of the reaction, which further undermined trust in the efficacy of the multilateral system. The Trump administration has gone one step further, and has turned away from regional to unilateral acts of declaring trade wars, and doing bilateral deals that bypass and further undermine multilateral rules. And while this crisis of trade multilateralism leaves no one better off, its consequences are the most adverse and severe for developing countries and LDCs.

There are several other relevant examples of the growing use and misuse of the poverty narrative. Another form of instrumentalization of powerlessness by the rich is in the area of 'ethical trade'. It is no coincidence that the fight for better labour and environmental standards in the global south is often fought by trade unions in the global north, which are not always disinterested parties in the debate. Trade, moreover, is not the only area where we are witnessing an overuse and misuse of poverty narratives, and thereby a backlash against the power of the genuinely poor and powerless. Europe has seen this most visibly in the immigration debate. Chancellor Merkel's 'Wir schaffen das' in 2015 in some ways represented the epitome of the power of the powerless: the poor and the weak of all ilk were to be welcomed into Germany, with no questions asked and no border controls. Subsequent years have seen a massive reaction against this policy. The growing popularity of extremist nationalist parties within Germany and beyond, as well as the movement to the Right by centrist parties, form a part of this reaction. Not only has Merkel's own political star waned, but so has the liberalism she espoused. The biggest losses of this declining liberalism sadly accrue to people most in need of escape from dire economic or political conditions, as well as to the highly qualified emigrants who could bring gains to the German and European economies. Similar power reversals seem to be happening in other key aspects of political life. Battle lines that seemed to have closed over some pretty basic issues, such as gender discrimination and sexual harassment, seem to be reopening again.

1.3.4 *Chapter 5: Conclusion*

From the Victorian Age, with its Dickensian schools where children were caned, its poor-houses where the indigent were treated as criminals, and its colonies where developing countries were treated as the 'white man's burden', we have thankfully come a remarkably long way. The evolution of the poverty narrative is important as an illustration of how a very debilitating form of weakness can be overcome. Its beauty lies in the fact that it offers greater agency to the weak and marginalized by cleverly harnessing and exploiting the very sources of their weakness and marginalization. The problem, however, is that overuse and misuse risk blunting this weapon, with considerable cost to all parties.

Chapter 5 is divided into two parts. In the first part, I offer a brief summary of the main findings. I further explore the scenarios that would likely follow the use, overuse, and misuse of the poverty narrative in international trade negotiations. Drawing on the case studies, the concluding chapter offers some generalizations on how winning narratives can be constructed. The cases also point to the risks of using this potent instrument. Successful narratives tend to work like asset bubbles:[44] as an increasingly large number and diversity of actors becomes aware of their uses, the temptation to overuse and misuse them also increases. The bursting of the bubble generates costs for the system as a whole. In the case of the poverty and powerlessness narratives, these costs will likely be the greatest for the most vulnerable members of society, many of whom stood to benefit the most from the narrative. This risk holds true for the

---

[44] I am grateful to Daniel Drezner for this analogy.

specific case of poverty narratives in trade negotiations. But it also applies to the range of other examples of powerlessness that this book deals with.

Overuse and misuse of narratives of powerlessness and poverty generate costs at a very human level, and risk creating a climate of distrust and litigiousness. We are already in a world where male teachers prefer to keep their office doors open when tutoring female students, and where adults think twice before they engage in normal conversations with legal minors. The increasing propensity to try anyone judged to be an 'offender' of any kind by social media, outside of legal courtrooms and sometimes even after due process has cleared individuals of any accusations, exacerbates the toxicity of our social environment. We risk creating a society where economic and political interaction becomes increasingly tense and increasingly constrained. For instance, the time is perhaps not far off when, rather than give opportunities to empowered minorities and women, employers may prefer to avoid employing them in the first place. Such developments would unfortunately only parallel moves that are already taking place in international politics: as developing countries have come to exercise greater voice and effective veto, multilateral processes have deadlocked and rich countries have turned to other forums and other means to reach their ends. The power of the powerless, while potentially acting as a valuable equalizer, also risks creating more polarized politics where the divisions between the self-identified powerless and the 'othering' of the powerful becoming even more entrenched. And while misusers and overusers may manage to cope in this polarized world, the genuinely poor and vulnerable will get caught in the crossfire.[45]

Is it possible to find solutions that could preserve the progress that narratives akin to the poverty and powerless narratives have helped achieve, and curtail their overuse and misuse? Given the widespread misuse of the power of the powerless, I argue that institutional reform can provide only a part of the answer. In the case of the unintended consequences of the overuse of the poverty narrative, one can come up with some good ideas for reforming decision-making in the WTO so that the organization is able to overcome the tyrannies of the powerless that consensus-based diplomacy can entail, while simultaneously preventing a return to past practices that had marginalized many developing countries. But in cases of deliberate misuse and in dealing with the backlash against the empowerment of the poor that is already underway, even the most innovative voting system will not suffice. Rather, a fundamental shift in the narrative itself will be necessary. Claims to

---

[45] I first developed this argument in Narlikar (2015).

powerlessness, poverty, and victimhood cannot be taken at face value. This, in turn, requires a rethinking of the presumptions of powerlessness and victimhood.

In the second part of Chapter 5, I offer some general guidelines on how policy-makers might be able to use narratives as a vital instrument of public policy and diplomacy, taking into account the risk that narratives are mutable and can be manipulated. And while there are no easy answers, a better understanding of the theory and practice of how narratives work, develop, and dissipate may help us avoid some of the worst pitfalls. This is the central purpose of this book, and it works hand in hand with the goal of reaching a better empirical understanding of possible pathways to empowerment of the weak and marginalized. But, additionally, I hope that this book will challenge readers and leaders of all political persuasions to rethink some basic assumptions on power and powerlessness. Intellectually, this takes us into theoretical and policy questions about narratives which serve as the key intermediary variable between power asymmetries and negotiated outcomes. And at a practical level, this should encourage at least some readers to have a further think on the products they consume, the social media channels they use, and the pro-poor policies they support.

BIBLIOGRAPHY

Acharya, Amitav. 2004. 'How norms spread: Norm localization and institutional change in Asian regionalism.' *International Organization.* 58: 2. Pp. 239–275.

Akerlof, George. 2007. 'The missing motivation in macroeconomics.' *American Economic Review.* 97: 1. Pp. 5–36.

Akerlof, George and Robert Shiller. 2009. *Animal Spirits: How Human Psychology Drives the Economy, and Why it Matters for Global Capitalism.* Princeton, NJ: Princeton University Press.

Allison, Graham. 1971. *The Essence of Decision: Explaining the Cuban Missile Crisis.* Boston: Little, Brown.

Benwell, Richard. 2011. 'Canaries in the coalmines: Small states as climate change champions.' *The Round Table.* 100: 413. Pp. 199–211.

Bhagwati, Jagdish. 2004. *In Defence of Globalization.* Oxford: Oxford University Press.

Bruner, Jerome. 1998. 'What is a narrative fact?' *The Annals of the American Academy of Political and Social Science.* 560. Pp. 17–27.

Cohen, Raymond. 1991. *Negotiating across Cultures: International Communication in an Interdependent World.* Washington, D.C.: United States Institute of Peace.

Collier, Paul. 2016. 'The cultural foundations of economic failure: A conceptual toolkit.' *Journal of Economic Behavior and Organization.* 126: B. Pp. 5–24.

Cooper, Andrew. 2009. *Celebrity Diplomacy.* London: Routledge.

Drezner, Daniel W. 2017. *The Ideas Industry: How Pessimists, Partisans, and Plutocrats are Transforming the Marketplace of Ideas.* Oxford: Oxford University Press.

Finnemore, Martha. 1996. *National Interests in International Society*. Ithaca: Cornell University Press.

Fisher, Walter R. 1984. 'Narration as a human communication paradigm: The case of public moral argument.' *Communication Monographs*. 58: 1. Pp. 1–22.

Goldstein, Judith and Robert Keohane. 1993, *Ideas and Foreign Policy: Beliefs, Institutions and Political Change*. Ithaca: Cornell University Press.

Howe, Leo. 1998. 'Scrounger, worker, beggarman, cheat: The dynamics of unemployment and the politics of resistance in Belfast.' *The Journal of the Royal Anthropological Institute*. 4: 3. Pp. 531–550.

Janis, Irving L. 1972. *Victims of Groupthink; a Psychological Study of Foreign-Policy Decisions and Fiascoes*. Boston: Houghton, Mifflin.

Kahneman, Daniel and Tversky, Amos. 1979. 'Prospect theory: An analysis of decision under risk.' *Econometrica*. 47 (2). Pp. 263–279.

Katzenstein, Peter. 1996. *The Culture of National Security: Norms and Identity in World Politics*. New York: Columbia University Press.

Keck, Margaret and Kathryn Sikkink. 1998. *Activists Beyond Borders: Advocacy Networks in International Politics*. Ithaca: Cornell University Press.

Keohane, Robert O. 1971. 'The big influence of small allies.' *Foreign Policy*, 2. Pp. 161–182.

Klotz, Audie. 1995. *Norms in International Relations: The Struggle against Apartheid*. Ithaca: Cornell University Press.

Macintyre, Alasdair. 1981. *After Virtue: A Study in Moral Theory*. Notre Dame: Notre Dame Press.

Narlikar, Amrita. 2003. *International Trade and Developing Countries: Bargaining Coalitions in the GATT and WTO*. London: Routledge.

2007. 'All that glitters is not gold: India's rise to power.' *Third World Quarterly*. 28: 5. Pp. 983–996.

2015. 'The power paradox.' *Current History*. 114. Pp. 29–33.

2017. 'India's role in global governance: A modification?' *International Affairs*. 93: 1. Pp. 93–111.

Odell, John. 2010. 'Negotiating from weakness in international ngotiations.' *Journal of World Trade*. 44: 3. Pp. 545–566.

Odell, John and Susan Sell. 2006. 'Reframing the issue: The WTO coalition on intellectual property and public health, 2001.' In John Odell (ed.). *Negotiating Trade: Developing Countries in the WTO and NAFTA*. Cambridge: Cambridge University Press.

Olson, Mancur. 1965. *The Logic of Collective Action: Public Goods and the Theory of Goods*. Cambridge, MA: Harvard University Press.

Schelling, Thomas C. 1957. 'Bargaining from strength and weakness.' *Challenge*. 5: 4. Pp. 35–39.

Scott, James. 1985. *Weapons of the Weak: Everyday Forms of Peasant Resistance*. New Haven: Yale University Press.

Shiller, Robert. 2017. 'Narrative economics.' *American Economic Review*. 107: 4. Pp. 967–1004.

Simon, Herbert. 1955. 'A behavioural model of rational choice.' *Quarterly Journal of Economics*. 69:1. Pp. 99–118.

1972. 'Theories of bounded rationality.' In C. B. McGuire and Roy Radner (eds.). *Decision and Organization: A Volume in Order of Jacob Marschak.* Amsterdam: North-Holland Publication Co.

Tsebelis, George. 1995. 'Decision making in political systems: Veto players in presidentialism, parliamentarism, multicameralism and multipartyism.' *British Journal of Political Science.* 25: 3. Pp. 289–325.

Tversky, Amos and Daniel Kahneman. 1981. 'The framing of decisions and the psychology of choice.' *Science.* 211: 4481. Pp. 453–459.

UN General Assembly. 1970. Resolution adopted by the General Assembly 2626 (XXV), International Development Strategy for the Second United Nations Development Decade. 25th Session, Agenda Item 42, 24 October 1970. A/RES/25/2626. Accessed at www.un-documents.net/a25r2626.htm

Wendt, Alexander. 1992. 'Anarchy is what states make of it: The social construction of power politics.' *International Organization.* 46: 2. Pp. 391–425.

Zartman, I. William. 1985. 'Negotiating from asymmetry: The North-South stalemate.' *Negotiation Journal.* 1. Pp. 121–138.

1997. 'The structuralist dilemma in negotiation.' *Research on Negotiations in Organizations.* 6. Pp. 227–245.

Zürn, Michael. 2018. *A Theory of Global Governance.* Oxford: Oxford University Press.

2

The Disempowered Many
When the Weak Suffered What They Must

The creation of the post-war economic system was driven by many worthy intentions. Henry Morgenthau, US Secretary of the Treasury, had laid out an ambitious agenda as he took up the presidency of the Bretton Woods Conference:

> We are to concern ourselves here with essential steps in the creation of a dynamic world economy in which the people of every nation will be able to realize their potentialities in peace; will be able, through their industry, their inventiveness, their thrift, to raise their own standards of living and enjoy, increasingly, the fruits of material progress on an earth infinitely blessed with natural riches.[1]

The aim of the conference was to usher in an era of prosperity and peace. Morgenthau highlighted the indivisibility of both these goals. This, quite directly, led him to address the issue of poverty:

> Poverty, wherever it exists, is menacing to us all and undermines the well-being of each of us. It can no more be localized than war, but spreads and saps the economic strength of all the more-favoured areas of earth. We know now that the thread of economic life in every nation is inseparably woven into a fabric of world economy. Let any thread become frayed and the entire fabric is weakened. No nation, however great and strong, can remain, immune.

The lessons of the inter-war years and their follow-on effects were clear to Morgenthau, even as countries had indulged in beggar-thy-neighbour policies of competitive tariff escalation and currency depreciation. 'Economic aggression', he argued, 'can have no other offspring than war. It is as dangerous as it is futile'.[2]

---

[1] Morgenthau (1944).
[2] Ibid.

Here was a strong and convincing narrative, which emphasized a causal link between economic deprivation and war.[3] If countries were to avoid a recurrence of the disastrous events that had dominated the first half of the twentieth century, issues of poverty and powerlessness had to be seriously addressed. To some extent, the emerging system created provisions to enable countries to address internal problems of poverty, at least for the sake of domestic stability. But the issue of global poverty, and especially the poverty and powerlessness of developing countries, did not find much direct redress in the post-war system. This chapter focuses on the system of multilateral trade as it evolved, and the rather limited extent to which developing countries were able to shape it in their favour. Importantly, this was not for want of trying. Amidst the devastation caused by two world wars, the developed world was showing some willingness to learn. And riding the wave of decolonization themselves, developing countries seized the potential opportunity that was emerging, and exercised their voice with considerable flair. But as I show below, these exertions generated lacklustre results.

In Section 2.1, I analyse the ambitious negotiation process that was launched to construct a post-war multilateral trade order. From the perspective of developing countries, this was a promising effort, but ultimately failed in its purpose to create the ITO. In Section 2.2, I explore the continuous attempts by developing countries to integrate issues of development – obviously an area of the highest priority to them – into the GATT. In the counterfactual universe of the ITO, development would have been integral to the multilateral trading system; in the reality of the GATT, the successes that developing countries achieved on this were few, tightly circumscribed, and hard won. I investigate the Uruguay Round negotiations in Section 2.3, where developing countries found themselves even more disempowered. In Section 2.4, I trace the decision-making processes of the GATT. Although these processes suggested equal voice and representation for developed and developing countries via a one-member-one-vote system, in practice they tilted the balance towards the already powerful. Through much of the period that

[3] This causation was clearly outlined in Morgenthau's (1944) speech: 'All of us have seen the great economic tragedy of our time. We saw the world-wide depression of the 1930's. We saw currency disorders develop and spread from land to land, destroying the basis for international trade and international investment and even international faith. In their wake, we saw unemployment and wretchedness – idle tools, wasted wealth. We saw their victims fall prey, in places, to demagogues and dictators. We saw bewilderment and bitterness become the breeders of fascism and, finally, of war'. Nor was Morgenthau alone in making the causal link; indeed John Maynard Keynes had argued this with prophetic eloquence in 1919 in his *Economic Consequences of the Peace.*

I study in this chapter, the dominant narrative on poverty among nations was one that saw poverty primarily as a phenomenon of inefficient domestic policies, or worse. Developing countries asserted and re-asserted the adverse effects of colonialism that their economies still bore, often largely to deaf ears. The best route to poverty reduction and empowerment of developing countries, as per the dominant narrative, was trade liberalization and structural reform. We saw this narrative peak towards the end of the Uruguay Round negotiations, in parallel with the emerging heyday of the Washington Consensus.[4] Section 2.5 explores the extent to which the powerlessness of the small and poor extended to other areas of international negotiation as well as other aspects of political and social life.

2.1 FAIRY GODMOTHERS, DEVELOPING COUNTRIES, AND THE ITO NEGOTIATIONS

Developing countries had participated actively in the ITO negotiations, and there was good reason for them to feel some ownership of the process. True, the idea of a permanent body that would deal with trade matters had origins in the developed world, with the discussions in the 1940s going back most immediately to James Meade's 'Proposal for a Commercial Union' in 1942.[5] Anglo-American discussions had followed,[6] and the United States, under the chairmanship of William Clayton, Assistant Secretary of State, had then prepared 'Proposals for Expansion of World Trade and Employment'.[7] The draft had served as the starting point for the discussions of Preparatory Conference on Trade and Employment. This bilateral process however was soon expanded. In contrast to the negotiations for the establishment of the World Bank and the International Monetary Fund, which had taken place primarily

---

[4] It is worth noting that although this was the dominant narrative in the GATT and the Bretton Woods institutions, other international policy spaces offered several counter-narratives. The UN Conference on Trade and Development was a prime example of an arena where an alternative narrative prevailed (see Toye 2014). These alternative narratives leaked into GATT debates too, for instance via the demands for exceptionalism by the Informal Group of Developing Countries (Narlikar 2003), but did not enter the mainstream here. This flourishing of a pluralism of narratives across different international institutions may have been intellectually interesting. But, for practical purposes, it did not make a big difference to developing countries that were trying to secure better bargains for themselves and their people, and the arena for negotiation was the GATT.

[5] Meade (1942).
[6] Canadian External Relations Documents (1948b).
[7] US State Department (1945).

between 'one and a half countries',[8] that is the United States and the United Kingdom, and then presented for approval to the forty-four countries meeting at the Bretton Woods Conference in 1944, the process for negotiating the third pillar of the international economic system – trade – was broadened soon after the US–UK consultations. Seventeen parties (eighteen countries) were involved in preparing the document that served as the basis for the discussions in Havana, and they met in London, New York, and Geneva to develop the proposals further.[9] Of the fifty-eight countries eligible to vote in the Havana Conference, forty-one were developing countries.[10] The active participation of the global South in both the preparatory process and the final act of signing meant that, if agreement were to be reached in Havana, the global north would have to do a lot more to accommodate the global South (in contrast to the Bretton Woods negotiations).

In this section, I highlight the several provisions in the Havana Charter that were shaped by developing countries and incorporated their interests. I then investigate how developing countries were able to exercise this influence. I argue that this was partly a result of their persistence and strategy, but perhaps even more important were external structural conditions, especially the serious rifts between the United States and the United Kingdom that only deepened as the negotiations progressed. In the last part of this section, I summarize the causes of the stillbirth of the ITO. This is the subject of a

---

[8] Daunton (2010) points out that, due to its weakened financial position, the United Kingdom 'largely accepted the United States plan of Harry Dexter White rather than the proposals of John Maynard Keynes' (p. 52). Note that Eric Helleiner (2014, 2015) has challenged the received wisdom on this issue, and shed fascinating new light on the history of participation and activism by developing countries also in the Bretton Woods negotiations. But as far as the outcome of this rich process is concerned, Helleiner's analysis is similar to that of other scholars. He argues, 'These development aspirations embodied in the Bretton Woods agreements have been overlooked by much scholarship for a simple reason – they were largely abandoned by US policymakers after Roosevelt's death in April 1945. This is not the place to analyse this dramatic shift in US foreign policy, but its impact was to make the "actually-existing" Bretton Woods system much less supportive of state-led development strategies than had initially been intended. That support was eroded further when the Bretton Woods institutions became leading advocates of neo-liberal policy advice later in the post-war period'. See Helleiner (2015), p. 39.

[9] These participants were Australia, Belgium-Luxembourg Economic Union, Brazil, Canada, Chile, China, Cuba, Czechoslovakia, France, India, Lebanon, Netherlands, New Zealand, Norway, Union of South Africa, United Kingdom, and United States. Note that this group, albeit far from universal, was more inclusive than the bilateral Anglo-American club, and brought together a good mix of countries at different levels of development and from different regions.

[10] Breda dos Santos (2016).

rich debate among historians. I sift through this debate to analyse what the
final outcome meant for developing countries. Here was a fortuitous mix of
circumstances that could have served as a remarkable opportunity for developing countries. But with the failure of the ITO, this early opportunity failed to
materialize, setting the stage for the next few decades in which the global
south would be largely on the defensive.

2.1.1 *The Pro-poor Sensitivity of the Havana Charter*

There are contrasting interpretations by historians on how pro-poor/pro-South
the Havana Charter was.[11] Norma Breda dos Santos, for example, focuses on
the role of the Latin American countries in the ITO negotiations, which
constituted almost one-third of the potential membership and often acted
together as a coalition.[12] She argues that power asymmetries undermined
the ability of this group to negotiate effectively, and the final outcome was
unfavourable to them. Richard Toye, however, argues that, had the ITO not
been stillborn, it would have produced a 'more inclusive, productive, orderly
and just world economy than that which emerged'.[13] The Havana Charter
offered developing countries some important wins, which were especially
important in light of their weak bargaining position. The Canadian delegate
at the Havana conference, reporting back to his government at the time,
described the Charter on balance as

> a bold compromise, flexible enough to take care of varying needs of different
> economic philosophies and of different stages of economic development, yet
> sufficiently true to the principles of multilateral trade to give rise to the hope
> that the Organization, when it is set up, will prove to be one of the most

---

[11] To some extent, the differences in these interpretations, and the historical accounts from
different negotiators they rely on, may be attributed to a Rashomon effect. Plus it is always
somewhat problematic to judge what counts as a 'success' or a 'failure' in a negotiation, given
that it is difficult to know what any negotiating party's 'true' preferences are. Even with revealed
preferences, depending on the context, negotiators sometimes deliberately come up with
unrealistically high opening demands as a bargaining strategy. Also, different sides speak to
different audiences as they try to legitimize their actions. For instance, negotiators may choose
to oversell the concessions that they themselves have made to argue that the final deal is fair to
all parties. Or politicians may choose to underplay the concessions they made when speaking to
domestic audiences. For the purposes of this book, I adopt the (imperfect) solution of
comparing the final outcome against the stated opening demands of the negotiation party, and
also the extent to which different parties made concessions.
[12] Breda dos Santos (2016).
[13] Toye (2003), p. 283.

successful and most enduring of all the intergovernmental organizations established during the last few years.[14]

Compromise and concessions were made on all sides to produce the charter. Breda dos Santos is right to point to the concessions that the Latin American group ended up having to make towards this. Toye also recognizes the pressures that developing countries more generally encountered, or as they were known at the time, the 'underdeveloped countries':

> The United States had, with increasing success, used divide-and-rule tactics against the developing countries, securing their opposition to each other's more extreme amendments. As Wilcox noted, 'the irony of this whole situation is that the underdeveloped countries, which at first were expected to have an articulate and effective bloc, have no effective bloc because their interests are too divergent to keep them together even on development matters' ... Therefore, at this time, in contrast to later decades, they were bought off relatively cheaply.[15]

That said, and especially in contrast to the Bretton Woods negotiations, developing countries managed to exercise more influence than their small economic size and limited technical capacities would normally have allowed for.[16] They couched their demands by drawing attention to the challenges they faced due to conditions of structural weakness, and insisted on the right to use protectionism in order to further their own development. The representative of El Salvador summarized the position of the 'underdeveloped' countries as being guided by the principle of 'unequal treatment for unequally developed countries'.[17] The confidential report of the Canadian delegate back to his government provides us with an insight into the difficulty that the persistence of developing countries (both as a group and in sub-groups) caused for their counterparts from developed countries. Writing after the conference in Havana, his report stated:

> These three months proved that the Conference was held not only in the wrong place but also at the wrong time. The Latin-American countries had become disturbed over the implications for them of the Marshall Plan. They

---

[14] Canadian External Relations Document (1948b), paragraph 14. Naturally, one must take primary sources too with a pinch of salt. For example, delegates to conferences are likely to have an incentive to present their endeavours as successes to their governments.

[15] Toye (2003), p. 298.

[16] On the limitations and challenges facing developing countries, particularly the Latin American group, see Breda dos Santos (2016).

[17] UN Conference on Trade and Employment (1947), p. 6.

felt the fairy godmother of the North was deserting them in favour of Europe. Their acquaintance with socialist ideas had converted them to a form of international socialism in which the richer countries were under an obligation to the poorer countries to promote the economic development of these countries and to raise their standard of living up to that of the richer countries. Some of them even went so far as to deny the right of the richer countries to assist in the reconstruction of the European countries because these countries had once enjoyed prosperity at the expense of the under-developed countries.[18]

The Latin American grouping was not the only one making demands to promote development in poor countries. Summary minutes of a meeting, which formed a part of the preparatory conference, report India's stated position as follows:

> … the obligation of countries with undeveloped economies to develop their resources could only be fulfilled by instruments such as developmental tariffs and quantitative controls, and by adequate safeguards. India was wedded to economic planning as opposed to free enterprise … . The creation of temporary unemployment was unavoidable in economic progress, though the ultimate result was greater employment. A developing country was thus likely to cause immediate unemployment in other countries in the industries it was developing. Nevertheless, if the industries or services for development were properly selected, no real unemployment should result. Developed countries should be obliged to make reasonable adjustments in their own industries.[19]

The developing world not only created a nuisance value for the North; rather, the Havana Charter came to reflect several of their priorities. Largely in keeping with their demands, the Charter came to incorporate an entire chapter – Chapter II – on employment.[20] On the particularly contested issue

---

[18] Canadian External Relations Document (1948b), paragraph 23.

[19] UN Economic and Social Council (1946), p. 4.

[20] Australia had led the charge on this issue (both for itself, and also speaking on behalf of developing countries in the early part of the negotiations), and its demands went further than Britain's. Daunton (2010) summarizes these as: 'If "dependent countries" – primary producers such as Australia – were required to abandon economic protectionism, they needed assurance that other countries fulfilled their "basic obligation" to maintain effective demand. Failure to do so should permit the complainant to take action, under the authority of the ITO to prevent unilateralism, against the culprit in order to prevent the spread of depression' (p. 67). For the different trade-offs between free trade and other competing goals, see Daunton (2012). Also see Ruggie (1982) on how the post-war negotiators, particularly from the United States and Britain, envisaged the relationship between domestic stability and international cooperation via 'the compromise of embedded liberalism: unlike the economic nationalism of the thirties, it would

of the use of Quantitative Restrictions, on which a showdown had been likely, developing countries again largely got their way in Article 13.[21] In fact, this article was located within Chapter III, which was explicitly dedicated to the issue of 'Economic Development and Reconstruction' – admittedly issues that were critical to Britain and Europe in the aftermath of the war, but were also important for the developing world. In terms of decision-making processes, developing countries found themselves considerably better off in comparison to the Bretton Woods institutions. Article 79 of the Havana Charter provided for a one-member-one-vote system with majority voting. As a result of some hard bargaining on the part of the developing world, and especially the Latin American group, plus India and China, the global North also had to make some compromises on the 'vexed question' of the Executive Board. True, having an Executive Board per se diminished the power of large numbers that the global South could have enjoyed. But the ITO negotiators agreed to open up the membership of this Executive Board to ensure not only a seat for countries of 'chief economic importance' but also broader geographical representation as well as an additional criterion that different levels of economic development would be represented.[22] Brazil joined India and China 'in stressing that population should be a determining factor nearly equal in importance to the share of a country in international trade'. Together, they were able to have this criterion also included in the Havana Charter.[23] In terms of the mandate of the ITO (as well as the special considerations it allowed to developing countries) and also decision-making processes, and in spite of serious power asymmetries, the global South seemed to have sealed quite a respectable deal for itself in Havana.

2.1.2 *How the Developing Countries Managed to Come So Far*

Three sets of explanations help us better understand why the cause of developing countries found a good reception in the ITO negotiations: power political, institutional, and agency-driven.

Among the power political considerations that played an important role in framing the ITO negotiations, two were key: the Cold War, and a rift between

---

be multilateral in character; unlike the liberalism of the gold standard and free trade, its multilateralism would be predicated upon domestic interventionism' (p. 36).

[21] E.g., Article 13(7) provided extensive exemptions for countries wishing to establish measures towards economic development or reconstruction, see UN Conference on Trade and Employment (1948). Also see Toye (2003, 2012).

[22] UN Conference on Trade and Employment (1948), Article 78 and Annex L.

[23] UN Conference on Trade and Employment (1948), Annex L, paragraph 2 (b).

the Americans and the British. The first influence played out in important and contradictory ways. At least until the Havana Charter negotiations were completed, the Cold War increased the willingness of the United States to accept deviations from its free trade principles. For example, Thomas Zeiler has argued that the United States was willing to make concessions because it was concerned that 'the Soviets would make political capital out of a break-down in Cuba'.[24] Additionally, and in contrast to the case of the Bretton Woods negotiations, there were greater divisions between the United Kingdom and the United States on trade issues. Martin Daunton writes that the British had been in a weaker position in the Bretton Woods negotiations and therefore acquiesced to American demands more readily; they now decided to reopen some of the questions of 1944 involving debtor countries via the trade route.[25] Towards this, the British had hoped to use developing countries to limit the power of the Americans, and to enhance their own influence. In fact, '... rather than taming the American elephant, the British found they had unleashed many other animals in the zoo'.[26] The Americans preferred to make concessions to developing countries, and only 'some tactical comprom-ises' to bring the British on board. Richard Toye has traced the history of how the British found themselves isolated in the endgame: 'The value of what Britain had received was debatable, and, undoubtedly left it with little cred-ibility in Havana'.[27] Recognizing its isolation, Britain ultimately gave in, albeit only begrudgingly.[28] For our purposes, Cold War considerations that had

---

[24] Zeiler (1999), p. 138. Note that there is a debate among historians on the extent to which the Cold War contributed to the willingness of the United States to make concessions and secure a deal in Havana. Richard Toye (2003), in contrast to Zeiler, offers the following explanation: '... the outcome of the conference was substantially a product of the US decision to extend its concept of multilateralism so as to allow a wide range of countries to help to design the new organization, rather than hoping that they would accede, passively, to a US blueprint. As decolonization added to the numbers of independent countries available to take part in the negotiations, and as – partly in consequence – the concept of economic underdevelopment gained a new importance in international affairs, there was increased pressure for the ITO to be designed with the needs of poor countries in mind. This was apparent even before the outbreak in earnest of the cold war in early 1947. Furthermore, granting special treatment to underdeveloped countries inevitably involved sacrificing some of the interests of developed countries' (p. 284). But the debate is mainly about the weightage to attach to the Cold war as an explanation for US actions; Toye also recognizes that the Cold War context mattered.

[25] Daunton (2010).

[26] Daunton (2010), p. 66.

[27] Toye (2003), p. 300.

[28] 'If we were to stand out at this stage, we should do so practically alone. The Americans would undoubtedly be able to cast the odium of breakdown on us and thereby gain credit with all the under-developed countries, including nearly all the Latin Americans and probably India and Ceylon as well' (British Memorandum 1948).

heightened American willingness to make concessions, as well as the divisions between the United States and Britain, together produced an important impact on the ITO negotiation process: they created valuable negotiating space for developing countries.

Add to these factors the peculiarities of the institutional setting, and developing countries found themselves equipped to punch significantly above their weight. Institutionally, unlike the Bretton Woods negotiations, the ITO negotiations came to include developing countries relatively early on in the process. At the conference itself the British had pushed for the idea that everyone invited to Havana should be able to show their legislatures and publics that they had exercised a voice. The Americans then decided to go one step further. They abandoned the idea of weighted voting, and argued in favour of one-member-one-vote to secure greater support for the ITO.[29] The Canadian delegate also reports that although the big players had made this compromise in the spirit of 'clearing the air and improving the atmosphere' at the conference, in fact, this move 'had the reverse effect. It made the majority more conscious of their numerical strength and encouraged them to hope for more concessions'.[30] That the conference for the signing of the Final Act took place at Havana also worked to the advantage of developing countries, especially the Latin American Group. The Canadian delegate, for example, reported, 'The fact that the Conference was being held in a Latin-American country gave them a great advantage. They were able to unite on the issue of the recognition of Spanish as one of the working languages of the Conference. They made full use of their numerical advantage'.[31]

Finally, to develop the point highlighted in the last quote, developing countries exploited this negotiating space and institutional setting with skill and persistence. They made their claims to special treatment on multiple

---

[29] Daunton (2010).

[30] Canadian External Relations Document (1948b), paragraph 33.

[31] Canadian External Relations Document (1948b), paragraph 22. As alluded to earlier, this account stands in contrast to the analysis provided by Norma Breda dos Santos (2016). Breda dos Santos argues that the Latin American delegations found themselves considerably disadvantaged due to the fact that most of them had not been privy to the preparatory conferences prior to Havana, their small delegation size, lack of technical knowledge, and the fact that the official working language was English. These difficulties were probably very real. But the reactions of the developed countries (e.g., of the British and Canadian reports at the time) reveal the considerable disruption that the Southern players managed to nevertheless cause them, and also successfully extract concessions in their own favour. Other historical accounts, for instance by Toye (2003) and Daunton (2010), reinforce the impression that, at least on balance, developing countries did not come out too badly from the Havana conference.

grounds, drawing on their unique experiences and priorities.[32] Even as they did so, they worked in blocs and coalitions. For example, the Latin American countries worked together as a 'caucus' in the Havana conference.[33] Other developing countries further backed their demands to use exceptional measures for economic development.[34] They were also seen as being allied together by their negotiating counterparts, and indeed even against the 'older established world traders'.[35] Banding together, they generated results, and they did this by appealing to high principle. For example, in a communique to his heads of state abroad, the Canadian State Secretary explained how agreement was finally reached on the one-member-one-vote system as a result of the collective action of developing countries:

> The principle on which voting on the Organization should be based had not been decided at Geneva, though all the members of major economic importance favoured the system of weighted voting, on the grounds that the International Trade Organization was an organization similar to the I.L.O., in which those members called upon to play an important role should have a preponderant voice. At Havana, however, *the pressure from the very great number of smaller countries was too strong* to permit the adoption of any system other than that of one state ore vote. Much was made of the claim that this was the only 'democratic' method and the only one which fully respected the sovereignty of each member.[36]

Through collective action and forceful argumentation, developing countries were able to secure a Havana Charter that took their concerns seriously, sometimes even at the expense of British interests and American ideals. Had the ITO actually emerged from the Havana Charter, the history of the post-war economic system might have looked quite different.[37] But then, the reality of American domestic politics and Cold War priorities intervened.

2.1.3 *Why the ITO Remained a Might-Have-Been*

In April 1949 President Truman sent the Charter to the Hill to secure approval of US participation. Given, however, that the US Congress was already preoccupied with foreign policy measures to deal with the Cold War, the

---

[32] E.g., Daunton (2010) for an overview of the positions adopted by developing countries.
[33] E.g., Breda dos Santos (2016).
[34] Canadian External Relations Document (1948b).
[35] British Memorandum (1948).
[36] Canadian External Relations Document (1948a), paragraph 11, emphasis added.
[37] For some interesting counterfactuals, see Toye (2003, 2012).

administration agreed with Congressional leaders to a further postponement. In April and May 1950 the House Committee on Foreign Affairs held hearings on the joint resolution, but the issue was not brought to the floor of the House. In December 1950, the President decided to withdraw the Charter from Congress. In 1951, Secretary Acheson confirmed that the Charter would not be resubmitted to the Congress.[38] Without the United States as a signatory, the ITO had little chance of surviving. Two reasons were especially important as to why the ITO died its quiet and unmarked death: the intensification of the Cold War and US domestic politics.

The Cold War context mattered, and its effect was different from the early phase of the negotiations. Initially, as highlighted in Section 2.1.2, it had encouraged the United States to act in a conciliatory way. This, in turn, had worked to the advantage of the developing world. Subsequently, though, as the Cold War intensified, the priorities of US negotiators changed to more immediate foreign policy concerns. In the words of William Diebold, 'By the end of 1950, when the ITO was dropped ... Americans, and their United Nations allies, were fighting in Korea. General Eisenhower was getting ready to take command of a new allied headquarters in Europe ... The aspirations of 1945 seemed more remote than ever. The Charter was adrift in a world for which it was never made'.[39] But even if the imperatives of the Cold War had not intervened to shift American priorities, it is doubtful whether the Charter could have passed the controversies it got embroiled in domestically.

William Clayton, in the foreword to Clair Wilcox's book, had written that the Charter would come up for approval in Congress in 1949. Until this happened, he hoped that the American people 'will study it, criticize it, analyse it, and finally decide to give it support'.[40] A diversity of interests did indeed scrutinize it and coalesced around two clusters, both of which vigorously opposed the creation of the ITO. In the words of William Diebold, 'the ITO was whipsawed between the protectionists and the perfectionists'.[41] The 'protectionists' comprised protected industries that were concerned about the impact of competing cheaper products, but they also took issue with 'the more broadly conceived disadvantages of the ITO – its one-sidedness, its alleged support for governmental control and planning, the freedom of most countries to use escape clauses'.[42] These, in fact, were also arguments used by the

---

[38] Diebold (1952).
[39] Diebold (1952), p. 6.
[40] Clayton (1949), p. xi.
[41] Diebold (1952), p. 24.
[42] Diebold (1952), p. 25.

'perfectionists' – those who believed that the Havana Charter had ended up making too many compromises. These concessions had been necessary to secure support internationally, but turned out to be unpalatable domestically, and ultimately fatal in a two-level game.

It is important to bear in mind that many of the compromises and concessions, which the 'perfectionists' objected to, had been made by the United States to secure the support of the 'Third World'.[43] Developing countries had managed to find the necessary negotiating space facilitated by the Cold War and Anglo-American differences, and exploited it with considerable agency. But the gains proved to be short-lived, not only because of opposition from business interests within the United States, but also a parallel lack of enthusiasm from the intellectual community. 'Professional economists and academic people concerned with foreign affairs for the most part favoured the ITO', wrote William Diebold, 'but usually with explicit recognition of its limitations principally because the other possible alternatives were so unattractive. This somewhat reserved attitude, stemming from the Charter's mix of high principle with detailed compromises that were distasteful, even if necessary, checked the growth of enthusiastic activity among independent liberals'.[44] The fact that the compromises leading up to the Havana Charter involved issues of economic development was not a coincidence. The absence of a widely-accepted narrative on poverty and development at the time, or indeed even an epistemic consensus,[45] rendered these exceptions, loopholes, and special provisions 'distasteful'.

With the failure of the ITO, the interim General Agreement on Tariffs and Trade (GATT) emerged as the *de facto* fallback. The GATT had been signed by twenty-three countries in 1947,[46] and had come into effect on 1 January 1948. Conceived as a provisional agreement to facilitate tariff reductions, the

---

[43] Toye (2003).

[44] Diebold (1952), p. 10.

[45] Intellectual opinion on this was divided. Besides the liberal view that Diebold (1952) refers to in the context of the United States, the United Kingdom argued for higher level of economic intervention under the influence of Keynsian ideas (Daunton 2010; Ruggie 1982), while the Latin American countries had, since the 1930s, been emphasizing the importance of central governments in promoting industrialization and escaping underdevelopment (Breda dos Santos 2016). Others, such as India, also offered variants of ideas that also favoured a greater role for state-led planning. For a rich account of the intellectual debates at the time, see Toye and Toye (2004).

[46] The original contracting parties to the GATT were: Australia, Belgium, Brazil, Burma, Canada, Ceylon, Chile, China, Cuba, Czechoslovakia, France, India, Lebanon, Luxemburg, Netherlands, New Zealand, Norway, Pakistan, Southern Rhodesia, Syria, South Africa, United Kingdom, and United States.

GATT was supposed to provide a necessary and minimum framework for tariff reductions until the ITO had been created. This weak 'interim' agreement provided the basis for the workings of the multilateral trading system for almost fifty years, and for this the GATT deserves much credit.[47] But from the perspective of developing countries, much of their activism during the preparatory conferences and at the Havana Conference had come to very little.

The GATT comprised mainly the commercial policy chapter of the Havana Charter. Its focus was considerably narrower than the ITO's would have been. Its dispute settlement system was weak (respondents could block panel decisions), and it was not a formal organization: this deprived developing countries of some valuable institutional safeguards that could have mitigated potential abuses of power on the part of the rich. A significant loss to developing countries was that it lacked an economic development chapter. Insofar as the ITO would have incorporated some of their concerns – on the substance of the agreements as well as the mechanisms of participation – its failure was a serious blow to developing countries. They would end up spending the next few decades trying – often with only limited success – to reclaim this lost ground. The ultimate failure of the ITO, and the emergence of the GATT as its substitute – and all this in spite of the promise of the Havana Charter and the constant activism of developing countries that had contributed to the making of this promise – confirmed that bargaining from a position of weakness was incredibly debilitating.

2.2 THE STRUGGLE TO BRING DEVELOPMENT ISSUES INTO THE GATT

Developing countries faced considerable institutional odds in the GATT (more on this in Section 2.4). Nevertheless, they persisted through the decades to enhance the GATT's development-friendliness. In this section, I focus on the efforts of poor countries to mainstream their development concerns into the GATT via their calls for Special and Differential Treatment (S&D) in various forms.[48]

John Whalley defines S&D treatment as follows:

> The term S&D treatment refers to various rights and privileges given to developing country Contracting Parties to the GATT, not extended to

---

[47] Irwin (1995).
[48] This acronym changes to SDT in the Doha Round. Both S&D and SDT, however, represent the same genre of demands from developing countries.

developed countries. These reflect a long history of calls by developing countries for special treatment in global trade ... The term 'S&D' contains both an access component and a right-to-protect component.[49]

I provide a brief overview of the changes that developing countries were able to bring about in the system under the rubric of S&D, and what they actually added up to.[50] I further investigate the strategies that developing countries used towards making these gains, which also partly explain why their successes remained relatively modest.

2.2.1 *Landmark Achievements*

In the negotiations leading up to the Havana Charter, developing countries had contributed over 807 amendments on issues ranging from commodity price controls and quantitative restrictions for balance of payments, to longer deadlines for commitments and other exceptions.[51] When the commercial policy chapter of the Charter became the *de facto* basis for the post-war trading system, developing countries tried hard to re-orient the GATT towards development as they had envisaged it. They had three significant achievements to their credit: Article 18, Part IV, and the Enabling Clause.

The first change in the GATT was via Article 18, which was titled 'Governmental Assistance to Economic Development'.[52] The article was redrafted in 1955. The Report of the Review Working Party on Quantitative Restrictions took note of the general orientation of Article XVIII as follows:

The general concept of the new Article is that economic development is consistent with the objectives of the General Agreement and that the raising of the general standard of living of the underdeveloped countries which

[49] Whalley (1990), p. 1319.
[50] Note that in this exercise, I do not debate the merits of the demands of developing countries. Multilateral and regional schemes of preferential treatment for developing countries have proven to be rather controversial in terms of both concept and implementation, with several economists pointing to their deleterious effects on countries that employ them (e.g., Johnson 1967; Özden and Reinhardt 2005; Panagariya 2002; Whalley 1990). As Richard Toye puts it rather pithily though, '... the fact that countries may not always make best use of the freedom to do intelligent things is no reason for not granting it' (Toye 2003, p. 305). I would go a step further to argue a libertarian case that even if countries seek the freedom to do unintelligent things (and cause no harm to others in the process), that is still no reason not to grant it! This book, however, is not about the normative case for or against development provisions, but about how developing countries have tried to push their own preferred agenda under conditions of asymmetric bargaining.
[51] Breda dos Santos et al. (2005).
[52] GATT (1947).

should be the result of economic development will facilitate the attainment of the objectives of the Agreement. In that sense, the new text represents a new and more positive approach to the problem of economic development and to the ways and means of reconciling the requirements of economic development with the obligations undertaken under the General Agreement regarding the conduct of commercial policy.[53]

Article 18 was not only the GATT's first attempt to accommodate the concerns of developing countries;[54] rather, 'the modified Article XVIII relevantly constitutes the only instance that gathered the contracting parties in an effort to amend the General Agreement. In addition, the new text implied the "incorporation within the terms of GATT itself of the infant industry protection view of economic development".[55] The most important clause here was Article 18B – 'the balance-of-payments escape clause for developing countries . . .',[56] which had less onerous criteria for application for developing countries in comparison to Article 12 criteria for developed countries. Also, whereas Articles 18A and 18C 'both involve compensation and retaliation', it was Article 18B that came to be 'associated with developing countries' special right to protect'.[57]

The second significant win for developing countries was the GATT decision in 1957 to appoint an expert panel to investigate 'in particular the failure of the trade of less developed countries to develop as rapidly as that of industrialized countries, excessive short-term fluctuations in prices of primary products, and widespread resort to agricultural protection'.[58] The fact that such a report was commissioned at all is indicative of the impact that the activism that developing countries had already begun to generate (more on this in Section 2.2.2). The Haberler Report was duly published in the following year.[59] This detailed report gave recognition, backing, and considerable legitimacy to both the 'access' and the 'right-to-protect' components of the S&D demands that developing countries had been pushing for. For example, the report was rather damning on the different forms of agricultural protectionism that were being exercised by the developed countries: access to these markets for developing countries had to be improved. On the positive

---

[53] GATT Analytic Index (1994a).

[54] Whalley (1990), p. 1320.

[55] Breda dos Santos et al. (2005), p. 641; Howse and Trebilock (1999).

[56] Whalley (1990), p. 1320.

[57] Whalley (1990), p. 1322.

[58] GATT Analytic Index (1994b).

[59] Haberler et al. (1958).

attention in the report regarding the right of developing countries to protect their own markets, Paragraph 345 provides a good example:

> We recognize that there are special considerations affecting the position of under-developed primary producing countries which justify a rather greater use of trade controls by them than by the highly industrialized countries. Industries may need special promotion during the first stages of industrialization ... Special measures to promote industry may be desirable in order to bring into productive employment labour which is under-employed in agriculture. Where the whole or the greater part of a luxury product comes from imports, the restriction of such imports may be administratively the best way of discouraging luxury consumption and promote savings. Under-developed primary producing countries may be more likely to be in genuine balance-of-payments difficulties than the majority of highly industrialized countries, in which case they will need more often to control imports on these grounds. Finally, insofar as import restrictions can turn the international terms of trade in favour of the restricting countries, it can be argued that poorer countries should have a somewhat greater freedom in their use than richer countries.[60]

The Haberler Report proved influential, and the contracting parties to the GATT took several decisions and issued declarations,[61] which culminated in the addition of Part IV. This new and important addition to the GATT on Trade and Development was presented at a Special Session of the Contracting Parties, in the presence of representatives of the press, amidst fanfare and many laudatory statements on 8 February 1965. The Committee on Trade and Development was also to be established at this session, which would be in charge of implementation. The Chairman, Ambassador Julio Lacarte, reported the following to the meeting:

> ... the Ministers had recognized that there was need for an adequate legal and institutional framework to enable the CONTRACTING PARTIES to discharge their responsibilities in connection with the work of expanding the trade of less-developed countries. To meet this need a new Part to the GATT had been drawn up. This new Part showed clearly that the promotion of the trade of less-developed countries and the provision of increased access for their products in world markets were among the primary objectives of the CONTRACTING PARTIES. These objectives were now set forth in a new Article XXXVI. Article XXXVII laid down the commitments in the field of

---

[60] Haberler et al. (1958), p. 125.
[61] For a helpful summary of these steps plus references to relevant documents, see GATT Analytic Index (1994b).

commercial policy which contracting parties would accept in order to promote these objectives. Article XXXVIII provided for joint action by the contracting parties, both within the framework of the GATT and in collaboration with other intergovernmental bodies, to further the objectives.[62]

The reaction of the contracting parties, including those from the developing world, was overall positive.[63] The tenor of Part IV was indeed sympathetic to the concerns that developing countries had expressed, especially in recognizing the principle that 'There is need for positive efforts designed to ensure that less-developed contracting parties secure a share in the growth in international trade commensurate with the needs of their economic development'.[64] Part IV also offered the first official recognition of the principle of non-reciprocity.[65] But two caveats are in order. First, the commitments outlined in Article 37 were best-endeavour and not binding ones. Second, despite the recognition of non-reciprocity, as pointed out by John Whalley, Part IV did 'not provide a GATT Article I exception for preferences, as had been argued for at the time'.[66]

The third landmark win for developing countries was indeed a long-awaited one on the issue of preferences. At the second session of the UN Conference on Trade and Development, held in New Delhi in 1968, the United States agreed to participate in a global system of preferences, and on the condition that they 'be limited to tariffs, should be temporary, should be based on voluntary adherence, and should be extended by all of the developed countries to all of the developing countries on an MFN basis'.[67] The important contribution – the 'novelty' of the Globalized System of Preferences (GSP) – was that it tried to 'generalize', in a non-discriminatory way, the 'patchwork of preferences' that only a few rich countries had until then granted to the former colonies.[68] To make the GSP compatible with the GATT (Most Favoured Nation (MFN) status was a fundamental principle of the system, which disallowed discrimination between members), a 10-year waiver was agreed to in 1971.

---

[62] GATT (1965).
[63] Ibid.
[64] GATT (1947), Part IV, Art. XXXVI, paragraph 3.
[65] Whalley (1990). GATT (1947), Part IV, Art. XXXVI, paragraph 8 stated, 'The developed contracting parties do not expect reciprocity for commitments made by them in trade negotiations to reduce or remove tariffs and other barriers to the trade of less-developed contracting parties'.
[66] Whalley (1990), p. 1320.
[67] Ibid.
[68] Tobin and Busch (2019), p. 137.

The conclusion of the Tokyo Round of trade negotiations in 1979 institutionalized the exception to Article 1 on a permanent basis, and also provided the legal basis for GSP schemes. The Framework Agreement on 'Differential and More Favourable Treatment, Reciprocity, and Fuller Participation of Developing Countries', also known as the Enabling Clause, stated in Paragraph 1: 'Notwithstanding the provisions of Article I of the General Agreement, contracting parties may accord differential and more favourable treatment to developing countries, without according such treatment to other contracting parties'.[69] It further recognized the LDCs as a separate category, and confirmed in Paragraph 6 the following:

> Having regard to the special economic difficulties and the particular development, financial and trade needs of the least developed countries, the developed countries shall exercise the utmost restraint in seeking any concessions or contributions for commitments made by them to reduce or remove tariffs and other barriers to the trade of such countries, and the least-developed countries shall not be expected to make concessions or contributions that are inconsistent with the recognition of their particular situation and problems.[70]

The above successes, culminating in the Enabling Clause, were not to be scoffed at. But on balance, they were still quite modest, in comparison to not only what the developing countries had demanded, but also what they would have achieved had the ITO been formed. Three problems were especially serious. First, the Enabling Clause allowed the provision of S&D measures for developing countries, but it did not require them. Preferences offered by the rich to the poor under GSP, for instance, bar a low threshold notification requirement, were offered unilaterally and could also be withdrawn unilaterally. Second, the Enabling Clause had facilitated the provision of S&D, but it had also introduced the principle of Graduation. Article 7 stated:

> Less-developed contracting parties expect that their capacity to make contributions or negotiated concessions or take other mutually agreed action under the provisions and procedures of the General Agreement would improve with the progressive development of their economies and improvement in their trade situation and they would accordingly expect to participate more fully in the framework of rights and obligations under the General Agreement.[71]

[69] GATT (1979).
[70] Ibid.
[71] Ibid.

The ambiguity created between the seemingly open-ended nature of the S&D that was allowed and the expectation of graduation, both incorporated within the Enabling Clause, would turn out to be a source of considerable irritation and conflict between the rich countries and the rising powers.[72] Finally, there was no way to get around the fact that development provisions in the GATT had appeared as a belated afterthought, rather than an integral part of the entire project. Hence, more immediately, the best-endeavour nature of GSP. But more fundamentally, this also meant that all the hard-won gains of developing countries would likely continue to be exceptions that proved an accepted 'rule': development and poverty reduction were not systemic concerns, and the responsibility for addressing them lay primarily with the poor themselves.

2.2.2 *Explaining the Successes, and Also Their Limitations*

There were two key factors that contributedto developing countries getting as far as they did in building the development dimension back into the GATT. First, developing countries framed their demands in terms of fairness and equity considerations, all the while making content-rich and detailed proposals. Second, when they found that the GATT was not proving to be so conducive a forum for their demands, they created new forums and tapped into parallel ones to support their cause.

Within the GATT, developing country contracting parties refused to be sidelined by institutional constraints. They presented proposals to argue their case, which were often admirably detailed, but even more interesting in the framing that they used. India's representative to the GATT, Sir Raghavan Pillai, for example, while arguing a case for special treatment for developing countries, used a resounding and powerful frame of powerlessness. Trade could produce win–win situations, but only if it provided the necessary conditions to accommodate and address conditions of poverty and under-development in the global South:

> ... among the contracting parties there are countries which are industrially and economically advanced and others with a backward economy and a very low standard of living. If we wish to retain both classes of countries within one common fold, there will have to be greater flexibility in the provisions

---

[72] It is not a coincidence that the United States has made S&D a core point in recent years as it seeks to reform the WTO.

that are to apply to all of them. *Equality of treatment is equitable only among equals. A weakling cannot carry the same load as a giant.*

... There is no bigger obstacle to the advancement of international trade than the poverty of underdeveloped countries ...

International trade is not an end in itself. It is but a means to greater prosperity ... The GATT cannot of course solve the kind of problem which underdeveloped countries with their rising populations and low standards of living have to face. The effort must inevitably be their own. What the GATT can do, and must do, is to give them the fullest scope and freedom to fulfil their economic programmes, which I maintain will bring prosperity not only to them but to all those who trade with them.[73]

Brazil, while sometimes emphasizing different priorities, also took a similar general line of argumentation:

If the objective of international economic co-operation is really the attainment of higher standards of living for all, and not simply the maintenance of high standards for a few, the special case of the late-comers in the process of development must be fully considered and greater flexibility and adaptation introduced into the General Agreement. My delegation recognizes that freedom of trade in a world of economic equals, with full international mobility of factors, would be an ideal to be gradually attained through patient effort and concerted action. But it also feels that given the present world economic structure, and in the absence of international investment in adequate magnitudes, *it would be against the most legitimate interests of the underdeveloped countries to accept the same set of rules that suits the convenience of developed countries, for the regulation of their own trade.*[74]

Besides mobilizing the forces of moralization and rhetoric, and appealing to issues of legitimacy and equality within the GATT, developing countries also worked outside the institution. Recognizing that progress within the GATT was slow, they created the UNCTAD in 1964. 'The United Nations, which had declared the 1960s to be the Decade of Development, would be the tool for prosperity and reform of the GATT system'.[75] They persisted in their efforts to reorient global governance towards development issues, for instance via the call for a New International Economic Order (NIEO) in the UNCTAD in the 1970s. This ambitious programme envisaged fundamental changes to the functioning of the world economy based on distributive justice.[76] These efforts

---

[73] GATT (1954), emphasis added.
[74] GATT (1953), emphasis added.
[75] Zeiler (2012), p. 109.
[76] UN General Assembly (1974).

represented an early and impressive form of forum-shopping,[77] in which developing countries utilized whichever forum that worked to their advantage, and tried to create synergies across the institutions. For example, they created and effectively utilized the UNCTAD in 1968 to get a system of preferences, which was then brought into the GATT system via the 1971 waiver and subsequently the Enabling Clause.

Through both framing and forum-shopping, developing countries were able to take some small but important steps towards building a promising narrative about the responsibility of international institutions to alleviate global poverty. But these steps fell short of establishing this narrative as a dominant one for at least two reasons.

First, although developing countries had pushed for S&D with considerable consistency, theirs was not the only intellectual approach on the table. Rather, two conflicting epistemic models were at work, one supported by the developed world and the other by developing countries. Breda dos Santos et al. summarize the battle of intellectual ideas as follows:

> The cleavage between developed and developing countries was primarily shaped by the conflict of two contending approaches of political economy. The first approach is based on the non-discriminatory and liberal ideas that reflect David Ricardo's theory of comparative advantage. The second approach opposes the notion of comparative advantage to the idea that developing countries experience detrimental terms of trade in relation to developed countries, and that they should therefore boost changes in their trade patterns by restricting the amount of imported industrialized products, diversifying their national production and promoting export of industrialized products. One of the main proponents of this last strand is the Argentinian economist Raul Prebisch. The Havana negotiations can thus be said to coincide with the onset of this clash of economic views in international negotiations.[78]

These differences were fundamental and, in the phase that the ITO was being negotiated, it was not obvious around which of these two intellectual poles would the different parties coalesce. The differences also translated into public debate. Developing countries were building up a narrative that drew a direct link between special development provisions for themselves on the

---

[77] On forum-shopping, see Busch (2007).

[78] Of course, there were also important differences within the North and the South (for instance between Harry Dexter White and John Maynard Keynes). But Breda dos Santos et al. (2005) are right to identify the broad brush intellectual differences between developed and developing worlds.

one hand and fairness and legitimacy considerations on the other (i.e., if one wanted to establish a fair and legitimate economic system, special provisions would have to be built in). There was strong support for the idea of collective responsibility for global poverty and also some optimism for finding global solutions. Gunnar Myrdal, for example, in his Nobel Prize lecture commented on 'the new awareness of the poverty in underdeveloped countries' that was 'bound to be morally disturbing in the Western world, where, particularly since Enlightenment, the ideal of greater equality has had an honored place in social philosophy'. He further pointed to 'a new element in Western thinking' that derived from the end of colonialism; now 'much of the writings of economists in that early stage of the postwar era, as in many cases even later, became focused upon urging the politicians and the general public in the developed countries to be prepared to come forward with technical assistance, capital aid, and commercial concessions'.[79] But there were others in academia and policy who expressed a deep scepticism of this view.[80] A vitriolic critic of the southern/developmentalist narrative was Harvard academic, Robert Tucker. Speaking disparagingly of the 'new political sensibility', Tucker countered Myrdal: 'In fact, there is little evidence for asserting so broad an association and a good deal of evidence that points to a quite different conclusion'.[81]

A report in the *New York Times* on the UNCTAD in 1964 walked a precarious balance between the two narratives as it navigated between the 'admonition' that George Ball, US Under Secretary of State, had delivered to developing countries in his speech versus the reporter's own view that developed countries had an 'obligation' to help developing countries.[82] Similarly, the American delegate's speech at the ECOSOC in 1975 on the agenda to establish the NIEO was framed politely, but in parts also adopted quite an irritable and impatient tone: 'It is too late in the day to accept that any single state or any bloc of states can arrogate unto itself all wisdom and all power in the ordering of our economic system. It is indeed much too late in the day to forget that judgements and opinions can be wrong as well as right ...'.[83]

Second, although developing countries coordinated their strategies and presented joint proposals, for instance via the Informal Group of Developing Countries,[84] they were not a cohesive bloc in the GATT when it came to

---

[79] Myrdal (1975).
[80] For a helpful overview of the reactions that the NIEO generated, see Cooper (1977).
[81] Tucker (1975).
[82] *New York Times* (1964).
[83] Ferguson, Jr. (1975).
[84] Narlikar (2003).

implementing S&D. There were fundamental divisions between the former colonies (which received some preferences from the European countries and Britain) and the Latin American countries that did not have access to this preferential treatment. Even though they made a conscious effort to unify their positions, the developed countries often had a more unified stance. When it came down to implementing the nitty-gritty of their shared idea of special treatment in the name of development, coalitions of developing countries did not prove to be effective at the time.[85]

Amidst polarized perspectives, conflicting narratives, and divided southern coalitions, it is possible to see why the gains that developing countries achieved were ultimately rather limited in this phase. But the situation was about to get even worse in the Uruguay Round.

2.3 THE FAILED PROMISE OF THE URUGUAY ROUND

The Uruguay Round was the longest lasting round of negotiations in the GATT, and took eight years to complete. By the time the round was concluded in 1994, not only had the multilateral trading system expanded in its range of coverage and members, but a new organization – the World Trade Organization – had been created. The expansion of mandate occurred, however, largely in areas of interest to developed countries. The importance accorded to development concerns diminished. In this section, I first highlight the main outcomes of the Uruguay Round, and then explain why the results turned out to be unfavourable to developing countries.

2.3.1 *The Results of the Uruguay Round*

After an attempted but failed start in 1982, the new round was launched in 1986 at Punta del Este. Known as the Uruguay Round, it saw the significant expansion of the agenda of the GATT.[86]

Developing countries had resisted the launch of a new round in the first place, and then vehemently fought against the inclusion of these new issues (of services, TRIPS, and TRIMS). Despite their resistance, the Uruguay Round was completed, and these new issues were included within the mandate of the trade regime. The concessions that the countries of the global south made were deep and wide-ranging. They agreed not only to tariff reductions, but also to abide by a broad swathe of new rules on customs

---

[85] Breda dos Santos et al. (2005).
[86] For a helpful summary of the Uruguay Round negotiations, see Preeg (2012).

valuation, import licensing, technical barriers to trade, sanitary and phytosa-
nitary standards. These commitments required developing countries to reform
their domestic regulatory environment – in some cases, fundamentally so.
Although the pursuit of some of these reforms made sense, the Uruguay
Round did not take into account the costs that the implementation of these
agreements brought. And the costs were significant in many cases.[87] The fact
that the final agreement was signed as a 'Single Undertaking' meant that
countries could not pick and choose most of their obligations. And while all
contracting parties would be bound to the new regulations, developing countries found themselves worse off for two reasons. First, they incurred costs that
they could ill-afford, given the smaller size of their economies, as well as the
diversion of scarce resources away from key areas such as education and
health. Second, for many developd countries, adherence to the new standards
meant 'no more than an obligation to apply their domestic regulations fairly at
the border . . . for the least developed countries they require first the establishment of such systems – or the conversion of indigenous systems – to the system
recognized by international conventions'.[88] Finally, the Single Undertaking
also created the World Trade Organization. On the one hand, and possibly in
the long run, this was a development that would align with the preference of
developing countries for authoritative regimes,[89] which could help level the
playing field. On the other hand though, they were now expected to take on a
qualitatively higher level of obligations, that were legally enforceable with the
creation of 'the strongest dispute settlement mechanism in the history of
international law'.[90]

---

[87] E.g., Finger and Schuler (1999) offered first approximations of the costs of implementing the
SPS, IPR, and customs reform for developing countries: 'To gain acceptance for its meat,
vegetables and fruits in industrial country markets, Argentina spent over $80 million to achieve
higher levels of plant and animal sanitation. Hungary spent over $40 million to upgrade the
level of sanitation of its slaughterhouses alone. Mexico spent over $30 million to upgrade
intellectual property laws and enforcement that began at a higher level than are in place in
most least developed countries, customs reform projects can easily cost $20 million. Those
figures, for just three of the six Uruguay Round Agreements that involve restructuring of
domestic regulations, come to $130 million. One hundred and thirty million dollars is more
than the annual development budget for seven of the twelve least developed countries for
which we could find a figure for that part of the budget' (p. 25). These estimates were with
reference to the more advanced of the developing countries; for the LDCs, the authors point
out that costs would be higher still, not least because their starting points would be further away
from the required standards.
[88] Ibid., p. 22.
[89] Krasner (1985).
[90] Ostry (2004), p. 272. Ostry goes so far as to say of the deal that they were offered on a 'take-it-or-
leave-it' basis: 'They took it, but it is safe to say, without a full comprehension of the profoundly

In return for making these concessions – many of which took the shape of bound commitments – developing countries got tariff reductions for their exports to northern markets. Plus they obtained some limited concessions on agriculture and textiles, including the assurance of further negotiations on agriculture in 2000 via the built-in agenda. They were promised technical assistance for some of the implementation issues highlighted in the previous paragraph. An important point to note though is that, despite the fact that developing countries 'accepted bound commitments to implement, they received in exchange unbound promises of assistance to do so'.[91]

On balance, seen from the perspective of the developing world, the 'grand bargain' had turned out to be a 'bum deal'. Its consequences were to carry across the next decades, and 'Southern hostility was evident at every subsequent ministerial meeting'.[92] How did this happen?

2.3.2 *Explaining Why Developing Countries Landed the 'Bum Deal'*

Four factors explain why developing countries found themselves with such an unfavourable outcome at the end of the Uruguay Round negotiations: active but relatively ineffective coalitions, missing synergies between states and transnational social movements, diminished BATNA, and the triumphalism of the Washington Consensus in the years of the round that also infected the GATT. It was virtually impossible for developing countries to develop a winning narrative against these odds.

The potentially high stakes of the Uruguay Round – both in terms of losses as well as gains – led developing countries to organize themselves into coalitions. Working in coalitions in the GATT offered them at least two important advantages. First, collective action enhanced the legitimacy of their claims: there was strength in numbers, despite the fact that decisions in the GATT were arrived at via consensus (rather than majoritarian voting). Second, coalitions also enhanced their capacity to negotiate via information sharing and a potential division of labour.[93] Developing countries creatively formed a variety of coalitions in the Uruguay Round, which can be classified into two types: bloc-type and issue-based.[94] Members of a bloc-type coalition were

transformative implication of this new trading system (an incomprehension that was shared by their Northern negotiators)'.

[91] Finger (2001), p. 1102.
[92] Ostry (2004), p. 282.
[93] More on the constraints that developing countries faced in decision-making in Section 2.4.
[94] For a detailed analysis of coalition politics in the GATT and the WTO, see Narlikar (2012) and Narlikar (2003).

bound together by a set of ideas and identity, and went beyond immediate instrumentality;[95] issue-based coalitions were formed around a more focused, instrumental, and limited aim.[96] Despite their collective mobilization and activism in the pre-negotiation and negotiation phases of the Uruguay Round however, these coalitions generated few successes. The potential success of bloc-type coalitions was hampered by their heterogeneity. They usually brought together groups of countries that together constituted collective external weight, but were also affected by a diversity of interests. Often it was not difficult to buy members of such coalitions off through side-deals. Issue-based coalitions did not suffer from this problem, but still proved to be difficult to sustain when large and diversified economies (with numerous issue interests) were involved. When loyalties were shared across multiple coalitions in competing issue areas, they became difficult to sustain.[97] Very narrow and focused coalitions involving smaller economies overcame this set of problems, but these ended up lacking external weight. In the Uruguay Round, developing countries tried these various permutations, and unfortunately discovered the downsides of both coalition types the hard way. As the round progressed,

---

[95] The G10, formed in the pre-negotiation phase of the Uruguay Round, and led by Brazil and India, was a classic bloc-type coalition comprising developing countries. It resisted the launch of a new round, fought against the inclusion of the new issues into the regime, refused to cooperate with other coalitions representing other positions, and employed a strict distributive bargaining strategy.

[96] Almost a contemporary of the G10, the G20 was a pioneering issue-based coalition (not to be confused with the G20 on agriculture in the Doha negotiations, nor the Finance G20, nor the leaders' level G20 that was formed in the aftermath of the 2008 financial crisis). It began as a modest research initiative to investigate the implications of including services into the GATT. It initially comprised Bangladesh, Chile, Colombia, Hong Kong, Indonesia, Ivory Coast, Jamaica, Malaysia, Mexico, Pakistan, Philippines, Romania, Singapore, Sri Lanka, South Korea, Thailand, Turkey, Uruguay, Zambia, and Zaire. Developed countries also joined the coalition in the form of a G9: Australia, Austria, Canada, Finland, Iceland, New Zealand, Norway, Sweden, and Switzerland. Colombian and Swiss leadership earned the group the moniker of *Café au lait*. Eventually, the coalition included some forty-eight countries, and it was much more successful than the G10: its draft proposal provided the basis for the Punta del Este declaration that launched the Uruguay Round (and included services in the agenda). The successes of issue-based diplomacy were replicated to some extent by the Cairns Group of agriculture-exporting nations, and brought together developed and developing countries. At the time of its formation, it included Australia, New Zealand, Canada, and also Argentina, Brazil, Chile, Colombia, Hungary, Indonesia, Malaysia, Philippines, Thailand, and Uruguay (plus Fiji, which was not a contracting party to the GATT at the time). On the Cairns Group, see Higgott and Cooper (1990); Tussie (1993). The successes of the Cairns Group promoted a flurry of efforts towards further issue-based coalitions that transcended north–south boundaries. The record of these follow-on coalitions was ambiguous, at best, and this method of coalition formation also proved to be short-lived (Narlikar 2003, 2012).

[97] Hamilton and Whalley (1989).

their coalitions unravelled, and developing countries had little choice but to cave in the endgame.

Second, it is true there had been public demonstrations against encroachments of 'GATTzilla' on their sovereignty in developing countries. Civil society activists in the north were also protesting against the GATT. For example, as the Uruguay Round neared completion, 'environmental NGOs covered Swiss highway bridges with graffiti admonishing "GATT: No Patents on Life"'.[98] But transnational synergies that could harness and amplify the voice of civil society, and combine them with the voices of dissidence from state actors, were missing. Southern governments seemed unwilling or unable to tap into the domestic discontent and thereby hold the international negotiation in the GATT hostage. India is a case in point. Despite its vibrant democracy, and the organization of mass protests (e.g., 'Seed Satyagraha' that was organized against the intellectual property provisions that would directly affect India's farming sector),[99] India was just not in a position to go-it-alone against the emerging international consensus on the GATT, given especially its severe Balance of Payments crisis in 1991 that had left it obliged to take on structural reform.

Third, the bargaining position of developing countries was rendered unfavourable in the Uruguay Round due to a diminished BATNA. The 1982 debt crisis had already left many of them weakened. The end of the Cold War in 1989 further deprived them of the possibility to find a niche for themselves by playing the great powers off against each other. And while not all of them had given up on the ideals that had led them to set up the UNCTAD, it certainly became much more difficult for them to argue in favour of alternative narratives against an international context where 'the end of history'[100] and the 'unipolar moment'[101] had been declared.

Finally, and related to the above point, the Uruguay Round narrative was one that was significantly influenced by the Washington Consensus emanating out of the Bretton Woods institutions. As the IMF came up with increasingly intrusive conditionalities, the GATT too began to incline towards the embrace of measures that went behind states' borders. Trade liberalization, even in a moderate version of the Washington consensus – rather than the more extreme form that took the shape of 'neo-liberalism' and 'market fundamentalism' – was seen as a natural and necessary step for poverty reduction in

[98] Ostry (2004), p. 274.
[99] *SUNS Online* (1993).
[100] Fukuyama (1989).
[101] Krauthammer (1990).

poor countries.[102] It is interesting to see that only two years after the attempt to launch a new GATT round with an agenda, which was both expansive and intrusive, had failed, the Director-General of the GATT could still claim the following in a speech:

> There has been a long effort to convince developing countries that their own need for efficiency and growth requires fuller exposure of their economies to international competition. A growing number of them, overcoming their suspicion that the GATT system was tilted against them, have made and are still making big strides in opening their markets, not out of altruism but because they recognize that efficiency depends upon it ... This continuing pressure is the major gain from acceptance of market disciplines – even more than the improved access to export markets.[103]

Developing countries, as per this epistemic consensus, would be best served by opening up their markets, which in turn translated into a toning down of S&D measures that the GATT had facilitated for them in the past.[104]

A ten-point summary of the debate that was held at the fiftieth session of the contracting parties in December 1994, just before the WTO came into effect, showed the extent to which the Uruguay Round agreements were much less sympathetic to S&D approaches. For example, the summary acknowledged that growth had been uneven, with LDCs and Africa seeing a decrease in their trade shares. But it blamed the domestic policies of the countries concerned as much as external factors, arguing 'these different trends could not be attributed to the international environment alone' (3). It highlighted the Uruguay Round as a 'significant opportunity' for developing countries, given its inclusion of agriculture and textiles into the GATT system, also 'because the Round had dealt with internal policies (and not just border measures) that restricted trade' (4). In other words, the answer to the problems of development and poverty reduction lay mainly with the problematic domestic policies of developing countries, rather than external actors or the international rules. 'In future, developing countries would make greater commitments in the WTO ...' (9).[105]

---

[102] Offering his clarification on the Washington Consensus, and trying to address misuses of the term, John Williamson (2000) had argued: 'Trade liberalization, certainly in low-income, resource-poor countries, tends to be pro-poor because it increases the demand for unskilled labor and decreases the subsidies directed to import-competing industries that use large volumes of capital and employ small numbers of workers, many of them highly skilled', p. 257. Also see Williamson (1990).
[103] Dunkel (1984).
[104] It is worth reiterating that I am not making a case in favour of S&D, see fn 50.
[105] GATT Analytic Index (1994b), p. 1041.

2.4 TRYING TO GET A VOICE IN THE 'RICH MAN'S CLUB'

The limited ability of the GATT to deliver on the expectations of developing countries was reflected not only in negotiated outcomes. Rather, the skewed nature of decision-making processes exacerbated the difficulty of securing outcomes in favour of the weak and the powerless.[106] At first glance, this would appear to be strange: Article 25 of the GATT provided for a decision-making system in which each contracting party had one vote, and also stated that decisions would normally be taken by 'a majority of the votes cast'.[107] On paper, this gave developing countries a clear advantage as their numbers grew in the system. In practice, however, the GATT acquired the dubious distinction of being called a 'Rich Man's Club'.[108] There were four reasons for this.

First, in spite of the formal rules on voting, the norm in the GATT was that decisions were taken by consensus.[109] Consensus, in turn, meant that no party should object to the decision. In theory, such a system endowed veto power even to the smallest player. But developing countries found it difficult to put the consensus to effective use because it required an informed presence in Geneva, whereas developing countries sometimes lacked either the physical presence or technical capacity, and sometimes both. Finger and Schuler note that when the Uruguay Round began, twenty of the sixty-five developing country contracting parties did not have delegations in Geneva. Fifteen of the twenty at least had embassies in European capitals, and five had representatives based only in their delegation capitals. Developing country delegations were also 'notably smaller' than those of developed countries. It is difficult to see how their countries could have stood much of a chance against their

---

[106] This section draws on research first presented in Narlikar (2003).

[107] GATT (1947), Article 25 (4).

[108] References to criticism of the GATT on the grounds that it was a 'Rich Man's Club' recur through the records. For example, explaining his country's decision to join the GATT, the Minister of Commerce and Industry of Tanganyika stated: 'We were not deterred by the criticism which is usually levelled at the GATT that it is the 'rich man's club ... ' (GATT 1963). Similarly, in 1967, the ambassador of Ceylon had the following to say: 'As I remember hearing the distinguished Minister of Economic Affairs for the Netherlands indicating yesterday that GATT was not intended to be a rich man's club. It was primarily intended to bring order out of chaos in international trade. Still the accidents of history have tended to make GATT a policy forum from which the major industrialized nations have derived greater benefit than countries primarily dependent on agricultural products and the developing countries' (GATT 1967).

[109] The Agreement establishing the WTO (GATT 1994) refers to this practice in Article 9 (1): 'The WTO shall continue the practice of decision-making by consensus followed under GATT 1947'.

better-resourced northern counterparts.[110] In addition to these problems, consensus required an open show of hands, in contrast to secret ballot. Developing countries were sometimes reluctant to openly show dissent in such a setting for fear of reprisals in other areas (such as bilateral aid), and their silence was interpreted as a form of consent.

Second, to facilitate consensus-building, it was commonplace for the Director General to convene 'Green Room meetings' among the key players. The most important of these players were the Quad – the European Union, United States, Canada and Japan. Smaller economies were seldom invited to Green Room consultations. The Brazilian Ambassador, Rubens Ricupero, to the GATT during the Uruguay Round years, describes his first experience of attending a Green Room meeting with some twenty delegates in November 1987:

> It was a frightening experience for the newcomer, alone, without advisers, in an almost English Club atmosphere, where everyone addressed the others by their first name. Despite the codified language, however, it was not difficult to perceive how the dividing line closely followed the development level of the countries the delegates represented.[111]

Consensus forged behind closed doors in such a manner would then be presented at a meeting of all the contracting parties. The bias towards agreement was high at this stage, especially as developing countries were reluctant to risk the potential costs of breaking consensus.

Third, recall that the ITO experiment had failed, and the GATT had been adopted on a provisional basis. As such, it was never an actual organization, and it lacked an elaborate institutional structure. The peculiar historical trajectory of the GATT meant, even as the institution evolved, its secretariat remained small (especially in comparison to the UN, the IMF, or the World Bank) and its mandate was tightly circumscribed. This placed the onus of effective negotiation and implementation on the contracting parties themselves. Developing countries did not have recourse to technical assistance or other forms of support from the secretariat, and had to manage the best they could.

Fourth, negotiation practices also did not help the cause of the poor and the powerless. An important negotiation approach that was used in the GATT was the Principal Supplier Principle. A GATT document described this approach as follows:

---

[110] Finger and Schuler (1999).
[111] Ricupero (1998), p. 15.

Participating countries may request concessions on products of which they, individually or collectively, are or are likely to be the principal suppliers to the countries from which the concessions are asked. This rule shall not apply to prevent a country not a principal supplier from making a request, but the country concerned may invoke the principal supplier rule if the principal supplier of the product is not participating in the negotiations or is not a contracting party to the General Agreement.[112]

This principle automatically gave greater prominence and agency to the major markets. It came with an important benefit to small players: once major players had agreed on tariff reductions, MFN meant that those reductions would be multilateralized, that is extended to all contracting parties. Free-riding, as identified by Mancur Olson (see earlier discussion in Chapter 1) was rendered possible by this system. But free-riding also came with a cost of exclusion and marginalization from core decision-making processes for developing countries that were already finding it difficult to exercise their voice.

Together, as a result of the above four reasons, power asymmetries outside the GATT too often and too easily translated into power asymmetries within the institution. For all its apparent commitment to equal participation of all contracting parties, the GATT was not an easy institution for developing countries to work. And attempts by developing countries to move the action on trade to other forums also generated only limited results. Some of the UN bodies could help push for a more developmentalist narrative, but the GATT remained the real game in town for trade negotiations.[113] The fact that the WTO inherited most of the decision-making procedures of the GATT meant that there were few institutional reasons expect change.

2.5 OPPRESSION AND DISEMPOWERMENT OUTSIDE THE CORRIDORS OF THE RICH MAN'S CLUB

The GATT was not an isolated island where the poor and the weak found themselves disempowered. If anything, they were exposed to the vagaries of

---

[112] GATT (1956), Article 3.
[113] Ferguson Jr (1975), for example, while reacting to the call for a NIEO and setting out the American agenda for the ECOSOC, also tried to limit any forays of the UN General Assembly into trade negotiations. He argued, 'The U.N. General Assembly has not been much experienced in the world of global economics ... We, for ourselves, are certain that no one contemplates that it will be the General Assembly which itself negotiates commodity arrangements reflecting a general consensus, or that the General Assembly itself will undertake to negotiate trade reform or monetary reform, or that the General Assembly will itself undertake to fashion arrangements to assure the feeding of the world'.

brutal power politics even more so outside the GATT. Stephen Krasner had concluded his classic work, *Structural Conflict*, on a sombre note:

> Decolonization imbued Third World states with a level of de jure and de facto control which they could not have attained or defended through their national power capabilities. The principle of the sovereign equality of all states has legitimated Third World challenges to the dominant market-oriented regimes favoured by the North; international organizations created and funded by the North have become forums where such challenges can be voiced; the weakness and vulnerability of developing countries compels such challenges to be made. Yet, the exiguity of their national power resources precludes any decisive victory. They can attack and undermine existing international regimes but they cannot destroy or replace them. This paradox has been a basic source of tension between the North and the South. It cannot be mitigated by economic development alone. A few Third World states may resign themselves to, or accept, market-oriented regimes because they are very large or domestically agile. But most will not. The North–South conflict will be an enduring characteristic of the international system. There are some problems for which there are no solutions.[114]

The evidence provided in this chapter reinforces the analysis that Krasner had offered. Across multiple issue-areas and organizations, there were good reasons for the powerless to feel disgruntled. Even multilateral organizations like the UN Security Council, the IMF, and the World Bank had decision-making systems based on weighted voting, which automatically reduced the voice of the developing world. Others, such as the G7, operated as unapologetic clubs without even a pretence of inclusiveness.

Recall that, the marginalization of poor countries did not mean that poverty itself was being marginalized from intellectual debate or policy. Rather, considerations of how to make the system work for the poor played a key role in its setting up. International trade rules, especially from a British perspective, had to be such that they would allow and sustain the emergence of a welfare state. Several compromises towards embedding liberalism in a social context were made to help reconcile the differing views of the United States and the United Kingdom. But the central purpose of pro-poor measures built into the system was to address the problems of the war-torn economies of the West and ensuring domestic stability. Their main targets were not usually developing countries, many of which were still colonies or just coming out of decades and centuries of imperial rule, and lacked the state capacity that would have been necessary for the compromise of embedded liberalism to

---

[114] Krasner (1985), pp. 313–314.

really work for them. This feature persisted over the next five decades. Even as the system developed further and multiple poverty narratives interacted with each other, it was clear that addressing global poverty (and especially poverty in the global south) was not a primary goal of the leading international institutions.

Naturally, developing countries worked constantly to change this. They did so by exploiting the power of large numbers in majoritarian universal organizations, with favourable voting structures, like the UN General Assembly. Through the power of intellectual ideas (such as Dependency theory), moral argument (such as distributive justice), and via coalitions (such as the G77), developing countries persisted in their efforts, over time and across different issue areas. They further tried to build new institutions, like the UNCTAD, which were sympathetic to their concerns and also worked on the basis of one-member-one-vote decision-making systems. But these forums themselves lacked international clout, not least because they were seldom ones that developed countries were willing to entrust with key negotiation processes.

In effect, global poverty and powerlessness were not the focus of negotiation among equals. At most, these considerations entered the international realm via aid programmes of multilateral organizations and bilateral donors. The record was mixed.[115] And for all the varied (and sometimes worthy) considerations driving it through different periods of history, aid was a one-way street. It represented largesse that was granted by rich people to poor people. The rich debated and updated their programmes in light of previous experiences, and further adapted them to incorporate new strategic or moral imperatives. But reliant on the strategic choices and occasional good will of rich donors, developing countries were *recipients* – and little more than that.

2.6 CONCLUSION

This chapter has highlighted the rather mixed results that developing countries achieved in international trade negotiations, despite the creation of the post-war international economic system on relatively equal terms (and certainly an improvement on colonialism). Even among their limited gains though, the chapter highlighted some variation. The differences in the results they were able to produce offer some potentially important insights on the exercise of the power of powerlessness.

---

[115] Easterly (2003, 2006); Moyo (2009).

First, recall the might-have-beens of the Havana Charter. The ITO would have incorporated several development-friendly provisions (partly due to divisions between the United States and Britain and how the negotiations were structured, but also due to the effective activism of developing countries). The failure of the ITO to take off was due partly to the domestic unsustainability of the compromises that the United States had struck (especially in favour of developing countries), and also because of a factor unrelated to trade controversies, that is the onset of the Cold War. When the GATT emerged as the *de facto* institution instead of the ITO, many of the concessions that developing countries had received in the latter years of the negotiations to create a new trade organization were nullified. The dominant narrative associated with the GATT was one that worked in tandem with the Bretton Woods narrative. This narrative allowed space for monetary policy autonomy, fixed exchange rates, and capital controls to preserve domestic stability, but mainly catering to the needs of the global north. As John Ruggie recognized, 'The compromise of embedded liberalism has never been fully extended to the developing countries. They have been disproportionately subject to the orthodox stabilization measures of the IMF, often with no beneficial results in export earnings but substantial increases in import bills and consequent increases in domestic prices. Moreover, the liberalization produced by the GATT has benefited relatively few among them'.[116] And once this narrative was in place, producing a change in narrative would be an uphill task for developing countries.

Second, in order to reassert their own agenda in the GATT, developing countries tried two broad sets of strategies in the next few decades. On the one hand, within the GATT, they framed their demands not in terms of a complete overthrow of the existing rules, but amendments and exceptions. On the other hand, outside the GATT, they framed their demands in terms of radical reform. The call for the establishment of the NIEO was an example of this; the exercise in forum-shopping via the creation of the UNCTAD, which could serve as a potential BATNA, was another. The former set of demands generated at least some successes via the granting of S&D provisions (however limited). The latter set, however, proved to be less successful, and in fact seemed to exacerbate divisions, deepen polarization, and trigger stalemates.

Third, in the Uruguay Round, the narrative espoused by developing countries seemed to have even less traction. This was not for want of trying. But the inadequacies of their coalitions, and the unwillingness plus inability of developing countries to work in networks that could draw support from

---

[116] Ruggie (1982), pp. 413–414.

multiple other actors greatly limited the dissemination potential of their narrative. Worsening BATNAs due to the debt crisis and the end of the Cold War did not help their case. And the credibility of the intellectual ideas that had underpinned their narrative was declining against the increasing triumphalism of the Washington Consensus. There was little reason to hope for change.

BIBLIOGRAPHY

Breda dos Santos, Norma. 2016. 'Latin American countries and the establishment of the multilateral trading system: The Havana Conference (1947–48).' *Brazilian Journal of Political Economy*. 36: 2. Pp. 309–329.

Breda dos Santos, Norma, Rogerio Farias, and Raphael Cunha. 2005. 'Generalized system of preferences in general agreement on tariffs and trade/World Trade Organization: History and current issues.' *Journal of World Trade*. 39: 4. Pp. 637–370.

British Memorandum. 1948. Memorandum by the President of the Board of Trade: Cabinet. CP (48) 84. 12 March. http://filestore.nationalarchives.gov.uk/pdfs/large/cab-129-25.pdf. Pp. 146–151.

Busch, Marc. 2007. 'Overlapping institutions, forum shopping, and dispute settlement in international trade.' *International Organization*. 61: 4. Pp. 735–761.

Canadian External Relations Documents. 1948a. Secretary of State for External Affairs to heads of post abroad. Volume 14: 581. Circular Document No. A 131. Ottawa. 4 June. http://epe.lac-bac.gc.ca/100/206/301/faitc-aecic/history/2013-05-03/www.international.gc.ca/department/history-histoire/dcer/details-en.asp@intRefid=10321.

1948b. Chief Delegate, Delegation to United Nations Conference on Trade and Employment, to Secretary of State for External Affairs. Vol 14: 582. Dispatch 165. Berne. 13 July. http://epe.lac-bac.gc.ca/100/206/301/faitc-aecic/history/2013–05-03/www.international.gc.ca/department/history-histoire/dcer/details-en.asp@intRefid=10322.

Clayton, William. 1949. Foreword for Wilcox, Clair. A *Charter for World Trade*. New York: Macmillan.

Cooper, Richard N. 1977. 'A new international economic order for mutual gain.' *Foreign Policy*. 26: Spring. Pp. 66–120.

Daunton, Martin. 2010. From Bretton Woods to Havana: Multilateral deadlocks in historical perspective. In Amrita Narlikar (ed.). *Deadlocks in Multilateral Negotiations: Causes and Solutions*. Cambridge: Cambridge University Press.

2012. The inconsistent quartet: Free trade versus competing goals. In Amrita Narlikar, Martin Daunton and Robert M. Stern (eds). *The Oxford Handbook on the World Trade Organization*. Oxford: Oxford University Press.

Diebold, William Jr. 1952. 'The end of the I.T.O.' *Essays in International Finance*. 16.

Dunkel, Arthur. 1984. *International Trade and Economic Growth*. Address by Mr. Arthur Dunkel, Director-General, General Agreement on Tariffs and Trade, to the European-Atlantic Group, London, 20 February. GATT/1335.

Easterly, William. 2003. 'Can foreign aid buy growth?' *Journal of Economic Perspectives.* 17: 3. Pp. 23–48.

2006. *The White Man's Burden: Why the West's Efforts to Aid the Rest Have Done So Much Ill and So Little Good.* London: Penguin.

Ferguson, Jr., Clarence Clyde. 1975. 'US discusses approach to the seventh special session of the UN General Assembly.' Statement by Clarence Clyde Ferguson Jr., US Representative in the UN Economic and Social Council, made before the 59th Session of the ECOSOC on 4 July. *Department of State Bulletin*, 73: 1885, 11 August.

Finger, J. Michael. 2001. The Uruguay Round agreements: Problems for developing countries. *The World Economy.* 24: 9. Pp. 1097–1108.

Finger, J. Michael and Philip Schuler. 1999. Implementation of Uruguay Round commitments: The development challenge. World Bank Working Paper. No. 2215. Washington, D.C.: The World Bank.

Fukuyama, Francis. 1989. 'The End of History?' *The National Interest.* 16: 3. Pp. 1–18.

GATT. 1947. General Agreement on Tariffs and Trade. www.wto.org/english/docs_e/legal_e/gatt47.pdf.

1953. Speech by Mr. Joao Alberto Lins de Barros (Brazil). Delivered in Plenary Session. 18 September. Eighth Session of the Contracting Parties. GATT Press Release/ 125. 21 September. https://docs.wto.org/gattdocs/q/GG/GATT/125.PDF.

1954. Speech by Sir N. Raghavan Pillai (India). Delivered in Plenary Session, 9 November. Ninth Session of the Contracting Parties. GATT Press Release/ 185. 11 November. https://docs.wto.org/gattdocs/q/GG/GATT/185.PDF.

1956. The Rules and Procedures for the Tariff Negotiations Commencing on 18 January 1956. Tariff Conference. TN.56/4. www.wto.org/gatt_docs/English/SULPDF/90330319.pdf.

1963. Statement made by the Honourable Mr C.G. Kahaha, Minister for Commerce and Industry, Tanganyika. On 17 May 1963. Meeting of Ministers. GATT Press Release. GATT/772. https://docs.wto.org/gattdocs/q/GG/GATT/772.PDF.

1965. Second Special Session: Summary record of the fifth meeting, held at the Palais des Nations, on 8 February. 2SS/SR.5. www.wto.org/gatt_docs/English/SULPDF/90280219.pdf.

1967. Statement by H.E. Major-General, H.W.G. Wijeyekoon. Ambassador of Ceylon. At the Review of the Work of the Contracting Parties and Future Programme. On 24 November. W.24/60. 30 November.

1979. Decision on Differential and More Favourable Treatment, Reciprocity and Fuller Participation of Developing Countries. LT/TR/D/1. 28 November. www.wto.org/english/docs_e/legal_e/tokyo_enabling_e.pdf.

1994. Uruguay Round Agreements: Agreement Establishing the WTO. www.wto.org/english/docs_e/legal_e/04-wto_e.htm.

GATT Analytic Index. 1994a. 'Article XVIII: Governmental Assistance to Economic Development.' GATT Analytic Index. www.wto.org/english/res_e/publications_e/ai17_e/gatt1994_art18_gatt47.pdf.

1994b. 'Part IV: Trade and Development.' GATT Analytic Index. www.wto.org/english/res_e/booksp_e/gatt_ai_e/part4_e.pdf.

Haberler, Gottfried, Roberto da Oliveira Campos, James Meade, and Jan Tinbergen. 1958. *Trends in International Trade: Report by a Panel of Experts.* Geneva: GATT. www.wto.org/english/res_e/booksp_e/gatt_trends_in_international_trade.pdf.

Hamilton, Colleen and John Whalley. 1989. 'Coalitions in the Uruguay Round.' *Weltwirtschaftliches Archiv.* 125: 3. Pp. 547–556.

Helleiner, Eric. 2014. *Forgotten Foundations of Bretton Woods.* Ithaca: Cornell University Press.

2015. 'India and the neglected development dimensions of Bretton Woods.' *Economic and Political Weekly.* 1: 29. Pp. 31–39.

Higgott, Richard and Andrew Cooper. 1990. 'Middle power leadership and coalition building: Australia, the Cairns Group, and the Uruguay Round of Trade Negotiations.' *International Organization.* 44: 4. Pp. 589–632.

Howse, Robert and Michael Trebilock. 1999. *The Regulation of International Trade.* London: Routledge.

Irwin, Douglas. 1995. 'The GATT in historical perspective.' *American Economic Review.* 85: 2. Pp. 323–328.

Johnson, Harry. 1967. *Economic Policies towards Less Developed Countries.* Brookings: Washington, D.C.

Keynes, John Maynard. 1919. *Economic Consequences of the Peace.* London: Macmillan.

Krasner, Stephen D. 1985. *Structural Conflict: The Third World Against Global Liberalism.* Berkley: University of California Press.

Krauthammer, Charles. 1990. '"The Unipolar Moment". America and the World.' *Foreign Affairs.* 70: 1. Pp. 23–33.

Meade, James. 1942. A proposal for an international commercial union. In Susan Howson (ed.), *The Collected Papers of James Meade Vol. III: International Economics.* London: Unwin Hyman.

Morgenthau, Henry. 1944. Inaugural address (1 July). United Nations Monetary and Financial Conference: Bretton Woods, Final act and related documents, New Hampshire, July 1 to July 22, 1944. Washington: United States Government Printing Office, 1944. www.cvce.eu/content/publication/2003/12/12/34c4153e-6266-4e84-88d7-f655abf1395f/publishable_en.pdf.

Moyo, Dambisa. 2009. *Dead Aid: Why Aid Is Not Working and How There Is Another Way for Africa.* New York: Penguin.

Myrdal, Gunnar. 1975. 'The Equality Issue in World Development.' Nobel Prize Lecture. 17 March. www.nobelprize.org/prizes/economic-sciences/1974/myrdal/lecture/.

Narlikar, Amrita. 2003. *International Trade and Developing Countries: Developing Countries in the GATT and WTO.* London: Routledge.

2012. Collective agency, systemic consequences: Bargaining coalitions in the GATT and WTO. In Amrita Narlikar, Martin Daunton, and Robert M. Stern (eds). *The Oxford Handbook on the WTO.* Oxford: Oxford University Press.

New York Times. 1964. 'Mr Ball's Geneva Homily.' *New York Times Archives.* 26 March. P. 34.

Ostry, Sylvia. 2004. The future of the World Trading System: Beyond Doha. In John Kirton and Michael Trebilock (eds). *Hard Choices, Soft Law: Voluntary Standards in Global Trade.* London: Ashgate (republished 2016, London: Routledge).

Özden, Caglar and Eric Reinhardt. 2005. 'The perversity of preferences: GSP and developing country trade policies, 1976–2000.' *Journal of Development Economics.* 78: 1. Pp. 1–21.

Panagariya, Arvind. 2002. 'EU preferential trade arrangements and developing countries.' *The World Economy*. 25: 10. Pp. 1415–1432.

Preeg, Ernst. 2012. 'The Uruguay Round negotiations and the creation of the WTO.' In Amrita Narlikar, Martin Daunton, and Robert M. Stern (eds). *The Oxford Handbook on the WTO*. Oxford: Oxford University Press.

Ricupero, Rubens. 1998. 'Integration of developing countries into the multilateral trading system. In Jagdish Bhagwati and Mathias Hirsch (eds). *The Uruguay Round and Beyond: Essays in Honour of Arthur Dunkel*. Ann Arbor: University of Michigan Press.

Ruggie, John. 1982. 'International regimes, transactions and change: Embedded liberalism in the postwar economic order.' *International Organization*. 36: 2. Pp. 379–415.

SUNS Online. 1993. 'Indian Farmers rally against Dunkel draft and MNCs.' Special United Nations Service. 5 March. www.sunsonline.org/trade/areas/agricult/03051093.htm.

Tobin, Jennifer and Marc Busch. 2019. 'The disadvantage of membership: How joining the GATT/WTO undermines GSP.' *World Trade Review*. 18: 1. Pp. 133–160.

Toye, John. 2014. UNCTAD at Fifty: A Short History. UNCTAD/OSG/2014/1. Geneva: United Nations Conference on Trade and Development. https://unctad.org/en/PublicationsLibrary/osg2014d1_en.pdf.

Toye, John and Richard Toye. 2004. *The UN and Global Political Economy: Trade, Finance, and Development*. Bloomington: Indiana University Press.

Toye, Richard. 2003. 'Developing multilateralism: The Havana charter and the fight for the International Trade Organization, 1947–1948.' *International Historical Review*. 25: 2. Pp. 282–305.

　　2012. The international trade organisation. In Amrita Narlikar, Martin Daunton, and Robert M. Stern (eds). *The Oxford Handbook on the World Trade Organization*. Oxford: Oxford University Press.

Tucker, Robert. 1975. 'Egalitarianism and International Politics.' *Commentary*. September.

Tussie, Diana. 1993. 'Holding the balance: The Cairns Group in the Uruguay Round.' In Diana Tussie and David Glover (eds). *Developing Countries in World Trade: Policies and Bargaining Strategies*. Boulder: Lynne Rienner.

UN Conference on Trade and Employment. 1947. Heads of Delegations: Summary record of meeting. Havana. 24 December. E/cow.2/23. https://docs.wto.org/gatt docs/q/UN/ECONF2/23.PDF.

　　1948. Final Act and Related Documents. Havana. April. www.wto.org/english/docs_e/legal_e/havana_e.pdf.

UN Economic and Social Council. 1946. Preparatory Committee of the international conference on trade and employment. Committee I. Summary record of meetings (part two). London. 22 October. E/PC/T/CI/7. https://docs.wto.org/gattdocs/q/UN/EPCT/CI-7.PDF.

UN General Assembly. 1974. Resolution adopted by the General Assembly: 3201 (S-VI). Declaration on the Establishment of a New International Economic Order. A/RES/S-6/3201. 1 May. www.un-documents.net/s6r3201.htm.

US State Department. 1945. Proposals for Expansion of Trade and Employment. Developed by Technical Staff within the Government of the United States in

Preparation for an International. Conference on Trade and Employment and Presented for Consideration by the Peoples of the World. Publication 2411. November. https://fraser.stlouisfed.org/files/docs/historical/eccles/036_04_0003.pdf.

Whalley, John. 1990. 'Non-discriminatory discrimination: Special and differential treatment under the GATT for developing countries.' *The Economic Journal.* 100: 403. Pp. 1318–1328.

Williamson, John. 1990. 'What Washington means by policy reform.' In John William-son (ed.). *Latin American Adjustment: How Much Has Happened?* Washington D.C.: Institute for International Economics.

2000. 'What should the Bank think about the Washington Consensus?' *World Bank Research Observer.* 15: 2. Pp. 251–264.

Zeiler, Thomas. 1999. *Free Trade, Free World: The Advent of the GATT.* Chapel Hill: University of North Carolina Press.

2012. The expanding mandate of the GATT. In Amrita Narlikar, Martin Daunton and Robert Stern (eds). *The Oxford Handbook on the World Trade Organization.* Oxford: Oxford University Press.

3

Winning against the Odds

A *Growing Empowerment*

Even decades of activism by developing countries in the post-war economic system had generated lacklustre results, as illustrated in Chapter 2. But towards the end of the 1990s, a dramatic change seemed to get underway. The poverty narrative – as espoused by developing countries along with other actors – came to acquire a qualitatively new importance in international negotiations. This was reflected in negotiation processes as well as outcomes. In this chapter, I analyse the mechanisms whereby this happened. I argue that, although the narrative itself did not fundamentally change, the ways in which it was put into action did. I do this by focusing on four case studies, and also offer some further examples in other issue areas where a similar narrative of poverty and powerlessness seemed to be on a winning streak.

The first three sections of this chapter focus on three sets of negotiations in the WTO, which cluster around three landmark ministerial conferences in chronological order – Seattle (1999), Doha (2001), and Cancun (2003). Section 3.4 studies the influence of the poverty narrative on decision-making processes within the WTO. I provide an overview of parallel developments in other areas in Section 3.5. Section 3.6 offers some conclusions.

3.1 SEATTLE AND THE EMPOWERMENT OF NEW VETO-PLAYERS

The Seattle ministerial conference was expected to run reasonably smoothly. The process had been established at the previous ministerial conference in Geneva in 1998. A press release from the WTO had confidently announced on 28 June 1999, 'The WTO's 3rd Ministerial Conference, scheduled to be held 30 November–3 December 1999 in Seattle, Washington, *will launch* the next major world trade negotiations due to start early in 2000'.[1] Everything was supposed to run like clockwork. Even six days before the conference was scheduled to begin, US Trade Representative and soon-to-be chairperson of the ministerial, Charlene Barshefsky, stated at a press briefing: '... everyone knows that failure is not an option. So it will come together; I have a very high degree of confidence in that'.[2] In fact, the conference did not come together at all.

Seattle ended without even a joint ministerial declaration, let alone the launch of a new round. In contrast to the optimism she had displayed less than a week earlier, Barshefsky ended up having to make the following statement at the closing session of the conference, 'We found as time passed that divergences of opinion remained that would not be overcome rapidly. Our collective judgment, shared by the [WTO] Director-General, the Working Group Chairs and Co-Chairs, and the membership generally, was that it would be best to take a time out, consult with one another, and find creative means to finish the job'.[3] At the conference venue, major conflict had ensued among negotiators over substance and process. Outside, there were protests and riots. Newspaper commentary in the immediate aftermath was by-and-large negative, with the *Financial Times* summing up the seemingly tragic affair in the following words: 'The World Trade Organization talks in Seattle that ended at the weekend were supposed to usher in a new dawn for the global trade system. Instead, they turned into a nightmare. The meeting began with mass demonstrations and vandalism that devastated the city centre, degenerated into all-night feuding between ministers and finished in abject failure'.[4]

The *Economist* also saw the proceedings in Seattle as an unmitigated disaster. In a scathing article entitled 'Clueless in Seattle', the exasperation of the reporters was clear:

> In so many ways, the WTO protesters and the ministers who had to put up with them richly deserve each other. It is hard to say which was worse – watching the militant dunces parade their ignorance through the streets of Seattle, or listening to their lame-brained governments respond to the 'arguments'. No, take that back: the second was worse. At least the rioters had a good time. It was the politicians who made the biggest hash of things ...

---

[1] WTO (1999a). Emphasis added: note the confident language of 'will launch' in contrast, for instance, to 'would launch' or 'aim to launch'. The press pack that the WTO had prepared also reflected a similar confidence that a new round of negotiations would be launched, even though it highlighted some of the differences among members and the challenges facing the organization, WTO (1999b).

[2] White House press briefing (1999).

[3] WTO (1999e).

[4] Jonquières and Williams (1999).

... governments have not merely failed to make the case for free trade. They have pandered to their (unappeasable) critics, moved half-way to meet their demands and lent credence to their bogus fears. When it comes to trade, governments entertain no presumption that people might actually know for themselves what is best. Ever mindful of producer lobbies, governments downplay or deny the fact that freer trade raises incomes: that is why they must be on hand to ensure that trade is 'fair'. And rich-country governments themselves have given rise to legitimate fears that the WTO will take on a role beyond its proper competence. Calls for the body to develop a new agenda on the environment and on labour standards – demands that will push it into matters that, at best, belong in other forums, and which could easily end up hurting the poorest countries – have come mainly from the United States. By acknowledging the need for such an agenda, the administration has conceded much of the ground to its stone-throwing critics and undermined broader support for freedom to trade. 'Clueless' is putting it kindly.[5]

Analysts from academia shared some of the concerns that journalists were voicing. The implications of the 'battle of Seattle' were on the minds of trade analysts, even as they tackled the question of why the ministerial conference had collapsed so spectacularly. Weighing up what the Seattle moment could mean, Gary Hufbauer leaned towards the following assessment: '... ten years from now, Seattle could be seen as the turning point – the event that marked the end of the policy-driven open markets agenda for much of the world'.[6]

Seattle had indeed generated significant costs to the public purse, dented the credibility of a still young WTO, and risked turning out to be a critical step in the anti-globalization movement that could threaten the many achievements of the post-war economic system. But this gloomy reading represents only one side of the Seattle story. The other side, often overlooked, is more positive, where Seattle represents a significant step in the exercise and impact of the poverty narrative. We saw the poverty narrative acquire greater sway on two fronts: outside the official negotiations via the visibility and voice of NGOs that claimed to represent the victims of globalization, and within the official meeting rooms where developing countries put their collective foot down and refused to be coerced into accepting a consensus.

[5]   Economist (1999a). It is worth mentioning though that not all the NGOs in Seattle had an anti-trade agenda. For example, 20 per cent of the NGOs accredited to participate in the conference comprised business groups, among the 700 or so at the official conference venue. www.wto.org/english/thewto_e/minist_e/min99_e/english/ngo_e/ngo_e.htm.

[6]   Hufbauer (1999).

3.1.1 'The WTO Kills People: Kill the WTO': The Revolt on the Streets

'The WTO kills people; kill the WTO' was the slogan of the People's Global Action network, which had a clear anti-globalization agenda. Other signs and slogans on the streets of Seattle clearly displayed the concerns and anger of large groups of people.[7] Although neither the international technocrats nor the country representatives had been prepared for a blowback on the scale that they actually encountered at Seattle, they did have information that protests were planned. In a special report published just before the summit, the *Economist* noted that over 1,000 groups, with over 100,000 demonstrators, were expected – 'a rag-bag that includes trade unionists, environmentalists, aid lobbyists, consumer-rights campaigners, human-rights activists and even a group called "Alien Hand Signals"'.[8] And turn up in droves they did indeed, brandishing posters, mottos, and manifestos of 'Banish WTO: Wake up Muggles', 'Breaking the cycle of exploitation: Reform the WTO or replace it', 'Caution: WTO Ahead', 'City-wide walkout of workers and students against the World Trade Organization', 'Come to Seattle: Festival of resistance', 'Direct Action Network: Against Corporate Globalization', 'Join "No to WTO!" People's Assembly', and more.[9]

Depending on who is doing the reporting, one gets different responses on the impact of the protests. Those involved in the protests (naturally) tend to present the demonstrations as a clear triumph. For example, one group, which describes itself as a 'web toolbox and international network of artist-activist trainers whose mission is to make grassroots movements more creative and more effective', describes its own involvement in the protests in a 'case study' and offers the following assessment:

> ... Teamsters and turtles were literally dancing together in the streets. A few hours later, as the Seattle police unleashed a torrent of tear gas and pepper spray to crack the blockade, 50,000 labor marchers defied their own marshals and reinforced us with a sea of humanity. The biggest business meeting on

---

[7] For a collection of the different slogans and messages of some of the protestors, as well as a detailed time-line of the protests and interviews, see the Washington State Libraries' 'WTO Seattle Collection', accessible at http://content.lib.washington.edu/wtoweb/index.html.

[8] *Economist* (1999b).

[9] Posters and papers and other publicity materials were not the only ammunition that the protestors had. The demonstrations were not always peaceful, and the 'carnival against capitalism' also included anarchists and others of violent persuasions. The Report of Seattle City Council's WTO Accountability Committee (Seattle City Council 2000) gave the following verdict, 'During the WTO conference, legitimate protest activity by thousands on Seattle's streets became tangled with criminal acts of property destruction, vandalism, and assaults on police officers by a few persons in ways that may never be unraveled to everyone's satisfaction'.

Earth had been shut down, a tactical victory most thought impossible. And the rest, as they say, is history.

The impact of Seattle was enormous. It launched the global justice movement in the Global North. It showed that a people's victory against global capital was possible. It created a teachable moment – for the public, on the WTO and the dark side of corporate globalization, and also for the movement, showcasing direct and mass action tactics and a carnivalesque sensibility that are still influential today, as well as training a new wave of actionistas who have gone on to play critical roles across the next decade of progressive movements.[10]

Academic analyses are more sober on the impact that the protests had, at least in producing the outcome of the failure of the ministerial process itself. There were many inadequacies in the negotiation process, and enough discontent and anger among disillusioned members, to generate a collapse of the conference even without the mayhem on the streets. There is also some debate on the extent to which the Seattle protests really represented the emergence of a transnational social movement for global justice. Gillian Murphy and Steven Pfaff, for instance, argue that the Seattle protests were based more in national groups, and relied on local resources.[11] Levi and Murphy study the strategies used by 'coalitions of contention'. They focus specifically on three coalitions formed by non-state organizations: People for Fair Trade/Network Opposed to WTO, Direct Action Network, and the American Federation of Labour Congress of Industrial Organizations & affiliate King County Labour Council. These coalitions were focused on the WTO's ministerial conference, and based themselves in Seattle to prepare in advance of the meeting. An important point that Levi and Murphy investigate is the transformation of their agenda, even through the short course of the ministerial meeting, from the global to the local. These coalitions thus started out with global justice as their main cause, and the WTO as the primary target, but ended up focusing on civil liberties as their central cause and Seattle's government and police force as their primary targets.[12] Jan Aart Scholte highlights several reasons for limiting one's exuberance about the engagement of civil society that Seattle brought to the fore, including the fact that

> the people congregated in Seattle, Geneva, and Washington have come disproportionately from the North ... In terms of gender and race, women and people of colour have been severely underrepresented in the academic, business, and trade union sectors of global civil society. In addition, urban

[10] https://beautifultrouble.org/case/battle-in-seattle/
[11] Murphy and Pfaff (2005).
[12] Levi and Murphy (2006).

residents have tended to obtain far easier access to civic campaigns on global economic governance than people from the countryside.[13]

Altogether then, we have good reason to question even the limited impact that the Seattle protests had on the ministerial conference itself (let alone the wider issues of global justice that the activists hoped to address and seek redressal for), as well as the extent to which the demonstrators could legitimately claim to speak on behalf of the global poor. But even though their direct impact on the ministerial outcome was limited, and one can and should ask questions about their accountability and legitimacy, two significant contributions of the Seattle protests must be acknowledged.

First, in the high level of engagement of 'ordinary' citizens, Seattle was unprecedented. Almost three months prior to the ministerial meeting, at a press conference, the Director-General of the WTO, Mike Moore, had taken note of the remarkable activism at work: 'Ordinary people greeted the launch of the Uruguay Round with apathy, the possibility of launching a new round in Seattle will be met with far greater emotions, some positive, some not so positive ... This time we will not be able to complain about apathy'.[14] These citizens advanced a narrative that emphasized the inadequacies of the multi-lateral trading system because it left so many actors marginalized and their interests unrepresented. They argued that a fundamental change was necessary, even though they were divided on whether this would involve reforming the WTO or getting rid of it. And, unlike trade negotiators from developing countries who had long argued such a case within international institutions, they were making this argument publicly.

Second, even though there was enough trouble brewing inside the conference venue among members (as I outline in the next sub-section) and the breakdown cannot be attributed to the street protests alone, the inside and outside were not hermetically sealed from each other. The interactions between the two included, but went considerably beyond, the physical disruption and delays caused by blockades.[15] Two effects were especially important.

(a) Nicholas Bayne points out that 'the NGOs' activities did increase the tension between developed and developing countries, especially between the United States and the rest, and this made agreement more difficult'. This happened because the protestors, even when claiming to speak on

---

[13] Scholte (2000).

[14] WTO (1999c).

[15] An example of the disruption was the human chain that protestors formed around the venue, which prevented delegates from getting access to the conference. As a result, the opening ceremony could not take place.

behalf of not just the poor in the developed world but the global poor, came from NGOs that were based in developed countries. Both the European Union and the United States (albeit to different degrees and for different reasons) tried to conciliate the NGOs. In contrast, developing countries had little sympathy for the labour standards or environmental standards that some NGOs were pushing for. Bayne writes, 'Even the development NGOs based in the West were regarded with mixed feelings by the governments of poor countries, who wanted to define and promote their development interests themselves, not have others do it for them'.[16] The Indian Minister for Commerce and Industry, Murasoli Maran enunciated just such a position: 'The international civil society has shown keen interest in the activities of the WTO. While they have a vital role to play in any democratic polity, it is really for national governments to deal with civil society within their domestic domain'.[17] An unintended consequence of the protests outside was thus an exacerbation of tensions between developed country members and developing country members.

(b) Even though the protestors found themselves at odds with developing countries, the broad sweep of their agenda for global economic justice may have created a more enabling context for dissident negotiators from developing countries to also raise their voices in protest. And developing countries articulated their demands in Seattle, acted on them, and produced an effect, which they had just not managed before.

3.1.2 *A Coup from Within*

Most academic and policy analyses recognize that the Seattle protests were just the tip of the iceberg of challenges facing the WTO at the time. There were several underlying and more fundamental causes for the chaos that had resulted in the collapse of the WTO's third ministerial conference. They included poor preparatory processes;[18] fundamental disagreement among members on the scope of issues;[19] and inadequate negotiation[20] and

---

[16] Bayne (2000), pp. 137–138.
[17] WTO (1999d).
[18] This included the contested and delayed appointment of the Director-General, which not only took time away from the preparations but heightened the atmosphere of distrust within the organization. E.g., Bayne (2000); Bernal (1999).
[19] E.g., Bayne (2000); Japan Ministry of Economy, Trade and Industry (METI) (2000); Odell (2006); US General Accounting Office (2000).
[20] Odell (2009) focuses on several failures of the negotiation process, including a heavily bracketed chair's text and lack of effective mediation. Normally, the chair and ambassadors

decision-making processes.[21] Over 800 proposals had been submitted by members as part of the Seattle process (from August 1998 to November 1999).[22] Such a wide range of proposals naturally produced cross-cutting alignments and fault-lines.[23] But, amidst all these complications, a strong north–south dimension emerged in the negotiation, and developing countries came to exercise an extraordinary voice. They declared, 'We reject the approach that is being employed . . .' and effectively declared a coup from within the ranks of the organization.[24]

By-and-large, developing countries were opposed to the inclusion of the issues of environment and labour standards into the agenda of the WTO. A group among them had further argued that long-standing issues of the unkept promises and unanticipated costs of the Uruguay Round had to be addressed as a priority.[25] India had played a leading role in developing these positions. And, as it had done in the past, it once again appealed to issues of fairness and equity, particularly from the perspective of poor countries. Minister Maran, for example, had made a clear statement at the start of the conference on the issue of the unfulfilled promises of the last round, and the importance of ensuring redressal:[26]

> Our assessment has all along been that the Uruguay Round Agreements have not served all the membership well. There are critical gaps that need to be urgently addressed.
>
> Asymmetries and inequities in several of the agreements including those relating to anti-dumping, subsidies, intellectual property, TRIMs and the

---

work through multiple iterations of a draft text, trying to narrow down the differences and having a minimum number of points in square brackets that indicate points where disagreement still remains. The draft (WTO 1999h) that was sent to the ministers in Seattle was a 'sprawling' 34 pages long (Odell 2009) and contained 402 pairs of square brackets (VanGrasstek 2013). In the official history of the WTO, VanGrasstek describes this text as follows: 'Far from being a consensus document, it averaged about one pair of brackets for every two centimetres of text. It was as if the Geneva ambassadors had prepared a multiple-choice examination for the ministers, and this is a test that they would collectively fail' (p. 486).

[21] Pascal Lamy (1999), as EU Trade Commissioner at the Seattle ministerial, had the following indictment of WTO decision-making processes: 'We are deeply worried about the WTO process. The procedures are medieval, and I sympathise with Charlene Barshesky, who will need to be a magician to produce a deal out of all this'.

[22] All the proposals are available on the WTO's website at www.wto.org/english/thewto_e/minist_e/min99_e/min99_e.htm. The website also offers a helpful summary of proposals submitted in the second phase of the preparatory process (WTO 1999f).

[23] E.g., Bhagwati (2001); Schott (2000).

[24] Third World Network (1999a).

[25] WTO (1999g).

[26] WTO (1999d).

non-realization of expected benefits from agreements such as textiles and agriculture during implementation have been a matter of great concern. The special and differential treatment clauses have remained virtually inoperative ... It is for these reasons that many developing countries have highlighted implementational issues and concerns ... Addressing the implementation issues effectively upfront will alone ensure an image of fairness and equity to the WTO.

Recall some of the statements made by developing countries in the ITO negotiations, which had emphasized special development considerations for developing countries, and also the fact that similar demands had been enunciated in the GATT. Seattle included such demands, but also others. The framing was palpably stronger and angrier as it reflected the disappointment of developing countries with what they saw as the unfulfilled promises and unanticipated costs of the Uruguay Round.

In highlighting the 'implementation issues', India was not alone. Other developing countries were also concerned that implementing the Uruguay Round agreements had generated unanticipated costs for them, without having delivered the promised gains. A coalition of countries – the Like Minded Group – had been working since the Singapore ministerial conference in 1996 to bring these problems to the fore. Initially, this India-led coalition had focused mainly on avoiding the inclusion of the so-called Singapore issues (trade and investment, government procurement, competition policy, and trade facilitation) and labour standards into the WTO. In 1998, the coalition began to focus more directly on implementation issues; as a result of its activism, the Geneva ministerial declaration of 1998 included references to these concerns.[27] Especially in the run-up to the Seattle ministerial conference, the LMG became even more concerted in its efforts.[28] An important flip-side of trying to focus attention on the implementation issues was a continued and clear resistance to any attempts towards the inclusion of environmental and labour standards. Minister Maran from India led the charge on this in his opening speech at Seattle:

> ... The multilateral trading system has been designed to deal with issues involving trade and trade alone. India in good faith had agreed at Marrakesh to the establishment of a WTO Committee on Trade and Environment. We

---

[27] Especially paragraphs 8 and 9, WTO (1998).

[28] Narlikar and Odell (2006). Comprising eleven countries (original members were Cuba, Egypt, India, Indonesia, Malaysia, Pakistan, Tanzania, and Uganda; by the time of the Seattle meeting, it included Dominican Republic, Honduras, and Zimbabwe). The group continued to be active after Seattle too, both before and after the Doha ministerial conference in 2001.

would, however, strongly oppose any attempt to either change the Committee's structure or mandate which can be used for legitimizing unilateral trade restrictive measures. Attempts aimed at inclusion of environmental issues in future negotiations go beyond the competence of the multilateral trading system and have the potential to open the floodgates of protectionism.

On the issue of labour, India is fully committed to observance of labour standards and has ratified most ILO conventions. We also cherish all the values of democracy, workers' rights and good governance. These issues however are not under the purview of the WTO. At Singapore, we decided once and for all, that labour-related issues rightly belong to the ILO. India resolutely rejects renewed attempts to introduce these in the WTO in one form or another. Any further move will cause deep divisions and distrust that can only harm the formation of a consensus on our future work programme.

Against this unambiguous position (which India and other countries had maintained fairly consistently in the preparatory process, and also at the start of the conference on 30 November), Seattle generated an unpleasant surprise. US President Bill Clinton, even before arriving in Seattle, gave a phone interview to the *Seattle Post* Intelligencer on 30 November, in which he emphasized his desire to incorporate labour standards into future WTO agreements. In fact, he went a step further by indicating that he would 'favour a system in which sanctions would come for violating any provision of a trade agreement'.[29] This proposal was anathema to many developing countries. The *Washington Post* reported the reaction as follows:

> The interview became a sensation. 'Nobody believed their eyes' when they read Clinton's comments, said Anabel Gonzalez, Costa Rica's vice minister of foreign trade. Many developing countries seized on the comments as evidence that the United States planned to impose new protectionist measures in the guise of labor standards that were actually designed to keep the poorer countries poor.[30]

That this was not just a diplomatic slip became clear in a speech that Clinton made on 1 December at a WTO luncheon, when he dropped three bombshells.[31] First, he reiterated his support for a linkage between trade and labour standards, and that too within the context of the WTO:

> ... the WTO must make sure that open trade does indeed lift living standards – respects core labor standards that are essential not only to worker rights,

[29] Froning (1999).
[30] Kaiser and Burgess (1999).
[31] Clinton (1999).

but to human rights. That's why this year the United States has proposed that the WTO create a working group on trade and labor. To deny the importance of these issues in a global economy is to deny the dignity of work – the belief that honest labor fairly compensated gives meaning and structure to our lives. I hope we can affirm these values at this meeting.[32]

Second, Clinton also brought in the issue of environmental standards:

Now, we do not have a right to ask anybody to give up economic growth. But we do have a right to say, if we're prepared to help you finance a different path to growth, and we can prove to you – and you accept, on the evidence – that your growth will be faster, not smaller, that you'll have more good jobs, more new technology, a broader base for your economy – then I do believe we ought to have those kind of environmental standards. And we ought to do it in a voluntary way with available technologies. But we ought to put environment at the core of our trade concerns.

Third, from the perspective of developing countries, not only did Clinton pander to the protestors by offering them concessions on labour and environmental standards, but also by arguing in favour of a bigger voice for NGOs within the WTO: 'The sooner the WTO opens up the process, and lets people representing those who are outside in, the sooner we will see fewer demonstrations, more constructive debate, and a broader level of support in every country for the direction that every single person in this room knows that we ought to be taking into the twenty-first century'.

It is notable that Clinton framed his support for civil society representation in the WTO, and also the inclusion of labour and environmental standards, in terms of a poverty narrative: the claim underpinning his proposals was that if his ideas were to be adopted, the poor and marginalized would gain globally. But this did not go down well with poor countries, and the labour question in particular attracted severe resistance. The Egyptian trade minister, Yousef Boutros-Ghali, described Clinton's attempt to link trade with labour as 'nonsensical', and retorted, 'The question is why all of a sudden, when third world labor has proved to be competitive, why do industrial countries start feeling concerned about our workers? When all of a sudden there is a concern about the welfare of our workers, it is suspicious'. A senior negotiator from Pakistan is reported to have been even more direct: 'We will block consensus on every issue if the United States proposal goes ahead ... We will explode the meeting'.[33]

[32] Clinton (1999).
[33] Greenhouse and Kahn (1999).

The anger of developing countries was patently visible as the conference progressed. The process of decision-making – always a source of some bickering – proved to be the last straw when Charlene Barshefsky, now chairperson of the conference, declared her readiness to use exclusionary Green Room meetings to reach consensus. I discuss the specifics of decision-making in Section 3.4, and trace exactly how the attempt to further marginalize poor and powerless countries actually resulted in their exercising much greater voice. At this point, suffice it to note that on 2 December, three groups of developing countries rose back in anger. In three separate statements,[34] they took serious issue with the Seattle process.

The African trade ministers stated:

> There is no transparency in the proceedings and African countries are being marginalized and generally excluded on issues of vital importance for our peoples and their future. We are particularly concerned over the stated intentions to produce a ministerial text at any cost, including at the cost of procedures designed to secure participation and consensus.
>
> We reject the approach that is being employed and we must point out that under the present circumstances, we will not be able to join the consensus required to meet the objectives of this Ministerial Conference.

The ministers of CARICOM similarly declared, 'their strong conviction that, as long as due respect to the procedures and conditions of transparency, openness and participation that allow for adequately balanced results in respect of the interests of all members do not exist, we will not join the consensus to meet the objectives of this Ministerial Conference'. The Latin American and Caribbean countries, in their joint communique, were equally critical of the host country for the poor organization of the conference, and also of the conference and WTO authorities for lack of due process. To the entire membership of the organization, they announced, '... as long as due respect to the procedures and conditions of transparency, openness and participation that allow for adequately balanced results in respect of the interests of all members do not exist, we will not join the consensus required to meet the objectives of this Ministerial Conference'.

Notably, NGOs reinforced the narrative that the marginalization of developing countries from WTO processes was no longer acceptable. The Third World Network, for instance, put out the following statement:

> NGOs from developing countries are shocked and outraged at the way the WTO and the organizers have treated the developing-country Members of the WTO at the Seattle Ministerial.

---

[34] All three statements can be found in Third World Network (1999a).

What has been going on in Seattle is a scandal. Developing countries that form more than two-thirds of the membership of the WTO are being coerced and stampeded by the major powers, especially the host country the US, to agree to a Declaration which they were given very little opportunity to draft or to consider.[35]

On 3 December, at the concluding plenary session of the conference, Barshefsky had to admit defeat. The negotiations were brought to a halt. No new round had been launched, nor had there been a ministerial declaration. From the perspective of the global south that had repeatedly expressed extreme dissatisfaction with the substance and process, the failure of the ministerial was a remarkable and positive development.[36] The success moreover was not limited to the failure of a new round to launch; Seattle also triggered a fundamental reflection and debate on reform of the WTO, especially in terms of ensuring better representation and voice for developing countries (discussed further in Section 3.4).

3.1.3 *Explaining the Rise of the Powerless in Seattle*

Seattle was not the first time when developing countries had taken issue with both the substance and the process of the negotiations. Nor was it the first time that they had demanded that the system be reformed to work better for poor countries. But this time their activism generated clear and visible results. These included not only avoiding an unwanted agreement, but also precipitating a shock to the system that resulted in much soul-searching, updating, and reform in the years to come. Why were the powerless able to rise with such force in Seattle? In good measure, the power of the powerless in Seattle derived from their different handling of their own version of the poverty narrative.

---

[35] Third World Network (1999b).

[36] Much of the literature on negotiation is aimed at reaching breakthroughs, and suffers from an implicit normative bias that the purpose of all negotiation is 'Getting to Yes' (as per the title of the classic by Fisher and Ury 1997). In fact, however, depending on where one sits in a power relationship, to not get steamrolled into an agreement can sometimes be the preferred outcome (Narlikar 2010). In this sense, from the perspective of developing countries, several 'failures' of negotiations can be judged as successes. This holds true, however, only as long as deadlock does not become chronic. A condition of recurrent deadlock is rarely advantageous to developing countries, which have less 'go-it-alone power' (Gruber 2000) than developed countries. At the point of constant chronic deadlock, the mantra of 'no deal is better than this deal' – which was indeed cleverly used by developing countries in the early years of the Doha negotiations – can become a costly platitude.

In contrast to the Uruguay Round, the poverty narrative of Seattle was no longer simply about seeking Special and Differential Treatment (SDT) clauses of exemptions from the rules in order to secure some breathing space for the world's poor countries and peoples. Rather, it was about correcting (what they saw as) the harm done to them by the Uruguay Round. The causal narrative on the relationship between trade and poverty thus received an interesting twist, and an angry new frame, on this front in WTO debates. Many developing countries argued they had been short-changed in the 'grand bargain' of the Uruguay Round. Until the 'implementation issues' had been addressed, attempts to launch a new round with a wide scope were unacceptable. Process concerns also came to be included in this narrative, where developing countries refused to be sidelined. It is worth bearing in mind though that developing countries had tried to launch a fundamental challenge to the existing rules in the 1960s and 1970s (as discussed in Chapter 2), without generating a similar effect. Four factors explain why they were able to cause such a big reverberation in Seattle.

First, the international ideational context enabled the cause of poor empowerment. The East Asian financial crisis of 1998, and the counter-productive interventions by international organizations (particularly the IMF), had brought the Washington consensus into considerable discredit.[37] For developing countries that had long argued – usually to deaf ears – that trade liberalization might not automatically lead to growth and development for them, this questioning of market fundamentalism or neo-liberal orthodoxy provided an important opportunity. It helped create a context where their concerns about fairness and development had a greater possibility of at least getting a hearing, rather than just be derided as a cover for protecting crony capitalism and narrow special interests.

Attention to questions of global poverty had been growing in some years prior to the Seattle Ministerial, which had also served as a vital background against which the Millennium Development Goals (MDGs) were negotiated. David Hulme marks 1990 as a 'pivotal year': 'Against the backdrop of the end of the Cold War three influential "events" happened in the world of development ideas to bring poverty in from the cold'.[38] These three events were: (a) the publication of the World Bank's first World Development Report, 'which reviewed poverty reduction and indicated that poverty was now a rehabilitated concept, having previously been marginalized within the Bank', (b) the publication of the first Human Development Report by the United Nations

---

[37] E.g., Furman and Stiglitz (1998); Stiglitz (1999).
[38] Hulme (2009), p. 8.

Development Programme (UNDP), which 'amplified the message that poverty was on the agenda ... Policies need to pursue ends (improved lives) and not just means (economic growth)', and (c) the 'reactivation of UN summits and conferences', with four major conferences in 1990 itself and other prominent ones through the decade (ranging from the UN World Summit for Children in 1990, to the Earth Summit in Rio, International Conference on Food and Nutrition in Rome in 1992, World Summit on Social Development in Copenhagen in 1995, and so forth). Hulme traces the process of negotiation of the International Development Goals, IDGs (of the *Groupe de Réflexion*, which was established as a political grouping at the initiative of the OECD's Development Assistance Committee, DAC, to address the problem of declining aid flows), which worked in parallel to the UN processes that eventually led to the launching of the MDG. While Hulme brings to light the differences in the approaches of the two institutions, and also the audiences that they targeted, one takeaway point is important for our purposes: besides the OECD and the UN, numerous government agencies, NGOs, and leading politicians were involved in these processes. The debate was no longer limited to a narrow community of experts; rather, it was in the public policy realm. The empowerment of 'We the peoples' was beginning to be perceived as a priority for many actors: through clear goals – whether they were the narrow IDGs or the more evolved MDGs – people's lives could be improved and deserved to be improved.

Transnational social movements constituted the second crucial ingredient in the recipe to empower the powerless in Seattle. Again, this involvement of NGOs in Seattle was grounded in activism in other institutions and issue areas as well (e.g., Multilateral Agreement on Investment). More specifically with reference to Seattle though, as argued earlier in this chapter, the protests and demonstrations on the streets did not directly cause the breakdown of the ministerial process. But the indirect effect of civil society activism was significant, and on balance resulted in the further empowerment of developing countries. This claim needs some unpacking because there were several reasons to expect the exact opposite: the demonstrations outside could have resulted in a further undermining of the power of poor countries. After all, the transnational social movements that shook Seattle had developed a poverty narrative that was at cross-purposes with that of the developing countries. This alternative narrative had emphasized the importance of labour standards, environmental standards, and direct voice to non-state actors in the process. Especially with Clinton having supported NGOs on all three fronts, it was even more likely that the NGO narrative would acquire dominance in WTO debates. Additionally, Nicholas Bayne has argued, 'Many countries were so irritated by the obstructive demonstrators and the extreme NGOs that they did not want to give them the satisfaction of seeing the meeting fail'.[39] Under these circumstances, developing countries could have found themselves under even greater pressure than usual to make concessions, and cave in the endgame. That this did not happen was because even though the agendas of northern NGOs outside, and southern states inside, were sometimes in conflict, the overarching narrative that the system had failed to deliver for the world's poor was one that both sides shared. The dramatic events that were unfolding in the streets of Seattle were one sign of the dissatisfaction against the WTO; there was a complementarity in this message and the one that developing countries were putting out regarding their marginalization from the process (even though, ironically, the human chain around the convention centre had contributed to the physical lack of access to the negotiations for some member countries). Interestingly, thus, in spite of their concrete differences, northern non-state actors and southern states found their shared dissatisfactions indirectly reinforcing and enabling each other against a common enemy (i.e., the WTO and the neo-liberal order that its critics associated it with).

Third, by the time of the Seattle ministerial conference, developing countries had accumulated valuable experience in coalition formation within the context of the WTO as well as through the history of the GATT. The Like Minded Group was an important example of how developing countries worked together on implementation concerns, presenting detailed technical proposals in arguing their case. On matters of process, we have seen that developing countries presented joint statements from the regional groupings that condemned the exclusionary tactics that were being employed. Having experienced the costs of disunity in the past, these coalitions also attempted to signal their commitment to stand together in the endgame. The statements by the three regional groupings, clearly stating that they would not be able to join consensus unless more inclusive processes were used, were concrete actions that locked in their own positions and made them more resistant to divisive tactics by outside parties. At this stage, it is unlikely that such efforts at collective action might have sufficed on their own. But they served as the key additional instrument in the hands of developing countries themselves, which allowed them to harness the first two advantages of a supportive ideational context, plus a coincidental broad alignment of their critique of

---

[39] Bayne (2000), p. 138.

the WTO with the fundamental questions that transnational social movements were also raising about the multilateral trading system.

Finally, while the narrative that developing countries advanced at Seattle
was not dramatically different from previous iterations, it was framed in
considerably angrier and emotive terms. Recall that more radical framing
had not proven to be successful in the past. But the frame used in Seattle
was not about a replacement of the WTO with an alternative institution (in
contrast to the creation of the UNCTAD as an alternative to the GATT). Nor
did it fundamentally question the mandate of the organization. Rather, the
new frame highlighted the failure of the multilateral trade regime to live up to
its *own* promises with respect to developing countries. Such framing may have
been especially effective when the legitimacy of the WTO was already under
challenge on the streets of Seattle.

Seattle represented the potential start of a new empowerment. It was not
clear at the time whether these successes would be sustainable, or if they
would fizzle out. The next years would serve as a test: if the poor (countries or
people) were unable to develop their influence further, then we would know
that Seattle was just a product of an enabling context plus the short-lived
confluence of the agendas of two actors with fundamentally divergent interests. But if poverty remained, or grew, as a focus in the negotiation process,
and if the powerless continued to refer to their powerlessness to set the agenda
and achieve gains, then we would know that a winning narrative was emerging
emerged.

3.2 DOHA: MAINSTREAMING DEVELOPMENT INTO THE WTO

Seattle had shown that the poor finally – by virtue of being poor – had the
power to walk away and disrupt. The first test of whether this power could be
used to achieve positive outcomes came with the WTO's fourth ministerial
conference, which was held from 9 to 13 November 2001 in Doha, Qatar.

Doha was likely to be quite a different affair from Seattle. For one, it was a
less accessible location for protestors. A smaller number of NGOs was
accredited (776 in Seattle, 651 in Doha), and even fewer attended (686 in
Seattle, 370 in Doha).[40] Second, the conference took place only two months
after the terrorist attacks on the World Trade Centre in New York. Both factors
were likely to act as constraints on the exercise of their newfound power for
developing countries: (a) northern governments were now under less pressure

---

[40] Van den Bossche (2006).

in comparison to Seattle due to the limited political space for demonstrations and civil disobedience in Qatar and (b) the importance of showing international cooperation and unity in the face of 9/11 meant that developing countries could potentially be put under greater pressure to agree to a deal. Besides, WTO officials and northern governments had also learnt some lessons from Seattle: they were likely to avoid a re-enactment of the chaos that had followed from poor preparation, bracketed texts, and so forth. These altered circumstances make Doha a hard test case for the exercise of the power of the powerless.

It was a test that developing countries passed, on balance, with flying colours. The Doha ministerial conference was a successful one: ministers agreed to a joint declaration and also to the launch of a new round. The successes of the ministerial were moreover not achieved by trampling on the ambitions of the global south, as had often been the case in the past; developing countries, still using the poverty narrative that they had begun advancing in Seattle, were able to effectively shape the agenda to their advantage.

The biggest achievement of developing countries (and other development actors) was to put their own priority – development – at the core of the new trade round. This was reflected in the naming of the round too – the 'Doha Development Agenda' – a feat that would have been difficult to realize in the days of the GATT. Especially for a regime that had long and consistently claimed to be primarily about trade and had argued against mission creep, the importance of this step cannot be overemphasized. It effectively reflected a fundamental change in approach, an epistemic and normative admission that trade liberalization, with a largely one-size-fits all model, would not suffice, nor would it automatically lead to development. Rather, development had to be prioritized as a goal, and the concerns of developing countries had to be taken seriously. The ministerial declaration thus stated upfront in Paragraph 2:[41]

> The majority of WTO members are developing countries. We seek to place their needs and interests at the heart of the Work Programme adopted in this Declaration ... The majority of WTO members are developing countries. We seek to place their needs and interests at the heart of the Work Programme adopted in this Declaration.

Paragraph 3 paid special attention to the LDCs:

> We recognize the particular vulnerability of the least-developed countries and the special structural difficulties they face in the global economy. We are

---

[41] WTO (2001a).

committed to addressing the marginalization of least-developed countries in international trade and to improving their effective participation in the multilateral trading system.[42]

These were remarkable advancements, which stood out in stark contrast to the GATT, where the issue of development had appeared more as an afterthought via Part IV. References to development concerns did not, moreover, end with the preliminaries of the declaration; they recurred throughout the text. Multiple paragraphs are devoted explicitly to issues that developing countries and LDCs had long tried to mainstream into the WTO (e.g., paragraph 36 on trade, debt, and finance; paragraph 37 on technology transfer, paragraphs 38–41 on technical cooperation and capacity-building, paragraphs 42–43 on LDCs, and paragraph 44 on SDT). And within this big win of taking the WTO outside the comfort zone of narrowly defined trade issues, the achievements of developing countries on access to medicine were an especially important illustration of the exercise of the power of the powerless.

3.2.1 *TRIPS and Public Health*

The Agreement on Trade-Related Intellectual Property Rights (TRIPS), under the WTO umbrella, offers protection to owners of different types of intellectual property rights, including patents for medicines. The agreement is one that is widely regarded as skewed in favour of developed countries, and an especially costly result of the Uruguay Round negotiations for countries lower down the technology ladder. The implementation of their WTO obligations required developing countries to amend their intellectual property laws, and the TRIPS agreement was expected to significantly increase the prices of medicines. For developing countries, and especially for lower income households within them, which would have to spend a much higher percentage of their incomes on these expensive medicines, this was sometimes a life-or-death issue.[43] True, the agreement did provide for some flexibilities, and an important one is that countries can issue 'compulsory licenses' under conditions of national emergency, whereby generic drugs can be produced without permission from the patent-holder. But a central issue was whether developing

---

[42] Ibid.

[43] Scherer and Watal (2001). The authors point out that, given the importance of accessible, affordable medicines, many developed countries had also excluded pharmaceutical products from patent protection: 'Germany until 1968, Switzerland until 1977, Italy until 1978, Spain until 1992, Portugal until 1992, Norway until 1992, Finland until 1995 and Iceland until 1997' (p. 4).

countries would, in practice, be able to (or indeed be allowed to) make use of these flexibilities and safeguards.[44]

When developing countries (including South Africa, Brazil, Thailand, and others) tried to make use of the compulsory licensing provision to deal with the AIDS pandemic in the late 1990s, they encountered complaints, threats, and even legal action from pharmaceutical firms seeking to protect their patents. In the early phases of this fight, these pharmaceutical companies received backing from their governments, especially the United States.[45] Rather than bow down to these pressures, developing countries mobilized a powerful coalition of the weak. Working in co-operation with non-governmental organizations (NGOs), they were able to set the agenda for the TRIPS and Public Health Declaration, which was negotiated in 2001 and included as part of the Doha Ministerial Declaration. This declaration was quite far-reaching in confirming the principle that implementation of the TRIPS agreement could not come at the cost of measures to protect public health. Paragraph 4 stated:

> We agree that the TRIPS Agreement does not and should not prevent members from taking measures to protect public health. Accordingly, while reiterating our commitment to the TRIPS Agreement, we affirm that the Agreement can and should be interpreted and implemented in a manner supportive of WTO members' right to protect public health and, in particular, to promote access to medicines for all.
>
> In this connection, we reaffirm the right of WTO members to use, to the full, the provisions in the TRIPS Agreement, which provide flexibility for this purpose.

The declaration further recognized that 'Each member has the right to grant compulsory licences and the freedom to determine the grounds upon which such licences are granted' (paragraph 5b) and further that it was up to each member to determine what constituted a 'national emergency or other circumstances of extreme emergency' (paragraph 5c).

Finally, the declaration acknowledged under Paragraph 6 that countries lacking the capacity to manufacture generic drugs would not be able to make use of the flexibilities provided by compulsory licensing. It thereby instructed the TRIPS council to find an 'expeditious solution' to this problem.

All in all, this declaration represented a clear win for developing countries and poor populations who had been adversely affected by TRIPS,

---

[44] Hoen (2002).
[45] Hoen (2002); Morin (2011); Odell and Sell (2006); Sun (2004).

and quite a slap for the pharmaceutical firms and the governments that had
backed their cause.

3.2.2 *Explaining the Success of the Poverty Narrative in the TRIPS Negotiations*

In this negotiation, the poor countries, even as a coalition, had started off from
a bargaining position of extreme weakness. They were helpless, and they were
clear victims of unfair rules of the WTO. Very smartly, developing countries
drew attention to this fact. They reminded the world that they were not asking
for luxuries, they were asking for affordable life-saving drugs for the dying. This
narrative was a vital device in endowing their cause with a moral strength.
Neither rich countries nor rich firms could have used this strategy.[46] The poor
countries won precisely because they were poor. But one could well ask the
question why developing countries were able to exercise this agency *at this
point* and get a result that should have been morally compelling all along. The
answer lies in four factors.

The success that developing countries achieved on TRIPs and public
health was a product, first and foremost, of the specifics of a poverty narrative
that they developed. John Odell and Susan Sell highlight the importance of
framing in this debate. In the Uruguay Round, the United States and its
pharmaceutical lobbies had presented a moral case for the protection of
patents by framing intellectual piracy as theft. Stealing is wrong and, hence,
it was argued, the world needed a rigorous system of protection for intellectual
property rights. Now, the world's poor reframed the same issue with a different
reference point. Life-saving medicines were available, but pharmaceutical
firms were willing to let people die in order to retain their profit margins.
'Not only that, but Washington was also trying to use the WTO to discourage
countries from exercising the emergency exception to save lives'.[47] Jean-
Frederic Morin offers a similar analysis:

[46] In fact, the rich countries worked hard with counter-strategies and counter-proposals. For
helpful accounts of the negotiation proposals, and how the wording of the declaration was
finally arrived at, see Sun (2004) and Odell and Sell (2006).

[47] Odell and Sell (2006). Note that the theoretical approach that Odell and Sell employ is that of
'framing'. They define framing in the following way: 'People transform information into
knowledge sometimes by employing different normative frames (Comor 2001). Frames have
also been defined as "specific metaphors, symbolic representations and cognitive clues used to
render or cast behavior and events in an evaluative mode and to suggest alternative modes of
actions" (Zald 1996, p. 262). Explicitly ethical arguments can also be part of framing'. I would
however argue that their case is an illustration of not just 're-framing the issue'. Rather, what we
see in the transformation from 'patent rights should be upheld because it is wrong to steal' to

... the issue was framed in a simple and highly successful formula, equating patents with high prices, and therefore with the narrative of premature death. The public's perspective was influenced by strategic vilification that cast pharmaceutical companies as greedy multinationals, juxtaposed against images of dying poor people. Advocates portrayed the South African litigation as a battle between powerful transnational corporations on one side, defending excessive profit margins, and a weak state on the other side, defending human life.[48]

This dire situation just could not be allowed to continue. The Africa group, which played a leading role in developing this narrative, made the following statement establishing two causal relationships. First, avoidable deaths were being caused because people were being denied access to medicines. Second, these deaths were taking place despite the fact that TRIPS actually had provisions and exceptions that should have allowed the poor citizens of poor countries access to medicines. See, for example, the following statement:

> The death toll from preventable and treatable infectious diseases is unacceptably high. 11 million people, most of them in developing countries, die each year from such diseases. In the case of HIV/AIDS, a human tragedy of horrific dimensions is now at hand. In some countries in Africa, more than a quarter of the adult population has HIV. Life expectancy is projected to fall dramatically. In industrialized countries AIDS deaths have been significantly reduced partly because of the availability of life-saving medicines to many patients. Patients in developing countries also deserve access to medicines at affordable prices, to treat AIDS and other diseases. ...
>
> ... Members should reach a common understanding that asserts and confirms the balance in the TRIPs Agreement that recognizes the importance of patent protection and provides that Governments may adopt all appropriate measures to protect the health and lives of their people. This is the assurance and guarantee that Governments need, to enable them to adopt such measures, without fear of litigation (either at national level or at the WTO) or that bilateral pressures will be applied on them. The Africa Group is convinced that all members, as a matter of right and at their discretion, can take advantage of the existing provisions and safeguards in the Agreement.[49]

'patent rights should be relaxed to prevent unnecessary deaths' are causal stories that negotiators, business groups, civil society, and other actors told themselves and others as they advanced, defended, and legitimized their cases. These causal stories shared a strategic element with 'framing', but ran deeper and were more pervasive.

[48] Morin (2011), p. 234.
[49] Africa Group (2001).

Interestingly, even though the narrative was a highly emotive one, it showed moderation in terms of the changes it sought. The Africa group did not seek a complete overthrow of TRIPs or the WTO. Rather, it sought to contextualize TRIPs and reinterpret it, rather than aim for a complete rewriting of the agreement. The group thus stated, 'In the context of public health, patent rights should be exercised coherently to the mutual advantage of patent holders and the users of patented medicines, in a manner conducive to social and economic welfare and to balance rights and obligations'.[50] The narrative that linked TRIPS and public health offered an unusual mix of some soul-stirring passion (after all, it dealt with life and death issues) on the one hand, and level-headed and palatable policy prescription on the other. This mix worked to the advantage of the cause.

The second factor that facilitated the dominance of this narrative in Doha was that its proponents worked in coalitions. Some sixty states constituted this coalition, and the Africa group its core. Zimbabwe's Ambassador Boniface Chidyausiku played a leading role in getting the issue on the agenda of the WTO, especially in his role as chair of the Africa group and chair of the TRIPS council. As a result of his efforts, a special session of the TRIPS Council on access to medicine was agreed on. Besides the Africa Group, members of the coalition included Barbados, Bolivia, Brazil, Dominican Republic, Ecuador, Honduras, India, Indonesia, Jamaica, Pakistan, Paraguay, Philippines, Peru, Sri Lanka, Thailand, and Venezuela.[51] These countries brought together a range of complementary interests, from across the world regions. This organized collective action through a coalition mattered, especially for developing countries: members were able to pool their otherwise limited resources for developing detailed proposals, plus the power of large numbers helped them secure greater legitimacy for their agenda. Additionally though, the TRIPS and public health coalition showed itself to be adept at using a mixed negotiation strategy. This was evident not only in the relatively moderate narrative that it developed, as per the last point, but also in its willingness to make some concessions to negotiating counterparts outside (rather than all-or-nothing choices).[52]

Third, in terms of external facilitating circumstances, this WTO coalition was helped in its cause by increasing awareness across international

[50] Ibid.
[51] WTO (2001b, 2001c)
[52] On the difficulties that can arise when coalitions use a strict distributive strategy (i.e., with moves aimed only to divide rather than expand the pie), see Narlikar and Odell (2006). On the specific concessions that the TRIPS and public health coalition made in the negotiation, see Odell and Sell (2006).

organizations on the issue. In 1998, the World Intellectual Property Rights Organization (WIPO) and the UN High Commissioner on Human Rights had held a panel discussion on intellectual property and human rights, and had special attention to the issue of patents and drugs. The UN Sub-Commission on Human Rights took a series of steps, including resolutions and reports, to highlight the linkage between intellectual property and human rights. The World Health Assembly, organized by the World Health Organization in May 2001, focused on the issue of ensuring high and sustainable standards of treatment for AIDS patients.[53] In this context, Ambassador Chidyausiku's statement to the TRIPS Council in April 2001 had even greater resonance: 'Our intention is to bring into this Council an issue that has aroused public interest and is being actively debated outside this organization, but one which we cannot afford to ignore'.[54]

Finally, transnational social movements showed a high level of activism in this issue area. And contra to the polarization that we had seen in Seattle between northern NGOs and southern states, the issue of public health in poor countries brought an alignment in the interests of pro-development northern NGOs and southern governments. This civil society mobilization was useful in terms of not only technical support but also especially important in terms of building awareness among people and exercising pressure on governments. For example, Médecins Sans Frontières, Health Action International, and the Consumer Project on Technology organized an international meeting to discuss the use of compulsory licensing for access to AIDS medicines in 1999.[55] James Love attributes an impulse from Martin Khor (who led the Third World Network at the time) to Ambassador Chidyausiku on including access to medicines on the agenda of the Doha ministerial conference.[56] The turnaround in the backing that the United States and the European Union had initially given to their pharmaceutical firms (for instance over their legal action against South Africa) is also attributed to NGO activism.[57] Additionally, an epistemic community of scholars played a helpful role in both developing the narrative and sustaining it.[58]

---

[53] Sun (2004).
[54] Quoted in Hoen (2002), p. 38.
[55] Hoen (2002).
[56] Love (2011).
[57] Hoen (2002).
[58] Morin (2014) conducted a survey of 1,679 academics to carefully trace how the expert knowledge that researchers provided was amplified via NGOs and international organizations, and served to bring about a paradigm shift in how the protection of intellectual property was viewed. In contrast to the prior discourse that assumed a convergence of high IP standards

3.2.3 *Sustainability of Narrative and Follow-Through*

Success via the TRIPS and public health declaration at Doha did not mean that the problem had been fully resolved. Importantly though, the narrative that developing countries and NGOs had developed continued to exercise its impact in the next years. At a time when much of the Doha negotiations were deadlocked, negotiators continued to take concrete steps to improve accessibility of life-saving medicines for the poor. The Africa group provided sustained leadership on the issue of parallel imports of generics, just as it had done in 2001. In 2003, in August, members approved a waiver: countries would now be allowed to import generic drugs manufactured under compulsory licensing, if they lacked the capacity to manufacture the drugs themselves.[59] In 2005, members agreed that the 2003 amendment would be permanently incorporated into the TRIPS agreement, once two-thirds of the membership had given its approval. In 2017, on 23 January, the amendment entered into force.[60] This was the first time that a WTO accord had been amended. It is a testimony to the efforts that the global south (often in cooperation with non-state northern actors) invested, and their effective use of the poverty narrative.

Beyond the TRIPS and public health issue, and as with any negotiation, some compromises had to be made, also by developing countries. A significant loss from the perspective of the LMG, for example, was the launch of a new round in the first place, without tangible gains to correct the imbalances of the Uruguay round. Environmental concerns had appeared unexpectedly in the final text. Some ambiguity was inserted regarding the Singapore issues, but they were in fact not really taken off the table, contra the explicit resistance to them by most developing countries.[61] But none of these issues were potentially fatal, especially when compared against the overall gain of having a round that was dedicated to development concerns. The TRIPS and public health declaration had shown that it would be very difficult for the rich to walk over the poor. The extent to which these gains could be banked on in future negotiations was born out at the next ministerial conference.

(modelled on the European Union and the United States), the academic community instilled considerable scepticism. This scepticism has probably helped sustain the continued and effective impact of the poverty narrative in this field to the present day.

[59] WTO (2003a). The original agreement had allowed compulsory licensing predominantly for domestic purposes. This meant that these cheaper generics could not be exported, even if some of the world's poorest peoples might be in desperate need of them.

[60] WTO (2017a).

[61] Narlikar and Odell (2006).

3.3 CANCUN: COLLECTIVE BARGAINING COMES OF AGE

Both Seattle and Doha had seen different parts of the global south asserting their rights to be heard and to shape the agenda. The next test came at the Cancun ministerial conference, held from 10 to 14 September 2003. The DDA was scheduled to be completed by 2005, and developing countries could have been under immense pressure to make concessions in the spirit of reaching a timely compromise. In fact, however, Cancun marked another step in the self-assertiveness and self-empowerment of the poor. From the conference venue at the time, the Malaysian Trade and Industry Secretary Rafidah Aziz was quoted as saying: 'No more are we sitting outside in the corridors being given sweeteners. No more'.[62]

The defining theme of the Cancun conference was the emergence of coalitions of developing countries with unprecedented clout. In this section, I provide a brief overview of the coalitions themselves, analyse the two big issues on which mainly north–south battle lines came to be drawn, explain why the negotiations ended in yet another deadlock, and suggest what these developments added up to.

3.3.1 *The Emergence of 'Strong Coalitions' at Cancun*

With the launch of the Doha negotiations in 2001, coalition diplomacy by developing countries became more visible and more effective. The Africa Group, the African Caribbean Pacific (ACP) Group, the LDC group, the Small and Vulnerable Economies (SVE) group, and the Like Minded Group were all coalitions that were active in the preparatory process leading up to the Cancun ministerial conference, but whose roots pre-dated the Doha ministerial. To varying degrees, these coalitions had had their concerns incorporated into the DDA. Their purpose now was to ensure follow-through, especially amidst concerns that their issues could still get sidelined as the negotiations progressed. New coalitions were also emerging. Agriculture was one such issue area where developing countries feared collusion between the European Union and the United States would work. Especially amidst concerns that the European Union and the United States would again collude on the issue of agriculture, to the detriment of the developing world, two interesting coalitions of developing countries emerged: the G20[63] and

---

[62] Quoted in Mathiason (2003).
[63] This G20 is not to be confused with the finance/leader-level G20 forum, which brings together major economies from the global north and south, and covers a range of systemic issues. More on the G20 forum in Section 3.5.

the G33.[64] Additionally, in the run-up to Cancun, the Cotton-4 group had emerged.

The G20 was created at the Cancun Ministerial itself. Under the leadership of Brazil, India, and China, it brought together some twenty-two developing countries at the time, which wanted to hold the European Union and the United States to account on their prior reassurances regarding the opening up of their agricultural markets.[65] Another group of nearly thirty developing countries also came together in Cancun to defend their agricultural markets via a right to designate certain products as 'special products' (that would be exempt from tariff reduction) and a 'special safeguard mechanism' (to protect their markets against import surges). This group came to be known as the G33 (and is discussed in some detail in Chapter 4).

It is worth noting that neither coalition brought together 'natural allies'. Yes, they had some apparent similarities, both the G20 and the G33 combined large and small countries at different levels of development, were transregional, and even had overlapping memberships (e.g., India was a part of both coalitions). But the G20 had an agenda that focused on market-opening, while the G33 had a defensive agenda of protecting the agricultural markets of developing countries. The relative heterogeneity of their memberships led observers at the time to believe that these two coalitions – like others involving developing countries in the past – would collapse in the endgame. Representatives from developed countries predicted an unravelling of these coalitions, and journalists reporting euphorically of the self-assertiveness of the global south similarly asked the question: 'The true test is whether the G23 (*sic*) can survive. What inducements will be offered to buy up countries and what armtwisting might take place?'[66]

In fact, what actually transpired at Cancun was not only the survival of the G20 and the G33 in the face of several pressures, but also the emergence of a

[64] For an overview of the coalitions that emerged in the run-up to and at the Cancun ministerial conference, see Narlikar and Tussie (2004).

[65] Celso Amorim (2003), the Brazilian Foreign Minister and coordinator of the coalition, had given a damning critique of agricultural protectionism as practised in developed countries: '... no other area of trade is subject to such blatant discrimination as agriculture. Distortions in agricultural trade not only harm efficient exporters by denying them market opportunities. Domestic and export subsidies in developed countries depress prices and incomes throughout the world, cut into export earnings and increase food insecurity in developing countries. Their addictive nature does not contribute to productivity gains or the creation of wealth. They only generate dependence, on one side, and deprivation on the other'. For details of the original proposal by the G20, see WTO (2003b).

[66] Mathiason (2003). On the beliefs of the north about coalitions of the global south, see Narlikar and van Houten (2010).

meta-coalition – the so-called G90 (that combined the ACP, the LDC, and the Africa groups) along with 'alliances of sympathy' between different southern coalitions.[67] The head of Oxfam International was quoted as saying, 'A group of countries representing over half the world is now talking about social justice within the WTO. It's just unprecedented'.[68] Members of the coalitions at Cancun – marking a break with past coalitions – successfully resisted the strategy of divide and rule. This was true of large and seemingly heterogeneous coalitions like the G20 and the G33, and also true of smaller ones that were focused on a specific issue area and comprised more vulnerable countries (such as the LDC group or the Cotton-4).[69] They stood firm until the very end of the ministerial conference, which ended in deadlock.

There were several reasons why the Cancun coalitions were able to stand united and successfully push for their demands, even in the face of considerably bilateral pressure from rich countries as well as side deals that were offered to their members. These included the structures of the coalitions and internal bargaining processes within the coalition that allowed compensation and side payments to smaller members. The fact that the leading members of some prominent coalitions were major growth markets (i.e., Brazil, India, and China) meant promising BATNAs for their smaller southern allies (e.g., the rising powers could now serve as aid donors for smaller players, and reduce their dependence on developed country donors).[70] But at least as important was a shared narrative that united members of specific coalitions, and also created shared goals – possibly even an identity – across coalitions. Amorim summarized this in the following words as he recounted the lessons of Cancun for future negotiations:

> As coordinator of the Group of 22 developing countries that presented a united front on agriculture, I am convinced that Cancun will be remembered as the conference that signalled the emergence of a less autocratic multilateral trading system. In Brazil, and in a host of developing countries large and small – which represent 69% of the world's farmers – Cancun has been hailed as a turning point ...

---

[67] Narlikar and Tussie (2004).

[68] Mathiason (2003). For some excellent reporting from and commentary on Cancun, see the Guardian Archive (2003).

[69] The Cotton-4 was a nice example of David taking on Goliath at Cancun. In the run-up to the ministerial conference, four West African countries – Benin, Burkina Faso, Chad, and Mali – submitted proposals that demanded an end to cotton subsidies in the rich countries, and compensation until subsidies were brought to an end. See WTO (2003c).

[70] Narlikar and van Houten (2010), Narlikar and Tussie (2004).

... may we bear in mind the lessons of Cancun. The G-22 and other developing countries will not be reduced to the role of supporting actors in discussions that affect their development prospects. Consensus cannot be imposed through pre-cooked deals that disregard previous commitments and ignore the legitimate aspirations of the majority of the world's population. Trade must be a tool not only to create wealth but also to distribute it in a more equitable way.[71]

3.3.2 *Conflict over Issues*

Two especially controversial issues at Cancun were agriculture and the Singapore issues. On agriculture, both the G20 and the G33 sought the opening of agricultural markets in the European Union and the United States. This, they believed, was not only what had been agreed at Doha, but indeed represented the unfulfilled promise of the development gains from the Uruguay Round.[72] On the Singapore issues too, the position of the great majority of developing countries was clear, and it was in direct conflict with the European Union's position. At issue were differing interpretations by either side on what the wording of 'explicit consensus', agreed upon as a compromise at Doha, actually referred to.[73] When the European Union tried to put the Singapore issues on the negotiating table prior to Cancun, twelve developing countries carefully and systematically picked apart the European Union's submission. They highlighted that the European Union's assumptions – that negotiations on the Singapore issues would begin at Cancun, that these negotiations would be a part of a Single Undertaking, and that preparatory work on these should commence in advance of Cancun – were all incorrect. They further pointed out that the group was not alone in advancing such an interpretation; other developing countries – such as the Africa Group and the LDC group – had adopted similar positions on these controversial issues.[74]

The immediate cause for the breakdown of negotiations in Cancun was the persistent push from the European Union on the Singapore issues, and firm pushback from many developing countries. In his closing statement at Cancun, Pascal Lamy, the EU Trade Commissioner, defended his position:

> On Singapore issues, which are key to harnessing world trade, we played a
> constructive role, we moved on timing, on scope as well as on content of any

---

[71] Amorim (2003).
[72] E.g., Amorim (2003).
[73] Paragraphs 20, 23, 26, 27.
[74] WTO (2003d).

possible agreement. We moved before Doha, in Doha and since Doha and again in Cancun. After intensive talks these last days and in order to forge consensus, we even accepted the chair's proposal to drop two issues and retain trade facilitation (key to small and medium companies) and transparency in public procurement.[75]

That this 'concession' by the European Union on the final day of the conference did not go down well with developing countries is perhaps unsurprising. Prior attempts during the conference by the European Union to link agriculture subsidies with the Singapore issues had already 'inflamed' the situation, given that developing countries had already made their position clear on the matter. Several accounts point to the fundamental disagreement on the Singapore issues as the reason for the unsuccessful end to the conference. The Kenyan delegate, George Oduor, for instance, when asked who was to blame, is reported to have said:

> I would say it is those who have been trying to manipulate the process. Those who have been trying to manufacture consensus. The EU and the US, we believe ourselves, are to blame. The Singapore issues were at the centre of the deadlock, all of them. The developing countries say that they are not ready for any of them.[76]

Much finger-pointing occurred in the aftermath of the failure of Cancun. But despite the gloom that almost inevitably follows such negotiation breakdowns, a certain optimism was evident in newspaper reports at the time, as well as among developing countries and NGOs. South Africa's trade minister, for example, stated: 'This is the first time we have experienced a situation where, by combining our technical expertise, we can sit as equals at the table. This is a change in the quality of negotiations between developing and developed countries'.[77] The Third World Network also put out a statement at the end of the conference and commented, 'The developing countries have organized themselves better this time and have shown that they are not ready to be bullied into accepting decisions which they are against. The developed countries should respect this emergence of the developing countries in the

---

[75] Lamy (2003).

[76] Quoted in Elliott et al. (2003). It is worth mentioning though that even though the proximate cause for the breakdown of the negotiations lay in the deadlock on the Singapore issues, agriculture had posed an equally thorny problem. If the chair, for instance, had chosen to bring up agriculture at that point rather than Singapore issues, the negotiations would likely still have ended in failure, with a divide along similar north–south lines.

[77] Quoted in Elliott et al. (2003).

system and re-think the way they operate in what was once a rich man's exclusive club'.[78] The poor were no longer going to apologise for being poor or for asking for more. Developed countries and institutions would have to adapt to this newly empowered and assertive force in international negotiations.

3.4 ADAPTATIONS AND UPDATES TO WTO PROCESSES

Developing countries had always tried to exercise voice and agency in the multilateral trading system, albeit not always with the best results (as highlighted in Chapter 2). When the WTO was created, there was little indication that anything would change on this front. The agreement establishing the organization confirmed, 'The WTO shall continue the practice of decision-making by consensus followed under GATT 1947'. The accompanying footnote offered the following clarification: 'The body concerned shall be deemed to have decided by consensus on a matter submitted for its consideration, if no Member, present at the meeting when the decision is taken, formally objects to the proposed decision'. The agreement went on to state: 'Except as otherwise provided, where a decision cannot be arrived at by consensus, the matter at issue shall be decided by voting. At meetings of the Ministerial Conference and the General Council, each Member of the WTO shall have one vote'.[79] This suggests that, at least at the time of the establishment of the WTO, there was little sensitivity to issues of marginalization and exclusion on the part of developing countries (or indeed other actors). This also meant that the discontent that the global south had expressed in the workings of the 'Rich Man's Club' simmered away in the early years of the WTO. Seattle, and especially the anger about being sidelined from the process, which was expressed by representatives of developing countries, was in some ways just an explosion of these pent up grievances.

The grievances were many. Delegations from smaller developing countries lacked a presence in Geneva, or found their sparsely staffed missions overtaxed by the sheer number of meetings that they had to cover. Poor countries found it difficult to challenge an emerging 'consensus' that had already been built among the Quad in Green Room meetings. Informal meetings that underpinned the consensus-building process were not announced in advance, worked on an invitation only basis, and there were no minutes that interested

---

[78] Third World Network (2003).
[79] Article IX.1, GATT (1994).

members could follow up on. This lack of transparency in the proceedings was a source of much frustration and disappointment for the many countries left out in the cold.[80] Writing in 2002, international lawyer Richard Steinberg gave a pretty scathing assessment of consensus-based decision-making in the organization:

> ... the GATT/WTO consensus decision-making process is organized hypocrisy in the procedural context ... The procedural actions of consensus and the sovereign equality of states have served as an external display to domestic audiences to help legitimize WTO outcomes. The raw use of power that concluded the Uruguay Round may have exposed those actions, jeopardizing the legitimacy of GATT/WTO outcomes and the decision-making rules, but weaker countries cannot impose an alternative rule.[81,82]

Even prior to the Seattle conference itself, members had taken issue with the organization's decision-making processes. On 6 November 1999, eleven developing country members had sent a letter to the chairman of the General Council officially expressing their grievances.[83] When the same practices continued unchanged at the conference itself, developing countries finally 'revolted' and shook the organization out of its complacency.[84] The statements

---

[80] Kwa (2003); Narlikar (2001, 2005); WTO (2002).

[81] Steinberg (2002), p. 342.

[82] The WTO's secretariat could have potentially compensated for some of these limitations, at least in terms of capacity-building and technical assistance. But a conceit of the WTO has always been that it is a 'member-driven' organization (another characteristic that it inherited from the GATT), which limits the mandate of its secretariat. Plus, developing countries had questioned even the narrow role that the Secretariat had played in the workings of the organization, accusing it of bias at different levels and in different functions (Narlikar 2001). Steinberg reinforced this point in his analysis: 'The secretariat's bias in favor of great powers has been largely a result of who staffs it and the shadow of power under which it works. From its founding until 1999, every GATT and WTO Director-General was from Canada, Europe, or the United States, and most of the senior staff of the GATT/WTO secretariat have been nationals of powerful countries' (Steinberg 2002, p. 356).

[83] The letter stated: 'We have been unhappy about the manner in which relatively small groups are convened for substantive discussions with yourself or the Director General, on specific portions of the draft Ministerial Declaration – the so-called green room meetings. We believe the shortage of information and reporting to Members regarding these meetings, both before and after their occurrence, leads to unnecessary divisiveness and rancor. The process of invitation to the small meetings is also highly unsatisfactory. The interested delegations themselves must decide if they have enough interest or stake in a topic to participate in the small-group discussions, or even be informed that the meeting will take or has taken place' (reported by Khor 1999).

[84] Notably though, developing countries were already making some headway in reforming the functioning of the organization even prior to Seattle. In the bitterly fought contest over the appointment of the Director-General, the process was concluded only after a compromise was reached: the term would be divided between Mike Moore (from New Zealand) and Supachai

by groups of developing countries (cited in Section 3.1) were examples of the extent of resistance that the decision-making processes of the WTO encountered. Developing countries were backed in their critique by southern NGOs, with the Third World Network denouncing the 'undemocratic and bullying tactics at Seattle'.[85] The WTO rapidly adapted and updated in response to this severe critique.

Much effort was spent in improving the transparency of the consensus-building processes. The availability of meeting schedules and relevant documents is dramatically improved, not only in terms of internal transparency but also external transparency.[86] Small group meetings became open-ended, directed explicitly towards consensus-building and not informal decision-making, and members had the opportunity to self-select participation. Capacity-building, technical assistance, and training for developing countries became an integral part of the WTO system. And the reform measures did not stop there; rather, they extended to the heart of WTO's decision-making and developing countries came to share centre stage.

Over the years, especially as the economic presence of the BRICS grew, the old Quad was also transformed. The high table of negotiations ceased to be dominated by Canada, the European Union, the United States, and Japan. Instead, new permutations emerged: the 'New Quad' or the G4, the Five Interested Parties, the G6, and the G7. Constants in these changing groups, besides the United States and the European Union, were Brazil and India. At the July 2008 talks (more on these in Chapter 4), the WTO's G7 came to include China (besides the European Union, United States, Brazil, India, Australia, and Japan). Importantly, the enhanced inclusiveness of the WTO was not a form of tokenism: the new entrants to the core of decision-making were not shy of using their veto power.

Naturally, for inclusiveness to improve, even an expanded high table would not suffice. Over the years, awareness and sensitivity to this issue has grown in

---

Panitchpakdi (from Thailand), with each getting three years (non-renewable). Supachai became the first Director-General of the WTO to come from a developing country. This was a significant break from a norm that had lasted for over fifty years. After Supachai completed his term, Pascal Lamy (France) took over in 2005, but was succeeded but Roberto Azevedo from Brazil in 2013.

[85] Third World Network (1999b).

[86] When I first started studying the GATT and the WTO in the 1990s, it was not easy to gain access to official documents. In the last twenty years, the availability of this information has undergone a sea-change, with the WTO's own website offering serving as an invaluable resource. Plus, there are a variety of observer commentaries, which have been facilitated by this improved external transparency, and have also translated into a wealth of materials produced by journalists.

the organization. In the past, developing countries had worked in coalitions, which allowed them to pool resources and bargain collectively (incorporating the interests of smaller members of the coalition), and make the best that they could of the 'Rich Man's Club'. The impact of these coalitions was amplified once their leading members became key participants in small group negotiations. As decision-making processes evolved, the WTO began to give increasing and explicit institutional recognition and role to these coalitions.[87] Director-General Pascal Lamy developed a model of consultations towards consensus-seeking via 'concentric circles', which accorded a place to 'representatives of key groups' in Green Room meetings.[88] Director-General, Roberto Azevedo, in later phases of the negotiation, also showed sensitivity to this issue of representation and inclusiveness, and developed his own innovations for the Bali ministerial conference.[89] What all these different mechanisms added up to was one significant new result: poor countries and their concerns could no longer be sidelined in the WTO.

It is worth mentioning that all these changes occurred in practice, without a change in the formal agreements. The reason why they came about at this point in time – despite developing countries having pushed for them for over fifty years – had partly to do with a change in the structural balance of power. In 1997, for example, China was not a member of the WTO, while Brazil and India did not feature in the list of top twenty-five exporters. Today, all the BRICS are members of the organization. The Chinese economy is the world's second largest economy, India stands at sixth place, and Brazil at ninth (or fifth and seventh, respectively, if one counts the European Union as one

---

[87] WTO (2008, 2017b). This was in stark contrast to the early years of the WTO. Whilst investigating coalition trajectories in the organization, I can recall being told in the summer of 1997 by a WTO official that coalition and group bargaining was an activity that was confined to the UNCTAD; the WTO and its predecessor, in contrast, worked through consensus and its one-member-one-vote system. In fact, of course, coalitions were one of the few instruments that developing countries had available to them, both in the GATT and also the early years of the WTO. It was an instrument that developing countries prized, and were willing to speak about in interviews. And one could trace coalition activity through joint submissions that countries made, non-papers they produced, and through additional reports (such as via the 'North South Monitor' that was produced by the Special United Nations Service).

[88] See, for example, www.wto.org/english/tratop_e/dda_e/meet08_circles_popup_e.htm. Also, for interesting accounts by practitioners of how these processes worked, see Diego-Fernandez (2008) and Ismail (2009).

[89] Azevedo (in Elliott 2013) explained the process as follows in an interview: 'It doesn't mean we didn't have meetings of small groups, but we changed the participants to include those that had particularly difficulties in each issue. It was not a club that was deciding everything. We had all the interested parties in the inner circle, and this included big countries and small countries, developed countries and developing countries. It didn't matter what the size was: what mattered was the degree of sensitivity'.

entity). By dint of sheer economic clout, these particular voices from the developing world have begun to 'matter' as emerging markets. This begs the question: is the entry of the rising powers into the inner circle of decision-making simply a product of their growing economic clout? Or to put it even more crudely: international institutions only adapt their processes to changing balances of power, and therefore now choose to welcome hitherto poor countries once it is clear that they are on a trajectory to richness and power?

There is no doubt that power matters. But several other factors do too – and increasingly so in recent times. Brazil and India were frequently invited to Green Room meetings even in the days of the GATT, not because they were the economic giants that they subsequently became in the 2000s but because they worked closely with many other developing countries in coalitions. Even as they have graduated into a new Quad, they have continued to work closely in coalitions, which are often still south–south coalitions.[90] And they have continued to flag up the cause of poverty in the positions that they have taken – both because they must address the concerns of their own peoples, and also because they share these concerns with other developing countries and LDCs. This creates a virtuous cycle. When a country like India brings up the cause of agrarian poverty (in its own rural areas as well as in other developing countries) in a new Quad-type setting, this can help build up further legitimacy for a narrative that trade multilateralism must work for all members. When the LDCs and other middle-income developing countries also back the positions that Brazil or India take in small-group settings, this can increase the influence of both groups to mutual advantage.

Besides, the changes that have occurred in the WTO have not been directed only towards accommodating the rising powers. In substance (for instance, via acceptance of the principle of Less Than Full Reciprocity in the Doha negotiations)[91] as well as in process (for instance, via the attention that WTO officials and many delegations now give towards facilitating inclusiveness), different groupings of developing countries, including the LDCs, are no longer on the margins. This awareness and action in favour of improving transparency and inclusiveness extends towards external actors too. Seattle was a hard lesson for the WTO and its members to learn, but it is a lesson that has

[90] The Cairns Group of agricultural exporting nations, of which Brazil was a member, was an important exception to these south–south coalitions. It went back to the Uruguay Round, and continued to argue the case for the liberalization of agriculture markets. But balancing against its Cairns Group membership, Brazil also became a leading member of the G20. This coalition was politically more visible in the Doha negotiations, and its membership came from the global south.

[91] More on this in Chapter 4.

been learnt well. The Doha round has given us some nice illustrations of how effectively developing countries and NGOs can work together. The WTO Secretariat has also steadily been improving accessibility of information for insiders and outsiders, plus actively engages with the general public via multimedia information campaigns. The seriousness with which the organization engages in public dialogue, and the efforts that it has made to bring both the rising powers as well as other developing countries into the heart of decision-making, are signals that groups that were hitherto marginalized and powerless can no longer be ignored.

3.5 EMPOWERMENT BEYOND TRADE

While the previous sections have focused on empowerment of the poor in trade negotiations, the phenomenon has not been restricted to trade. Far from it. In this section, I explore two broad arenas where we see the power of the powerless at work: the first still within the realm of international economic negotiations at large, and the second in our daily lives.

3.5.1 *International Economic Negotiations*

As highlighted in Section 3.1, debates on development and poverty alleviation were getting underway across international forums and through the activism of multiple actors since around the turn of the decade. The UN was taking key steps via the MDGs and thereby providing a vital focal point for multiple actors. The WTO was contributing on this front via the DDA. Other international organizations were turning their attention and resources to the issue of poverty, and thereby marginalization and disempowerment in a broader sense. In 1998, the UN Office of the High Commissioner for Human Rights established the Special Rapporteur on extreme poverty and human rights[92] and the Special Rapporteur on the right to food in the year 2000.[93] Other appointments included the establishment of the Independent Expert on the effects of foreign debt and other related international financial obligations of states on the full enjoyment of all human rights, particularly economic, social, and cultural rights[94] and the Special Rapporteur on adequate housing as a component of the right to an adequate standard of

---

[92] 1998 (CHR res. 1998/25)/2017 (HRC res. 35/19).
[93] 2000 (CHR res. 2000/10)/2019 (HRC res. 40/7).
[94] 2000 (CHR res. 2000/82)/2017 (HRC res. 34/3).

living.[95] In fact, of the forty-four special procedures of the UN Office of the High Commissioner for Human Rights, only four pre-date 1990.[96] This expansion of the idea of human rights – and the conditions necessary for individuals to enjoy them – showed the growing centrality of powerlessness concerns in international politics.

Outside of the corridors of formal, institutionalized power, civil society along with 'a new cast of characters' was also turning its attention to issues of global poverty and development. In a Brookings report, the authors describe the emergence of a development community that had come to include 'megaphilanthropists', the corporate sector, new bilateral donors, celebrities, and the global public.[97] Activists were able to connect the local and the global, and also influence the officialdom within countries and in international organizations, more effectively than ever before.

Jubilee 2000 was an early case in point, where we saw an expanded network of actors harnessed the emerging poverty narrative, further advanced it, and contributed to its spread. Marshall and Keough write of Jubilee 2000: 'As the campaign harnessed the political power of millions of credible and informed people, one of its most significant achievements may have been the building of links between high-level officials and grassroots social activists'.[98] Founded in the United Kingdom in 1996 and drawing on the support of faith leaders and social activists, Jubilee 2000 sought debt relief for the world's poorest nations. It mobilized citizens across sixty-two countries, won the support of political leaders (e.g., Tony Blair and Gordon Brown, and subsequently also Bill Clinton), and garnered public attention also through the backing of religious leaders (e.g., Pope John Paul II and the Archbishop of Canterbury) and celebrities (e.g., Bono, Bob Geldof, Muhammed Ali). Its impact was significant not only in the creation of public awareness (the campaign secured twenty-four million signatures in support), but also in creating vital feedback loops with governments and international organizations. For example, the initiative, despite some tensions with international organizations, was able to exercise influence in the shaping of the World Bank's HIPC (Highly Indebted Poor Countries programme). Concrete monetary results included securing a G8 pledge of support of US$ 100 billion in debt relief, following the G8 summit in Cologne in 1999.[99]

---

[95] 2000 (CHR res. 2000/9)/2017 (HRC res. 34/9).
[96] UN Office of the High Commissioner for Human Rights (2019).
[97] Brainard and LaFleur (2008).
[98] Marshall and Keough (2004), p. 35.
[99] Busby (2007); Marshall and Keough (2004). Note that, at certain points in this chapter, I refer to the G7, rather than the G8. The two names of course refer to the same group, with and without Russia. Russia was a member from 2007 to 2014.

The narrative continued to grow with the help of networks through the 2000s, and to influence international trade and development negotiations. The World Social Forum met for the first time in June 2001 in Porto Alegre, bringing together a diverse group of activists around the slogan *Another world is possible*. *Make Poverty History* was another striking campaign that saw NGOs, celebrities, protestors, and other committed citizens, as well as government leaders and international institutions, coalesce around the G8 Gleneagles Summit in 2005.[100] As people sported their real or virtual white bands to declare their commitment to the cause, which in turn was closely linked with the eight Millennium Development Goals it is worth emphasizing that this was not just empty 'cheap talk'. Even though not all the goals of the campaign have been fulfilled, on balance the results are quite positive.[101] Assessing the results ten years after Gleneagles, Adrian Lovett (Europe's executive director of the *One Campaign*) outlined the following achievements:

> Perhaps the most profound change is in the perceived achievability of Make Poverty History's mission. In 2005, despite Nelson Mandela's insistence that extreme poverty could be overcome just like slavery and apartheid, many observers – and even some campaigners – assumed it was an unreachable pipedream.
> Ten years on, that aim of ensuring that nobody should live in absolute poverty by 2030 is set to be enshrined in the sustainable development goals, which will be signed by world leaders at the UN this September ...[102]

Following the financial crisis of 2008, the poverty narrative seemed to gain even further momentum. Related concerns about inequality, which had simmered away in academic journals, now entered public debate and shaped the poverty narrative further. The works of influential intellectuals (e.g., including Dani Rodrik, Abhijit Banerjee and Esther Duflo Joseph Stiglitz, Thomas Picketty, and Branko Milanovic[103]) brought the issue of poverty alleviation, and inequality in both the global south as well as the global north to the fore. Movements like 'Occupy Wall Street' that demanded fundamental changes in the financial system, in the name of the great majority of people ('We are the 99%')[104] further mobilized citizens, including those who were being directly affected by austerity policies as a response to the crisis.

---

[100] BBC (2005).
[101] E.g., Amos (2015).
[102] Lovett (2015).
[103] Rodrik (2011); Banerjee & Duflo (2011); Stiglitz (2012); Picketty (2014); Milanovic (2016).
[104] http://occupywallst.org/

The poverty narrative aimed not only at securing more equitable outcomes in favour of the powerless and the marginalized; it also targeted the workings of the system, and thereby sought a change in process. The poor were entitled to speak for themselves. We saw this position evolve in the case of the *Make Poverty History* campaign, which had its origins in the global north, and specifically the United Kingdom. Adrian Lovett offered the following reflection on the successes of the campaign:

> Networks like Avaaz and change.org, unheard of in 2005, have harnessed internet and social media platforms to put power in people's hands and turn leadership pyramids upside down.
>
> A growing movement of global citizens is forming. And that movement is more authentic and representative than ever, no longer directed from Washington, New York or London.[105]

Attention to the poverty narrative and related concerns about the legitimacy of global governance also led to other forms of institutional innovations. The Goldman Sachs study of 2003, *Dreaming with the BRICSs*, had predicted that in forty years, the four economies of Brazil, Russia, India, and China could together be bigger than the G6 (United States, Japan, United Kingdom, Germany, France, and Italy) combined.[106] The WTO had been ahead of the curve in offering a more prominent place to the rising powers, but the G8 also came to recognize how anachronistic its structure appeared amidst these global power shifts. The Heiligendamm process, named after the G8 Summit of Heiligendamm in Germany in 2007, sought to institutionalize the G8's dialogue to the five emerging markets (Brazil, China, India, Mexico, and South Africa) that Tony Blair had already initiated at Gleneagles two years earlier.[107] This was an important development for the G8 club on the one hand, but also an illustration of the still old-fashioned attitudes of the major economies: the emerging economies were good enough for sustained 'dialogue' in a G8+5 format, but not yet sufficiently seriously regarded to constitute a new grouping of a G13 with equal status with the G8. Against the backdrop of the poverty narrative, and most immediately in the aftermath of the financial crisis of 2008, this calculation changed.

The financial crisis had its roots in the United States, but threatened global disruption. A response coordinated among the G8 was unlikely to suffice. This led the mobilization of the G20: a group of finance ministers and central

---

[105] Lovett (2015).
[106] Wilson and Purushothaman (2003).
[107] G8 (2005, 2007).

bankers that had been meeting since 1999 (i.e., since the East Asian financial crisis in 1998),[108] but one which convened for the first time at the leaders' level in Washington D.C. in November 2008. The emergence of the G20 as a parallel, and potentially even a replacement, forum to the G7 in the aftermath of the financial crisis in 2008 was another indication of the growing centrality of the hitherto marginalized in international economic negotiations. In its original function, the G20 acted as an effective 'crisis committee'[109] with a limited but urgent mandate. The group brought together a critical mass of systemically significant economies, and had several advantages over the G8, not least the fact that together its members constitute over 80 per cent of world trade and two-thirds of the world's population. Also, in response to some severe criticism about its own legitimacy,[110] and perhaps also as a function of different international context that claimed to attach importance to inclusiveness, the G20 showed itself willing to improve its outreach processes. Via processes such as T20 (Think 20), C20 (Civil Society 20), B20 (Business 20), and so forth, the G20 created opportunities to gain inputs from non-state actors. Not only did the G20's new networked diplomacy offer more voice to non-state actors, but the group also included invited guests from non-member governments as well as heads of international organizations. This is not to suggest that the G20 is unproblematic – as with all forms of global governance, there are a variety of fronts on which it can be rightly challenged.[111] But, for all its limitations, it does represent a dramatic improvement on the structure of the G7.

In climate change negotiation too, we saw a change underway. COP 21 was held in Paris from 30 November to 12 December 2015. Climate change was an area that had seen high levels of civil society activism, in comparison to trade, finance, or security.[112] Finally, two groups of countries, which had traditionally

[108] Alexander (2014). Note that both the finance ministers–central bankers G20 and the leaders' level G20 are different from the coalition of the G20 that was formed at the Cancun ministerial conference in 2003.

[109] Cooper (2010).

[110] E.g., Aslund (2009).

[111] For example, the G20 needs to consider how it can take into account the voices of the many who are still outside (yes-bigger-than-G7-but-still-exclusive) club. Besides serious legitimacy concerns, the group also faces effectiveness challenges: it is not easy to reach agreement among twenty members that often diverge in terms of interests, and sometimes even world views. The G20 moreover is not an international organization and has few powers of implementation. For some of the critique that the group has encountered, see Harris Rimmer (2015); Narlikar (2017); and Sidiropoulos (2011).

[112] Bäckstrand et al. (2017) describe 'UN climate diplomacy' as 'pioneering in continuously seeking to facilitate access and inclusion of a growing range of non-state actors'.

found themselves at a disadvantage in the negotiation process, now began to make some vital gains.

The first of these was the group of developing countries. Different interpretations on how common but differentiated responsibilities were to be translated into actual mitigation measures had long been a source of deadlock between the global north and south. Finally, at the COP in Paris, developing countries got recognition for the importance of bottom-up processes (rather than binding emissions reductions imposed from the top and at the expense of development). The idea of 'Nationally Determined Contributions' was critical in building in the flexibilities that many developing countries had traditionally sought, and the absence of which had acted as a deterrent to agreement. In Paris, it was agreed that the NDCs 'would not be legally binding, although binding provisions (Art. 4) govern their content, timing, and revision'.[113] But given that the interests of the United States and developing countries were more or less aligned on this, one could argue that the resulting negotiation success was unsurprising. In contrast, the small island developing states worked under harder conditions.

The small island developing countries had cooperated as the Alliance of Small Island States (AOSIS) for over thirty years. This coalition comprised a heterogeneous group of forty-four countries. In contrast to developing countries such as India and China, whose large emissions make their participation indispensable to a deal and thereby impart them with considerable bargaining power, AOSIS members were in a very vulnerable position. This vulnerability derived from the fact that they would be the first and worst affected by climate change, and even major contributions from them would not make a significant difference towards mitigation. It was precisely this vulnerability that the AOSIS countries put to work through a variety of negotiation strategies. Richard Benwell hits the nail on the head in his analysis:

> In the climate regime, small states' main resource is the power of exhortation based on: warnings concerning an impending tragedy of the commons; historical responsibility; scientific principles; sovereign states' legal and moral right existence; and the right to sustainable development. The theme that unites these discursive strands is that as the principle victim of a common resource problem not of their own making, small states' power lies in their powerlessness.[114]

The small island states overcame capacity constraints – such as small delegation size – by pooling resources through their coalition. Their public and

[113] Christoff (2016).
[114] Benwell (2014), p. 73.

media engagement was innovative, for example via the underwater cabinet meeting organized by the Maldives in 2009.[115] They relied on scientific evidence, and they used moral suasion. In Paris, they also coordinated their positions with other countries (e.g., the LDCs, the High Ambition Coalition, and the Climate Vulnerable Forum), even while attempting to resist encroachment on their 'victim status'.[116]

As a result of these coordinated strategies, which were built on a narrative of their unique vulnerability and powerlessness,[117] the AOSIS countries made some significant gains in Paris. Their three wins were: (a) the agreement recognized their status without any 'watering down' (e.g., they were able to keep 'their special circumstances regarding flexibility in the reporting system and the new transparency framework, and avoiding any additional burden in terms of reporting activities');[118] (b) even though the agreement recognized the less than +2° warming target, it included their +1.5° as a long-term goal; and (c) it included the concept of 'Loss and Damage' on a permanent basis as a separate article (Article 8).[119] True, they had also argued for 'special provisions' to finance adaptation in the small island states, 'given the particular challenges and the attendant existential threat that climate change poses to our countries'.[120] On this, they failed to secure preferential access, so this was not an absolute win. But the deal they secured on this was also far from an absolute loss. For example, Article 9 (4) of the Paris Agreement states:

> The provision of scaled-up financial resources should aim to achieve a balance between adaptation and mitigation, taking into account country-driven strategies, and the priorities and needs of developing country Parties, especially those that are particularly vulnerable to the adverse effects of climate change and have significant capacity constraints, such as the least developed countries and small island developing states, considering the need for public and grant-based resources for adaptation.[121]

---

[115] *Wall Street Journal* (2009).
[116] Benwell (2014), p. 72; Ourbak and Magnan (2018).
[117] See e.g., AOSIS (2015).
[118] Ourbak and Magnan (2018), p. 2203.
[119] AOSIS (2015); Ourbak and Magnan (2018); UNFCCC (2015).
[120] AOSIS (2015).
[121] Article 9(9) further states: 'The institutions serving this Agreement, including the operating entities of the Financial Mechanism of the Convention, shall aim to ensure efficient access to financial resources through simplified approval procedures and enhanced readiness support for developing country Parties, in particular for the least developed countries and small island developing States, in the context of their national climate strategies and plans' UNFCCC (2015). To be recognized in the same category as the LDCs for the use of the financial mechanism by the small island developing states was no mean achievement.

The small island states had successfully harnessed their vulnerabilities and victimhood into their negotiation narrative, and converted them into bargaining strengths.

3.5.2 David Winning against Goliath in the Politics of the Everyday

The transformative impact of the power of the powerless is also borne out in some aspects of the daily lives of people. We see the powerlessness narrative now offering justice to the oppressed within and across societies.

Some remarkable power reversals have resulted through the acknowledgement of powerlessness. Women in India had been subject for centuries to demands for dowry, some of which would result in bride-burning and dowry deaths. Although the practice of dowry had been outlawed in India since 1961, the pernicious problem had persisted. A major amendment to the law was made in 1983, which put the law firmly on the side of women. For example, Section 498A of the Indian Penal Court stated in Article 2(iii):

> The Indian Evidence Act, 1872, is being amended to provide that where a woman has committed suicide within a period of seven years from the date of her marriage and it is shown that her husband or any relative of her husband had subjected her to cruelty, the Court may presume that such suicide had been abetted by her husband or by such relative of her husband (*vide* Clause 7 of the Bill).[122]

The result of Section 498A was to introduce a strong presumption of guilt against the powerful party – in such cases, the husband and his family – in favour of the woman. Such presumption is usually considered a necessary condition to allow hitherto marginalized minorities to stand up to their oppressors.

We see a similar evolution in attitudes towards cases of sexual harassment. The rise of #MeToo is an especially moving and dramatic illustration of the influence that narratives, worked through networks using a variety of social media platforms, can have in shaping and even changing societal norms. #MeToo had its origins with the decision of prominent celebrities in the film industry to finally take a public and collective stance, but the success of the movement was driven at least as much by the fact that it also appealed to women in less glamorous jobs who had been subject to similar extremes of the abuse of power.[123] In other sectors too, including academia, we saw positive

---

[122] Indian Penal Code (1983).
[123] As *Time Magazine* (2017) put it, 'When multiple harassment claims bring down a charmer like former *Today* show host Matt Lauer, women who thought they had no recourse see a new,

spill-over effects, for example via #WomenAlsoKnow. Gender equality and diversity – for long relegated at best to a polite tokenism – finally seem to be in with a chance.

'Ethical consumerism' also entered the mainstream. Especially in a world where gritty images of gruelling poverty in the south circulated with ease through Facebook, Twitter, and Instagram, the contrast in living standards between 'us and them' became even more shocking. Via movements that focused on labour standards and environmental standards, consumers began to show much greater concern for the working conditions of the global poor. In a study published in 2004, the authors found that one-third of the consumers were willing to pay even 10 per cent extra for 'sweat-free' products.[124] The popularity of such movements increased over the years. Universities and cities vied each other to get FairTrade accreditation: both my former universities acquired FairTrade status (Oxford in 2018; Cambridge in 2015), while students at both universities successfully lobbied their colleges to also become FairTrade colleges. The consumer choices of individuals based on their conscience seemed to be doubly empowering: individuals could now supposedly make a positive difference in the lives of poor families living in far-off places.[125]

Climate activism shows us a similar pattern. Already, as mentioned in the last section, developing countries acquired more voice and influence in the negotiations than ever before. But a different group of stakeholders has recently harnessed the same narrative of powerlessness with extraordinary effectiveness – schoolchildren who decided to take up strike action in the name of #FridaysForFuture. Analysing the phenomenon, Wahlström et al. write:

> The #FridaysForFuture climate protests mobilized more than 1.6 million people around the globe in March 2019. Through a school strike, a new generation has been galvanized, representing a historical turn in climate activism. This wave of climate protest mobilization is unique in its tactics, global scope and appeal to teenage school students. Media coverage of these

---

wide-open door. When a movie star says #MeToo, it becomes easier to believe the cook who's been quietly enduring for years'.

[124] Prasad et al. (2004). The study was based on a field experiment conducted in a department store in a working class community in southeast Michigan.

[125] Rather like the quality of mercy not being strained, 'it blessed him that gives and him that takes', crowdfunding via platforms like 'JustGiving' and 'GoFundMe' seemed to produce similar win-wins for both sides. Such forms of direct giving allowed individuals to bypass governmental and non-governmental agencies and middlemen, and feel reassured that their resources were reaching the targets for whom they were intended.

protests and high-level national and international political meetings involving the movement's icon, Greta Thunberg, illustrate a level of global attention that no previous youth movement has ever received.[126]

It is worth pointing out that Greta Thunberg's narrative was about crisis, but it was also about the powerless and the small striking back. In her speeches at the COP 24, she argued,

> Many people say that Sweden is just a small country and it doesn't matter what we do. But I've learned that you are never too small to make a difference and if a few children can get headlines all over the world just by not going to school then imagine what we could all do together if we really wanted to.

In the same speech, she also stood up against the powerful, by pitting the innocent voices of children like herself (plus the development priorities of developing countries) against the irresponsible voices of adults (plus selfish lifestyle choices of developed countries):

> You are not mature enough to tell it like it is. Even that burden you leave to us children. But I don't care about being popular. I care about climate justice and the Living Planet. Our civilization is being sacrificed for the opportunity with a very small number of people to continue making enormous amounts of money. Our biosphere is being sacrificed so that rich people in countries like mine can live in luxury. It is the sufferings of the many which pay for the luxuries of the few.[127]

With narratives that speak on behalf of a powerless or oppressed group, or have the powerless and oppressed groups speaking up for themselves and getting heard, and especially in an age of 'hashtag activism',[128] normal power relations seem to be finally breaking down.

3.6 CONCLUSION

Go with the developments that gained momentum especially around the start of the new millennium, and one could well be forgiven for believing that a liberal utopia was in the offing. The powerless were harnessing some of the most fundamental drawbacks that they had traditionally faced and converting them into a bargaining advantage. Backing this were two sets of movements. On the one hand, governments learnt that if they wanted to sell a deal to

---

[126] Wahlström et al. (2019).
[127] Thunberg (2018).
[128] Bonilla and Rosa (2015).

domestic and global audiences, pointing to the benefits it would bring to the poor and the marginalized was a promising way to win support. International institutions also made some serious efforts to build more inclusive processes to accommodate players that had traditionally stood at the periphery. On the other hand, the assertiveness of smaller players also grew as their BATNAs improved with the rise of the BRICS. Multiple actors saw that pointing to their weaknesses and limitations would no longer be a liability; rather, it might open access to resources and processes that had long been denied to them.

This empowerment was not limited to the fields of trade, or even international economic negotiations conceptualized more broadly. The poverty narrative that was enabling so many states and non-state actors internationally also opened up new negotiation spaces domestically within societies for individual citizens. And as multiple actor networks expanded the use of social media for the promotion of poverty and powerlessness narratives across different levels and issues, more and more individuals and organizations ended up supporting and disseminating these narratives even further.

In international politics as well as domestic, this new empowerment was also contributing to improvements in decision-making processes. Having larger numbers of actors in different settings, and offering inclusiveness to the hitherto excluded, would of course complicate and slow down decision-making processes. But one could also expect that decisions arrived at through a meticulous exercise in transparency and accountability would enjoy greater sustainability. A virtuous cycle of empowerment, democratization, and sustainability could follow, creating wins for all parties involved. But the question was, how far could this virtuous cycle be sustained?

BIBLIOGRAPHY

Africa Group. 2001. Africa Group Statement on TRIPs, Access to Medicine, and Public Health. Presented by the Delegation of Zimbabwe. 20 June. www.cptech.org/ip/wto/tc/africagroup.html.

Alexander, Nancy. 2014. 'Introduction to the G20.' Heinrich Böll Foundation: Global Economic Governance. Issue 1. July. https://us.boell.org/sites/default/files/alexander_new_introduction_g20_7-23-14.pdf.

Amorim, Celso. 2003. 'The Real Cancun.' *Wall Street Journal*. 23 September.

Amos, Felicity. 2015. Ten years after Make Poverty History: Did world leaders keep these 8 promises? www.one.org/us/blog/10-years-after-make-poverty-history-did-world-leaders-keep-these-8-promises/.

AOSIS (Alliance of Small Island States). 2015. AOSIS Opening Statement for 21st Conference of Parties to UNFCC. https://unfccc.int/sites/default/files/cop21cmp11_hls_speech_aosis_maldives.pdf.

Aslund, Anders. 2009. 'The G20 must be stopped.' *Financial Times*. 26 November.

Bäckstrand, Karin, Jonathan W. Kuyper, Björn-Ola Linnér, and Eva Lövbrand. 2017. 'Non-state actors in global climate governance: From Copenhagen to Paris and beyond.' *Environmental Politics.* 26: 4. Pp. 561–579.

Banerjee, Abhijit V. and Esther Duflo. 2011. *Poor Economics: A Radical Rethinking of the way to fight Global Poverty.* New York: Public Affairs.

Bayne, Nicholas. 2000. 'Why did Seattle fail? Globalization and the politics of trade.' *Government and Opposition.* 35: 2. Pp. 131–151.

BBC. 2005. Thousands flock to poverty march. 2 July. http://news.bbc.co.uk/2/hi/uk/4642053.stm.

Benwell, Richard. 2014. 'The canaries in the goldmine: Small states as climate change champions.' In Amrita Narlikar (ed.). *Small States in Multilateral Economic Negotiations.* London: Routledge. First published as part of centenary special issue of *The Round Table: Commonwealth Journal of International Affairs.* (413). 2011.

Bernal. Richard L. 1999. 'Sleepless in Seattle: The WTO Ministerial of 1999.' *Social and Economic Studies.* 48: 3. Pp. 61–84.

Bhagwati, Jagdish. 2001. 'After Seattle: Free trade and the WTO.' *International Affairs.* 77: 1. Pp 15–29.

Bonilla, Yarimar and Jonathan Rosa. 2015. '#Ferguson: Digital protest, hashtag ethnography, and the racial politics of social media in the United States.' *American Ethnologist.* 42: 1. Pp. 4–17.

Brainard, Lael and Vinca LaFleur. 2008. Making Poverty History? How activists, philanthropists and the public are changing global development. Report: Brookings Blum Roundtable 2007. Brookings Global Economy and Development. Washington D.C. February. www.brookings.edu/wp-content/uploads/2016/06/02_global_development_brainard.pdf.

Busby, Joshua William. 2007. 'Bono made Jesse Helms cry: Jubilee 2000, debt relief, and moral action in international politics.' *International Studies Quarterly.* 51: 2. Pp. 247–275.

Christoff, Peter. 2016. 'The promissory note: COP 21 and the Paris climate agreement.' Commentary. *Environmental Politics.* 25: 5. Pp. 765–787.

Clinton, Bill. 1999. Remarks by the President to the luncheon in honor of the Ministers attending the Meetings of the World Trade Organisation. 1 December. www.staff.city.ac.uk/p.willetts/PIE-DOCS/CLNT1299.HTM.

Cooper, Andrew. 2010. 'The G20 as an improvised crisis committee and/or a contested "Steering Committee".' *International Affairs.* 86: 3. Pp. 741–757.

Diego-Fernandez, Mateo. 2008. 'Trade negotiations make strange bedfellows.' *World Trade Review.* 7: 2. Pp. 423–453.

Economist. 1999a. 'Clueless in Seattle'. 4 December.

1999b. 'Special: World Trade: The Battle in Seattle.' 27 November.

Elliott, Larry. 2013. 'Bali Summit invigorated World Trade Organization, says Roberto Azevedo.' *The Guardian.* 18 December.

Elliott, Larry, Charlotte Denny, and David Munk. 2003. 'Blow to world economy as trade talks collapse.' *The Guardian.* 15 September.

Fisher, Roger and William Ury. 1997. *Getting to Yes: Negotiating an Agreement Without Giving In.* New York: Random House.

Froning, Denise. 1999. 'An absence of leadership: Clinton and the WTO.' Heritage Foundation Report. 10 December. www.heritage.org/trade/report/absence-leadership-clinton-and-the-wto.

Furman, Jason and Joseph Stiglitz. 1998. 'Economic crises: Evidence and insights from East Asia.' *Brookings Papers on Economic Activity*. No. 2. Pp. 1–114.

G8. 2005. Joint Declaration of the Heads of State and/or Government of Brazil, China, India, Mexico, and South Africa participating in the G8 Gleneagles Summit. www.g8.utoronto.ca/summit/2005gleneagles/plusfive.pdf

2007. Heiligendamm Process. www.g-8.de/nn_92160/Content/EN/Artikel/g8-summit/2007-06-08-heiligendamm-prozessen.html.

GATT. 1994. Uruguay Round Agreements: Agreement establishing the WTO. www.wto.org/english/docs_e/legal_e/04-wto_e.htm.

Greenhouse, Stephen and Joseph Kahn. 1999. 'US effort to add labour standards to agenda fails.' *New York Times*. 3 December. https://archive.nytimes.com/www.nytimes.com/library/world/global/120399wto-labor.html.

Gruber, Lloyd. 2000. *Ruling the World: Power Politics and the Rise of Supra-National Institutions*. New Jersey: Princeton.

Guardian Archive. 2003. Special Report: The WTO Summit in Cancun. www.theguardian.com/wto/cancun/0,13815,1018998,00.html.

Harris Rimmer, Susan (2015). 'A critique of Australia's G20 presidency and the Brisbane summit 2014.' *Global Summitry*. 1: 1. Pp. 41–63.

Hoen, Ellen 't. 2002. 'TRIPS, pharmaceutical patents, and access to essential medicines: A long way from Seattle to Doha.' *Chicago Journal of International Law*. 3 (1). Article 6. http://chicagounbound.uchicago.edu/cjil/vol3/iss1/6

Hufbauer, Gary F. 1999. 'World trade after Seattle: Implications for the United States.' Policy Brief. Peterson Institute for International Economics. 99-10. December. www.piie.com/publications/policy-briefs/world-trade-after-seattle-implications-united-states.

Hulme, David. 2009. 'The Millennium Development Goals (MDGs): A short history of the world's biggest promise.' BWPI Working Paper. No. 100. Brookings World Poverty Institute. September. www.unidev.info/Portals/0/pdf/bwpi-wp-10009.pdf.

Indian Penal Code, Amendment. 1983. Criminal Law (Second Amendment) Act, 1983 (46 of 1983). 26 December. www.498a.org/contents/amendments/Act%2046%20of%201983.pdf.

Ismail, Faizel. 2009. 'Reflections on the July 2008 collapse.' In Amrita Narlikar and Brendan Vickers (eds). *Leadership and Change in the Multilateral Trading System*. Leiden: Martinus Nijhoff.

Japan Ministry of Economy, Trade, and Industry (METI). 2000. 'The Seattle Ministerial Conference.' Chapter 17 in Report on the WTO Consistency of Trade Policies by Major Trading Partners. Industrial Structure Council. http://dl.ndl.go.jp/info:ndljp/pid/1286050/19.

Jonguières, Guy de and Frances Williams. 1999. 'A goal beyond reach: The unseemly collapse of the World Trade Organisation talks means that further liberalisation is becoming a distant prospect.' Commentary and Analysis. *Financial Times*. 6 December.

Kaiser, Robert and John Burgess. 1999. 'A Seattle primer: How not to hold WTO talks.' *Washington Post*. 12 December. www.washingtonpost.com/wp-srv/WPcap/1999-12/12/117r-121299-idx.html.

Khor, Martin. 1999. Letter sent by 11 Countries Criticising Green Room Processes (6 November). News Report. 15 November. www.globalpolicy.org/component/content/article/209/43577.html.

Kwa, Aileen. 2003. *Power Politics in the WTO*. Bangkok: Focus on the Global South. January. 2nd ed. https://focusweb.org/wp-content/uploads/2003/01/power-politics-in-the-WTO.pdf.

Lamy, Pascal. 1999. Speech at ministerial meeting, Seattle. Speech/99/203. 2 December. http://europa.eu/rapid/press-release_SPEECH-99-203_en.htm.

    2003. Speech. Press Conference closing the World Trade Organisation 5th Ministerial Conference. Cancun. 14 September. SPEECH/03/409. https://europa.eu/rapid/press-release_SPEECH-03-409_en.htm.

Levi, Margaret and Gillian Murphy. 2006. 'Coalitions of contention: The case of WTO protests in Seattle.' *Political Studies*. 54. Pp. 651–670.

Love, James. 2011. 'What the 2001 Doha Declaration changed.' 16 September. www.keionline.org/21680.

Lovett, Adrian. 2015. 'Make poverty history? A decade from Gleneagles, it is now a genuine possibility.' *The Guardian*. 6 July. www.theguardian.com/global-development/2015/jul/06/make-poverty-history-campaign-gleneagles-sustainable-development-goals.

Marshall, Katherine and Lucy Keough. 2004. *Mind, Heart and Soul in the Fight against Poverty*. Washington D.C.: World Bank. http://documents.worldbank.org/curated/en/220251468762875492/pdf/298790PAPER0Mind1heart010soul.pdf.

Mathiason, Nick. 2003. 'Poor rattle doors of WTO Club.' *The Guardian*. 14 September. www.theguardian.com/business/2003/sep/14/wto.politics.

Milanovic. Branko. 2016. *Global Inequality: A New Approach for the Age of Globalization*. Cambridge, MA: Harvard University Press.

Morin, Jean-Frederic. 2011. 'The life-cycle of transnational issues: Lessons from the access to medicines controversy.' *Global Society*. 25: 2. Pp. 227–247.

    2014. 'Paradigm shift in the global IP regime: The agency of academics.' *Review of International Political Economy*. 21: 2. Pp. 275–309.

Murphy, Gillian and Steven Pfaff. 2005. 'Thinking globally, acting locally? What the Seattle protests tell us about the global justice movement.' *Political Power and Social Theory*. 17. Pp. 151–176.

Narlikar, Amrita. 2001. 'WTO decision-making and developing countries.' Trade-Related Agenda, Development, and Equity (T.R.A.D.E) Working Paper. No. 11. Geneva: South Centre. November. www.iatp.org/sites/default/files/WTO_Decision-Making_and_Developing_Countries.htm.

    2005. *The World Trade Organization: A Very Short Introduction*. Oxford: Oxford University Press.

    2010. *Deadlocks in Multilateral Negotiations: Causes and Solutions*. Cambridge: Cambridge University Press.

    2017. 'Can the G20 save Globalisation?' *GIGA Focus*. No. 1. www.giga-hamburg.de/en/system/files/publications/gf_global_1701_en.pdf.

Narlikar, Amrita and Diana Tussie. 2004. 'The G20 at the Cancun Ministerial: Developing countries and their evolving coalitions.' *The World Economy*. 27: 7. Pp. 947–966.

Narlikar, Amrita and John Odell. 2006. 'The strict distributive strategy for a bargaining coalition: The like minded group in the World Trade Organization.' In John Odell (ed.). *Negotiating Trade: Developing Countries in the WTO and NAFTA*. Cambridge: Cambridge University Press.

Narlikar, Amrita and Peter van Houten. 2010. Know the enemy: Uncertainty and deadlock in the WTO. In Amrita Narlikar (ed.). *Deadlocks in Multilateral Negotiations: Causes and Solutions*. Cambridge: Cambridge University Press.

Odell, John. 2006. *Negotiating Trade: Developing Countries in the WTO and NAFTA*. Cambridge: Cambridge University Press.

2009. 'Breaking deadlocks in international institutional negotiations: The WTO, Seattle, and Doha.' *International Studies Quarterly*. 53. Pp. 273–299.

Odell, John and Susan Sell. 2006. Reframing the issue: The WTO coalition on intellectual property and public health, 2001. In John Odell (ed.). *Negotiating Trade: Developing Countries in the WTO and NAFTA*. Cambridge: Cambridge University Press.

Ourbak, Timothée and Alexandre K. Magnan. 2018. 'The Paris agreement and climate change negotiations: Small islands, big players.' *Regional Environmental Change*. 18: 8. Pp. 2201–2207.

Picketty, Thomas. 2014. *Capital in the Twenty-First Century*. Cambridge, MA: Harvard University Press.

Prasad, Monica, Howard Kimeldorf, Rachel Meyer, and Ian Robinson. 2004. 'Consumers of the world unite: A market-based response to sweatshops.' *Labor Studies Journal*. 29: 3. Pp. 57–80.

Rodrik, Dani. 2011. *The Globalization Paradox: Why Global Markets, States and Democracy Can't Coexist*. Oxford: Oxford University Press.

Scherer, F. M. and Jayashree Watal. 2001. Post-trips options for access to patented medicines in developing countries. CMH Working Paper series. Commission on Macroeconomics and Health: A WHO Commission examining the interrelation between investments in health, economic growth and poverty reduction. November. http://icrier.org/pdf/jayawatal%20.pdf.

Scholte, Jan Aart. 2000. 'Cautionary reflections on Seattle.' *Millennium*. 29: 1. Pp 115–121.

Schott, Jeffrey. 2000. *The WTO after Seattle*. Washington D.C.: Institute for International Economics.

Seattle City Council (2000). Report of Seattle City Council's WTO Accountability Committee. 14 September. http://depts.washington.edu/wtohist/documents/arcfinal.pdf.

Sidiropoulos, Elizabeth (2011). 'Legitimacy and credibility: Challenges of broadening the G20 agenda. In Wilhelm Hofmeister and Susanna Vogt (eds). *G20 – Perceptions and Perspectives for Global Governance*. Berlin: Konrad Adenauer Stiftung. www.kas.de/wf/en/33.29099/.

Steinberg, Richard. 2002. 'In the shadow of law or power? Consensus-based bargaining and outcomes in the WTO.' *International Organization*. 56: 2. Pp. 339–374.

Stiglitz, Joseph. 1999. 'Reforming the global economic architecture: Lessons from recent crisis.' *Journal of Finance*. 54: 4. Pp. 1508–1521.

2012. *The Price of Inequality*. New York: WW Norton.

Sun, Haochen. 2004. 'The road to Doha and beyond: Some reflections on the TRIPS agreement and public health.' *European Journal of International Law*. 15 (1). Pp. 123–150.

Third World Network. 1999a. 'Africa, Caribbean, Latin America protest no democracy at WTO.' African Trade Ministers' statement, Caribbean Community

(CARICOM) communique, Latin American and Caribbean countries' joint communique. 2 December. http://twn.my/title/deb5-cn.htm.

1999b. 'The Revolt of Developing Nations.' 3 December. http://twn.my/title/deb1-cn.htm.

2003. 'Statement by the Third World Network on the events of the final day of the Cancun Conference.' 14 September. www.twn.my/title/twninfo77.htm.

Thunberg, Greta. 2018. Speech: COP 24 Plenary Session. Katowice. Poland. 12 December. www.fridaysforfuture.org/greta-speeches#greta_speech_dec3_2018.

Time Magazine. 2017. '2017 Person of the year: The silence breakers.' https://time.com/time-person-of-the-year-2017-silence-breakers/

US General Accounting Office. 2000. 'Seattle Ministerial Conference: Outcomes and lessons learned.' Testimony by Susan S. Westin, Committee on Finance, US Senate. GAO/T-NSIAD-00-86. February. www.gao.gov/new.items/ns00086t.pdf.

UN Office of the High Commissioner for Human Rights. 2019. Special Procedures: Current and Former Mandate-Holders for Existing Mandates. www.ohchr.org/EN/HRBodies/SP/Pages/.aspx. Valid as of 1 May.

UNFCCC. 2015. *The Paris Agreement*. Paris: UN Framework Convention on Climate Change. https://unfccc.int/sites/default/files/english_paris_agreement.pdf.

Van den Bossche, Peter. 2006. 'NGO involvement in the WTO: A lawyer's perspective on a glass half-full or a glass half-empty?' Maastricht Faculty of Law Working Paper. 2006/10. http://digitalarchive.maastrichtuniversity.nl/fedora/get/guid:b69b60a9-1f56-465a-a57a-6aedca7822e5/ASSET1.

VanGrasstek. Craig. 2013. *The History and Future of the World Trade Organization*. Geneva: WTO.

Wahlström, Mattias, Piotr Kocyba, Michiel De Vydt and Joost de Moor (eds). (2019). Protest for a Future: Composition, Mobilization and Motives of the Participants in Fridays For Future Climate Protests on 15 March, 2019 in 13 European Cities. www.tu-chemnitz.de/phil/iesg/professuren/klome/forschung/ZAIP/Dokumente/Protest_for_a_future_GCS_Descriptive_Report.pdf.

Wall Street Journal. 2009. Maldives Underwater Cabinet Meeting: Video. 17 October. www.wsj.com/video/maldives-underwater-cabinet-meeting/AC96723D-AF29-4C86-AF19-4A56E102D218.html.

White House press briefing. 1999. Office of the Press Secretary: Press Briefing by Gene Sperling and Charlene Barshefsky. 24 November. https://clintonwhitehouse4.archives.gov/textonly/WH/New/WTO-Conf-1999/briefings/19991124-1245.html.

Wilson, Dominic and Roopa Purushothaman. 2003. *Dreaming with the BRICS: The Path to 2050*. Goldman Sachs, Global Economics, Paper no. 99. 1 October. www.goldmansachs.com/insights/archive/archive-pdfs/brics-dream.pdf.

WTO. 1998. Geneva Ministerial Declaration. Adopted on 20 May. www.wto.org/english/thewto_e/minist_e/min98_e/mindec_e.htm.

1999a. Press Release on the Ministerial. 28 June. www.wto.org/english/thewto_e/minist_e/min99_e/english/press_e/minrel_e.htm.

1999b. Press Pack: WTO 3rd Ministerial Conference, Seattle, 30 November–3 December. 28 November. www.wto.org/english/thewto_e/minist_e/min99_e/english/about_e/presspack_english.pdf.

1999c. Press Release: Moore spells out priorities for Seattle Ministerial Conference. Press/135. 2 September. www.wto.org/english/thewto_e/minist_e/min99_e/english/press_e/pres135_e.htm.

1999d. Statement by Murasoli Maran, Minister for Commerce and Industry, India. WT/MIN(99)/ST/16. 30 November.

1999e. '3 December: the final day and what happens next.' Briefing Note 3. 3 December. www.wto.org/english/thewto_e/minist_e/min99_e/english/about_e/resum03_e.htm.

1999f. *Preparation for the 1999 Ministerial Conference: Compilation of proposals submitted in phase 2 of the preparatory process.* Informal Note by the Secretariat. JOB(99)/4797/Rev 3. 18 November.

1999g. *Preparations for the 1999 Ministerial Conference: Implementation issues to be addressed before/ at Seattle.* Communication from Cuba, Dominican Republic, Egypt, El Salvador, Honduras, India, Indonesia, Malaysia, Nigeria, Pakistan, Sri Lanka and Uganda. WT/GC/W/354. 11 October.

1999h. 'Preparations for the 1999 Ministerial Conference: Draft Text.' JOB(99)/5868/Rev.1. 19 October. www.ictsd.org/sites/default/files/news/2012/12/WTO-MC3-declaration.pdf.

2001a. Doha Ministerial Declaration. Adopted on 14 November. WT/MIN(01)/DEC/1. 20 November.

2001b. TRIPS and Public Health: Paper submitted by a group of developing countries to the TRIPS Council for the special discussion on intellectual property and access to medicine. Submission by the Africa Group, Barbados, Bolivia, Brazil, Dominican Republic, Ecuador, Honduras, India, Indonesia, Jamaica, Pakistan, Paraguay, Philippines, Peru, Sri Lanka, Thailand and Venezuela. IP/C/W/296. 20 June. www.wto.org/english/tratop_e/trips_e/paper_develop_w296_e.htm.

2001c. Draft Ministerial Declaration on the TRIPS agreement and Public Health: Proposal from a group of developing countries. Submission by the African Group, Bangladesh, Barbados, Bolivia, Brazil, Cuba, Dominican Republic, Ecuador, Haiti, Honduras, India, Indonesia, Jamaica, Pakistan, Paraguay, Philippines, Peru, Sri Lanka, Thailand and Venezuela. IP/C/W/312, WT/GC/W/450. 4 October. www.wto.org/english/tratop_e/trips_e/mindecdraft_w312_e.htm#Top.

2002. Summary Report. Internal Transparency and Decision-Making processes at the WTO: Critical Issues and Recommendations. WTO NGO Symposium. 1 May. www.wto.org/english/tratop_e/dda_e/summary_report_intern_transp.doc.

2003a. Implementation of paragraph 6 of the Doha Declaration on the TRIPS Agreement and Public Health: Decision of the General Council of 30 August of 2003. WT/L/540. 1 September.

2003b. Agriculture – Framework Proposal. Joint Proposal by Argentina, Bolivia, Brazil, Chile, China, Colombia, Costa Rica, Cuba, Ecuador, El Salvador, Guatemala, India, Mexico, Pakistan, Paraguay, Peru, Philippines, South Africa, Thailand and Venezuela. WT/MIN(03)/W/6. 4 September.

2003c. Poverty Reduction: Sectoral Initiative in Favour of Cotton. Joint Proposal by Benin, Burkina Faso, Chad and Mali dated 28 July. WT/MIN(03)/W/2. 15 August.

2003d. Comments on the EC Communication (WT/GC/491) on the Modalities for the Singapore Issues: Communication from Bangladesh, Cuba, Egypt, India, Indonesia, Kenya, Malaysia, Nigeria, Pakistan, Venezuela, Zambia and Zimbabwe dated 4 July. WT/GC/W/501. 8 July.

2008. Groups in the WTO. www.wto.org/english/tratop_e/dda_e/meet08_brief08_e .doc.

2017a. Press Release: WTO IP rules amended to ease poor countries' access to affordable medicines. 23 January.

2017b. Groups in the Negotiations. 24 June. www.wto.org/english/tratop_e/dda_e/ negotiating_groups_e.htm.

4

When Fair Is Foul and Foul Is Fair
Overuse and Misuse of the Poverty Narrative

The previous two chapters (Chapters 2 and 3) illustrated how a narrative about poverty and victimhood has facilitated a newfound edge for developing countries and marginalized groups in different bargaining situations. As such, the narrative – admittedly duly adapted, re-framed, and differently disseminated, but more or less the same narrative – has turned out to be a game-changer and has in some instances fundamentally overturned power asymmetries. But, as with most things in life, there can be too much of a good thing. Plus, improved ways of using a narrative about poverty and powerlessness have not been limited to the neediest. This chapter provides illustrations of the increasingly indiscriminate overuse and deliberate misuse of poverty narratives by the less rich and the rich, respectively.

The first case that I explore in this chapter relates to agricultural liberalization in the WTO. Debates underpinning this set of the negotiations reveal an overuse of the poverty narrative – often under the frame of food security or food sovereignty – by some rising powers, especially India. This has worked to the detriment of all parties, including the rising powers themselves. My second case study revolves around special concessions for LDCs. We find that rich countries respond to and reinforce the special pleading of LDCs, sometimes in an opportunistic manner. If, by evoking it, the developed world could facilitate a better distribution of the gains of globalization to also include the LDCs, this would still justify an expanded use of the poverty narrative by the rich in favour of poor countries. But such is not always the case. Developed countries sometimes explicitly and paradoxically appeal to the very cause of poverty alleviation in order to refuse concessions even towards this small group of the world's poorest countries. The middle-income developing countries have also been using the cause of the poorest of the poor to their own advantage. This is a misuse of the power of the powerless by the rich and the powerful. The third case goes a step further. It investigates the politics that underpins President Trump's trade wars. Although framed in terms of protecting the interests of America's own poor, Trump's trade measures may turn out to be a war against the global poor as well as the groups in America that they claim to defend. This is a clear perversion of the original motivation behind the poverty narrative that had empowered so many developing countries and their peoples. The analysis, however, does not join the Trump-bashing polemic that has come to dominate public debate. Rather, it sheds new light on how the tariff wars of today, although being waged in the name of those who feel left behind in the United States, are in fact a next step in the life of the evolving poverty narrative. The fourth case on negotiation and decision-making processes of the WTO provides a further illustration of how the overuse and misuse of the poverty narrative risk undermining its original purpose and recent gains.

The central point that emerges from these cases is a sombre one. The poverty narrative, because of its many demonstrated wins, has been appropriated and hijacked by multiple players. As more and more states and people learn to effectively play the role of the powerless victim, the poverty narrative is attracting a major backlash. There is a tragic irony to this: as the (still relatively newly discovered) power of the powerless loses credibility through overuse and misuse, the biggest losses accrue to the neediest and the poorest. The potential damage to the international system of rules is also severe.

4.1 AGRICULTURE, FOOD SECURITY, AND THE CASE OF INDIA

In Chapter 3, we saw that the global south had finally managed to place the cause of development at the heart of the WTO with the launch of the Doha Development Agenda. We now turn to the next phase of the use of the poverty narrative during the Doha negotiations. Agriculture and food security provide us with an interesting case of how a poverty narrative, which had initially been articulated to the advantage of developing countries, subsequently became a costly liability for all. India was a major protagonist in this debate, having led the charge on including agricultural liberalization along with food security concerns in the DDA. The second part of this section thus focuses on India.

4.1.1 *The Increasing Complexity of Agricultural Trade Liberalization*

As discussed in Chapters 2 and 3, agriculture was always a difficult issue to mainstream into the rules of the GATT. Narrow special interests in this sector were deeply entrenched, having enjoyed decades of protection from their governments. Plus, the close linkage between land use and culture made this a politically charged issue.[1] Against this background, the inclusion of agriculture as part of the Doha negotiations constituted a double victory for developing countries. First, the DDA was mandated to facilitate agricultural liberalization, and thus catered to a cause that many developing countries (including those that belonged to the Cairns Group – a coalition that dates back to the Uruguay Round and brings together developed and developing countries) had espoused since the Uruguay Round. Paragraph 13 of the Doha Ministerial Declaration duly stated the following, indicative of an 'offensive'[2] agenda:

> Building on the work carried out to date and without prejudging the outcome of the negotiations we commit ourselves to comprehensive negotiations aimed at: substantial improvements in market access; reductions of, with a view to phasing out, all forms of export subsidies; and substantial reductions in trade-distorting domestic support.

Second, the Doha mandate also recognized the competing demands of countries with more 'defensive' (i.e., protecting one's own markets) interests in agriculture. The same paragraph thus also stated:

> We agree that special and differential treatment for developing countries shall be an integral part of all elements of the negotiations and shall be embodied in the schedules of concessions and commitments and as appropriate in the rules and disciplines to be negotiated, so as to be operationally effective and to enable developing countries to effectively take account of their development needs, including food security and rural development.[3]

The agenda for agricultural reform – one of the most difficult issues for the multilateral trading regime to tackle – would thus now require the liberalization of agricultural markets to facilitate export opportunities (especially for developing countries) and simultaneously also their protection in the interest of food security, development, and 'non-trade' concerns.[4] Together these

---

[1] Davis (2003); Laborde and Martin (2012).
[2] The use of the term 'offensive' may appear slightly peculiar. But in the context of the WTO, it refers to interests driven by the search for new markets, and 'defensive' refers to protection of one's own market.
[3] WTO (2001).
[4] Recognition of some of these contradictory goals was also present in the Uruguay Round and the resulting agreements. For example, the Agreement on Agriculture (AoA) was accompanied by a Decision on Measures Concerning the Possible Negative Effects of the Reform Programme on Least-Developed and Net Food-Importing Developing Countries. But with the launch of the DDA (where agriculture was now included as part of the single undertaking and the negotiations had an explicit development focus), this tightrope act became more real, more immediate, and tougher.

measures were aimed at tackling the problem of oversupply and depressed prices, while at the same time also targeting the problem of undersupply and high prices. Action on both problems was necessary to address the issue of price volatility. Working simultaneously on the two fronts could have been just the right strategy. The protection of their own agricultural markets by rich countries had fed 'a vicious circle in which other countries demand their "policy space" which further leads to a less stable and reliable world market'.[5] Market opening in one set of economies could potentially now facilitate opening in the other by creating more give-and-take, and thereby systemic gains. And yet, agriculture catalysed competing and divergent interests, with considerable venom, for three reasons.

First, the well-intended attempt to balance the offensive and defensive interests of members proved problematic. Through much of the Uruguay Round, the primary push on agriculture had come from the agriculture-exporting nations. The Cairns Group had led this initiative, and comprised members which had found themselves unable to compete in an international market distorted by European and American subsidies and other support mechanisms for their own farmers. An important reason for the eventual breakthrough was that the European Union and the United States had also come to realize that their subsidy wars were unsustainable, and thus found their interests reasonably aligned with those of the Cairns Group. Although the Uruguay Round was able to include this issue, getting meaningful progress, even on this offensive agenda alone, was going to be a mammoth task. The DDA bravely took on this challenge, and was supported and pushed to maintain momentum in this direction via the G20 coalition (which was formed at the Cancun ministerial meeting, as discussed in Chapter 3). And negotiators at Doha also added the defensive agenda to this demanding programme.

The defensive agenda, which sought legitimate protection of agricultural markets, had not enjoyed the same prominence as the offensive agenda for liberalization in the Uruguay Round. The results at Marrakesh reflected this. The Agreement on Agriculture (AoA) focused primarily on addressing distortions (market access, domestic support, export subsidies) in the sector. Article 16 and the accompanying 'Decision on Measures Concerning the Possible Negative Effects of the Reform Programme on Least-Developed and Net Food-Importing Developing Countries' constituted exceptions to the rule. In contrast, the Doha ministerial declaration put the offensive and defensive interests

---

[5] Matthews (2014).

on agriculture on a relatively equal footing. It extended the possibility of the use of some market interventions by all countries (not just the LDCs or net food-importing developing countries) via the following inclusion in paragraph 13: 'We take note of the non-trade concerns reflected in the negotiating proposals submitted by Members and confirm that non-trade concerns will be taken into account in the negotiations as provided for in the Agreement on Agriculture'. This agenda thus also catered to the demands of some OECD countries.[6]

Besides attending to the demands of food exporting countries, as well as non-trade concerns (of developed and developing countries), in a round that claimed to prioritize development, the defensive concerns of LDCs and other developing countries had to be central. This was reflected in SDT provisions (e.g., paragraph 44 of the Doha Ministerial Declaration reaffirmed that 'provisions for special and differential treatment are an integral part of the WTO Agreements', while issue-specific clauses reiterated this, and paragraph 50 emphasized the importance of building SDT into the negotiation process); recognition of Less Than Full Reciprocity (e.g., in paragraph 16 on non-agricultural market access); and also agriculture-specific clauses (paragraphs 13 and 14) that reflected the development priorities of developing countries and SDT requirements in the original mandate. As the round progressed, developing countries pressed harder for these issues to be taken seriously, particularly the adverse impact that indiscriminate market opening of their own agricultural markets could have on their farming-dependant populations. The G33 coalition was formed in Cancun in 2003 to specifically address this

---

[6] The G10 coalition on non-trade concerns, for instance, comprised Iceland, Israel, Japan, South Korea, Liechtenstein, Mauritius, Norway, Switzerland, Chinese Taipei – all OECD countries except for Chinese Taipei. This coalition argued along the following lines (WTO 2005):

'3. During the negotiations, many Members have referred to a number of non-trade concerns of relevance to their reform process. These include food security, rural development and the viability of rural areas, various environmental concerns such as biological diversity, agricultural landscapes and land conservation (which includes flood control, landslide prevention and combating soil erosion and desertification), and cultural heritage and identity. An essential commonality of these NTCs is that their safeguarding to a large extent is dependent on domestic production.

4. Food security is a typical example. The relationship between domestic agriculture and national food security is well established. It is a fundamental objective of every country to ensure stable supplies of food, and most governments have opted for a certain degree of domestic agricultural production, in conjunction with imports and stockholding, to ensure such supplies. In order to reduce the risks that are often associated with an excessive reliance on world markets, many countries with a low self-sufficiency in agricultural products judge as essential a certain degree of domestic agricultural food production'.

The coalition justified its agenda in terms of fairness and equitability, and also referred to 'disadvantaged production conditions', thereby working through a narrative that showed some affinity to the narratives developed by poor countries.

agenda. The dramatic spike in food prices in 2007–2008 helped further focus the attention of trade negotiators on the problem of food and nutrition. A new understanding emerged that 'markets must be regulated not just for the abundance that marked the 1980s and 1990s, but also for periods of scant, and unpredictable, supply'.[7] From the perspective of especially poor and vulnerable economies, as well as higher-income developing countries with large agriculture-dependent poor populations, this growing international awareness was of critical importance to their cause.

Inclusive framing to ensure stakes for a larger number of parties should have facilitated negotiation breakthroughs, not impeded them. What was not anticipated at the time though was the increasing likelihood of a clash between countries espousing these two different approaches, both of which had been legitimized by the DDA.[8] Those responding to demands for greater access to their markets would not grant these easily on a unilateral basis, and would run into conflict with counterparts who refused to open up their own markets (sometimes with equally convincing arguments about non-trade concerns). The fact that both offensive and defensive claims were legitimized by the Doha mandate (and the legitimization of defensive claims included not only the food security and livelihood concerns of poor countries but also the non-trade concerns of rich countries) meant that no one would give in easily.

Second, the DDA's attention to defensive concerns within the WTO was reinforced by the activism of development NGOs and other transnational actors. In 1996, the transnational social movement, La Via Campesina,[9] had advanced its concept of food sovereignty.[10] The Human Rights Commission created the office of the Special Rapporteur on the Right to Food in 2000.[11] In providing the justification for this step, the Commission stated that it considered it 'intolerable that 825 million people, most of them women and

---

[7]   Chatterjee and Murphy (2013), p. 5.
[8]   As economists often like to point out, even unilateral trade liberalization works to the advantage of the liberalizing economy. But reality usually strikes via political economy considerations, and hence the need for a multilateral trade organization in the first place.
[9]   La Via Campesina defines itself as 'an international movement bringing together millions of peasants, small and medium size farmers, landless people, rural women and youth, indigenous people, migrants and agricultural workers from around the world. Built on a strong sense of unity, solidarity between these groups, it defends peasant agriculture for food sovereignty as a way to promote social justice and dignity and strongly opposes corporate driven agriculture that destroys social relations and nature'. https://viacampesina.org/en/international-peasants-voice/. Friends of the Earth International is another example of an NGO that played an important role in this agenda-setting process, see Friends of the Earth International (2003).
[10] Agarwal (2014).
[11] Office of the High Commissioner for Human Rights (2000).

children, throughout the world and particularly in developing countries, do not have enough food to meet their basic nutritional needs, which infringes their fundamental human rights and at the same time can generate additional pressures upon the environment in ecologically fragile areas'.[12] While this attention to the issue of hunger and nutrition was urgently needed, it did not always follow through with a focus on the multiple measures that would be necessary to achieve food security. The conflation between the two concepts of food security and sovereignty contributed to confusion and misunderstandings.[13] A debate between the Director General of the WTO at the time, Pascal Lamy, and the Special Rapporteur on the Right to Food, Olivier de Schutter, was indicative of the polarization between the trade community and the development community at large.[14] At least some developing countries with a more defensive agenda drew succour from de Schutter's argumentation (e.g., Tanzania, Bolivia, Cuba, India, Ecuador, and Mauritius).[15] As the fault-lines deepened, many 'well-intentioned civil society voices' also chose to 'dismiss the WTO, to call for limits on trade, and to hold up the mirage of self-sufficiency as an effective global food security strategy'.[16]

Third, divergent interests found expression in not only the voices of member countries, but also bargaining coalitions. The WTO's website lists sixteen coalitions that were active in the DDA.[17] The Doha coalitions showed different degrees of formalization, and were active in different phases of the round. The activism of these coalitions could have resulted in a simplification of negotiation positions due to the reduction in the number of actors. In fact, already difficult two-level games got even more complicated,[18] and resulted in more entrenched positions and further polarization. More follows on this issue in Section 4.4. At this point, suffice it to note that the G33 coalition provides us with a good example of how collectively, too, developing countries adopted distributive strategies in the name of their poor:

> ... the objective reality of agriculture in most parts of the developing world where the central preoccupation of the hundreds of millions of people

---

[12] Office of the High Commissioner for Human Rights (2000).

[13] For a good overview on this debate, see Clapp (2015a).

[14] WTO (2009a).

[15] WTO (2009b).

[16] Matthews (2014).

[17] ACP group, African group, Asian developing members, MERCOSUR, G90, LDCs, Small Vulnerable Economies, Article 12 members, Low income economies in transition, Cairns Group, Tropical Products, G10, G20, G33, Cotton-4, Pacific Group. List (updated 18 December 2017). www.wto.org/english/tratop_e/agric_e/negoti_groups_e.htm.

[18] Narlikar and van Houten (2010); Young (2010).

engaged in agriculture is that of survival, not trade ... It is important that the SSM is not viewed primarily through the prism of commerce. The correct perspective is to view it as an instrument which allows developing countries to address their central concerns of food and livelihood security and rural development while undertaking liberalization commitments. It needs to be emphasized that in most developing countries, agriculture which provides the bulk of employment, is not a commercial activity per se, but a way of life. Most agriculture production in such countries involves small land holdings mainly producing for self consumption. Subsistence agriculture is deeply mired in the vicious cycle of low investment and growth. Such agriculture is also deeply connected with issues of poverty alleviation as about 75 per cent of the world's poor live in rural areas where agriculture is the main economic activity. The last decade has witnessed many disquieting developments in developing country agriculture which reflect the interplay between economic liberalization and the crisis of subsistence agriculture. Greater openness to international markets has brought incessant price fluctuations which adversely impact on the food security of the poorest sections of the population. The World Bank has estimated that due to high food and oil prices in 2007 and 2008, the number of people living in extreme poverty may have increased by 130–150 million. Frequent food riots and farmer suicides have reflected the violent face of this crisis. Greater reliance on imports has also led to large scale displacement of local crops in several countries with the attendant impact on rural employment and food security. Several crops which are environmentally well-suited to particular agro-climatic zones have also been displaced by cheaper imports.[19]

The consistency and persistence with which this argument was made suggests that it went beyond being 'just' a strategic narrative and was increasingly taking the shape of a norm. And its most avid defender was India.

4.1.2 *India's Negotiation Stance and Contribution to Deadlock*

India epitomized the challenges and contradictions just highlighted. In the DDA negotiations, it took on a dual role. On the one hand, it was a founding member of the G20 coalition. As discussed in Chapter 3, the main purpose of this coalition was to seek agricultural liberalization in the markets of rich countries. This was clearly presented as intrinsic to the cause of development. But additionally, India was an active member of the G33, which sought to protect the markets of developing countries from import surges via a special safeguard mechanism. And while India was not the only country that

---

[19] WTO (2010), paragraphs 4 and 5.

belonged to both the G20 and the G33,[20] it was the only one that chose to take a leading role in both coalitions.

In the early years of the round, developing countries managed to show some unity across their defensive versus offensive interests: they demanded greater access in the markets of developed countries (as per the agenda of the G20) but also argued for the protection of their own markets (as per the G33's agenda). A demand for concessions from the other side while refusing to make any oneself was an unlikely recipe for a negotiation breakthrough, especially when the demandeurs were the rising powers. Hence, for example, when talks broke down in the summer of 2006, US Secretary for Agriculture, Mike Johanns, had no qualms in pointing the finger to the larger developing countries:

> Now advanced developing countries are world class competitors. This would be China, this would be India, this would be Brazil, this would be other countries around the world that quite honestly can compete with anybody very effectively. Yet in the proposal that they tabled, it essentially blocked 95 to 98 percent of their market . . . So in the end, what we were faced with is this: we've got a very bold proposal already, we've announced our willingness to be flexible but we're still not seeing the market access that is necessary for world trade.[21]

Interestingly, developing countries did not deny these accusations. India was unambiguous in its rebuttal. Minister Kamal Nath is reported to have spoken of 'big gaps in mind-sets' at a press conference. Already, the poverty narrative was evolving – at least from the perspective of the Indian side – into a non-negotiable and inalienable norm. Nath thus argued: 'If the developed countries want to view this round as a market access round for themselves, which is going to impinge upon the livelihood of our farmers and is going to hurt our industry, then we made very clear there is and can be no further movement in these negotiations'.[22] Despite the emergence of increasingly entrenched normative positions,[23] members persisted in their efforts to secure agreement over the DDA.

Two years later, a significant possibility for a breakthrough emerged in July 2008. Backing the persistent efforts of developing countries to secure development-oriented outcomes soon was an important change in context:

---

[20] China, Cuba, Ecuador, Guatemala, Indonesia, Nigeria, Pakistan, Venezuela, and Zimbabwe were also members of both coalitions.
[21] USTR (2006).
[22] BBC (2006).
[23] See Clapp (2015b) for an excellent account on norm contestation in agriculture.

soaring food prices. On the one hand, the increase in food prices resulted in a variety of new protectionist challenges to the system (such as export controls), which in turn exacerbated the problem of price spikes.[24] On the other hand though, these high prices also made it politically feasible for developed countries to limit the domestic support subsidies they paid to their own farmers – governments could potentially argue that given the increase in food prices, subsidies were no longer necessary. About forty delegations met in Geneva, for a series of meetings that lasted from 21 to 30 July. Seven countries constituted the high-table of the negotiations (European Union, United States, Australia, Japan, Brazil, China, and India). The United States offered to cap its Overall Trade Distorting Support (OTDS) at $15 billion. As this figure was almost twice the value of subsidies that the United States had actually applied in 2007 (i.e., $7–8 billion), developing countries demanded more significant cuts. After much haggling, the United States agreed to reduce its OTDS to $14.5 billion, and made some further demands in return (including a peace clause). The ceiling on the OTDS, despite some attempts to caricature it as an empty offer, was not insignificant; it would have served as a valuable buffer against demands for increased protectionism by farmers whenever prices plummeted again in the future. A package deal, comprising different aspects of the DDA (including Non-Agricultural Market Access, NAMA) emerged via this give-and-take, plus the good offices of Director General Lamy. Brazil – a founding and leading member of the G20, and also India's close ally in the WTO – signalled its willingness to accept this package. Paul Blustein describes the strife that followed in the following words:

> The drama intensified when Amorim, the gray-bearded, sixty-six-year-old elder statesman of the group, delivered his overall verdict on Lamy's paper: 'As a package, I can swallow it', he said, to the shock of Nath, who couldn't believe that his erstwhile G20 comrade in arms was failing to back him up. At last, the inherent contradictions in the Brazilian–Indian alliance were coming to the fore – the offensive interests in agriculture of Brazil, and the defensive interests in agriculture of India, which had been apparent for all to see when the G20 was first formed in 2003. As far as Amorim was concerned, he was committing no breach of G20 unity by backing Lamy's proposal; the group's main purpose had always been securing reductions in rich-country subsidies and trade barriers, and individual members were supposed to decide themselves whether or not they favoured loopholes for developing countries such as special products and the SSM. Brazil's interests naturally

---

[24] Chatterjee and Murphy (2013); Martin and Anderson (2012).

lay on the side of greater market access, and Amorim wasn't going to oppose a package that could deliver substantial benefits to his nation's farm sector.[25]

In contrast to Brazil, India took a much more severe stance. Kamal Nath, in response to Lamy's paper,[26] is reported to have said, 'I reject everything'. He was also the only member of the core group of seven in the July talks 'who was firmly saying no' until the end of the discussions.[27] His objections were several – not only on the issue of the OTDS (Nath is reported to have 'famously called on the US to effectively cut its domestic subsidies by agreeing to reduce its OTDS to $7 billion minus one dollar'[28]), but also the SSM. In cooperation with China, and its G33 allies, India demanded a lower 'trigger' mechanism (than the proposed 40 per cent import surge over a three-year average), and also a higher level of percentage points by which countries using the SSM could raise protectionist barriers. Brazil was brought to align with the Indian position under pressure from its allies (which were also G33 members). The G20 coalition did not collapse in July 2008, even though it came close to breaking point.

For the failure of the July negotiations, newspaper reports at the time laid the blame primarily on the rising powers for the resulting deadlock, particularly India. Alan Beattie, writing in the *Financial Times* at the start of the July talks, had already pointed to the potential recalcitrance of the Indian delegation.[29] After the collapse of the talks, an editorial in the *Financial Times* attributed the proximate cause of failure to 'a stand-off between the US, India and China over rules protecting small farmers from surges in food imports'.[30] In an edition of the newspaper on the previous day, Beattie had provided his answer to the question of why the talks had broken down:

> Fundamentally, the same problems that have bedevilled the talks for years: the desire of some big emerging market countries, particularly India and

[25] Blustein (2009), pp. 265–267; also see Ismail (2009).

[26] The paper – a one-pager – apparently put together by Lamy, in consultation with chairpersons of the relevant WTO bodies, and taking into account the positions of the key players, was circulated on 25 July 2008.

[27] Ibid., p. 265.

[28] Khor (2008).

[29] Writing on 21 July, Beattie (2008a) reported: 'Mr Nath, who has more than once been instrumental in causing ministerial meetings in the Doha round to collapse, is for the moment being represented by G. K. Pillai, his deputy at the commerce ministry, nicknamed "Dr No" by one business lobbyist for his intransigent negotiating style. Observers close to the Indian delegation said there seemed to be an atmosphere of willingness to compromise, but warned that this might merely be political positioning to shift the blame if the talks collapsed'.

[30] *Financial Times* (2008).

China, to retain the right to protect farmers and manufacturers they say are vulnerable to international competition. On the other side, the US – and to some extent the EU – have demanded access to those markets in return for cutting their own support for farmers. All sides could not agree an acceptable trade-off.[31]

In other words, at least a major reason for the deadlock was to be found in the overuse of the poverty narrative by the rising powers, especially those with a defensive interest in agriculture. The extent to which this was the case was reflected in an opening statement that Kamal Nath had made on 23 July, still relatively early in the talks:

> As far as developing country agriculture is concerned, the challenges are well known. Most of Indian agriculture is subsistence level agriculture. For us, agriculture involves the livelihoods of the poorest farmers who number in the hundreds of millions. We cannot have a development Round without an outcome which provides full comfort to livelihood and food security concerns in developing countries. There has been some progress in discussions on SPs and SSM but important gaps still remain. The poor of the world will not forgive us if we compromise on these concerns. These concerns are too vital to be the subject of trade-offs.[32] A successful outcome will require a full addressal of these concerns.
>
> We are not at all happy about the SSM proposal. All manner of objections are being raised to our right to safeguard livelihood concerns of hundreds of millions. Are we expected to standby, see a surge in imports and do nothing? Do we give developed countries the unfettered right to continue subsidizing and then dumping those subsidies on us, jeopardizing lives of billions? The position of developed countries is utterly self-righteous: they have enjoyed their SSG (and want to continue it) but our SSM must be subject to all sorts of shackles and restraints. This self-righteousness will not do. If it means no deal, so be it.[33]

The negotiation ended in deadlock, for which India bore a good share of the responsibility. By contributing to an increasingly moralistic and normative framing of the poverty narrative, India ended up exacerbating the polarization in the DDA negotiations. A changing balance of power in its favour improved its BATNA, and allowed it to play even harder ball than before. While the price spike for food created potential opportunities for countries to limit their

---

[31] Beattie (2008b).

[32] This was a big claim to make; the livelihood and food security concerns of India's farmers, Nath seemed to be arguing, were non-negotiable.

[33] WTO (2008).

subsidies' programmes, it also provided legitimization for those with a defensive agenda as well as those who were fundamentally sceptical about the ability of even well-regulated international markets to deliver to the poor. Public transnational concern about food security – a concept that had come to be mistakenly conflated with food sovereignty – created a supportive context for India's cause of protecting its own agrarian market. Its participation and leadership in the two coalitions of the G20 and G33 allowed India to exercise pressure on Brazil and dissuade it from compromising (contra Brazil's export-oriented interests). And all this it did in the name of the poor – not only its own poor, but also 'the poor of the world' whom Kamal Nath had referred to in his speech.[34]

Had this been just a negotiating ploy – high opening demands to be followed by some concessions in a longer-term game – all of the above might have eventually generated a breakthrough that was tilted on the side of India and other developing countries. But this was not the case. India contributed significantly to the breakdown of the negotiations in 2008, and it persisted with similar strategies in the years that followed. At the Bali Ministerial Conference in 2013, it was not the only voice but certainly a leading one of opposition against an emerging consensus. When negotiators in Bali attempted to create

---

[34] As it so happens India's repeated pointing to the concerns of its poor farmers was not unfounded. The productivity of its agricultural sector was a serious problem. The WTO Secretariat's report as part of India's 2015 trade policy review reported that agriculture was a sector with higher levels of tariffs in comparison to industrial products – whereas the average for non-agricultural products was 9.5 per cent, for agricultural products it was 36.4 per cent. Bound tariff rates in agriculture were also much higher than applied rates, leaving water in the tariffs and the risk of tariff unpredictability. Most central government subsidies also targeted agriculture, plus fertilizers and petroleum. Despite all the protection afforded to the sector, its contribution to India's GDP was small – around 18 per cent since 2011, even though it occupied 56 per cent of the total workforce (WTO, 2015b). There were several structural bottlenecks that made reform of this sector difficult. But an important reason was the weakness also of India's manufacturing base (which even as late as 2015 contributed to only 13 per cent of India's GDP). This mattered in its own right, but also because it also had adverse implications for agricultural sector reform: a weak industrial sector meant that there were few avenues open to those transitioning out of a reforming agrarian sector. The services sector contributed to about 50 per cent of India's GDP, but jobs in high-tech or outsourcing services were not easy for rural populations with lower levels of literacy to enter. In the absence of a major (and politically challenging) reform drive, which would target infrastructure, manufacturing, welfare measures, education and training, and more, Minister Kamal Nath's angry rhetoric had some legitimate cause: were the millions of small farmers in India subject to sudden import surges, they would be deprived of their livelihoods with no alternative means of survival available to them. The point of the exercise here is not to assess the legitimacy of India's claims. Rather, our main purpose is to investigate how far countries have come with their use of the poverty narrative as part of their negotiation strategy, and the successes and failures that it has generated.

a 'package' deal across issue-areas (a standard compromise-building tactic that helps ensure that there is some gains for all parties involved), India's Commerce Minister, Anand Sharma, expressed scathing scepticism. He did so again in the name of not only his own country but developing countries at large. And like his predecessor, he framed agriculture and food security in normative and non-negotiable terms:

> We have a half-baked agricultural package, statements of pious intent for Least Developed Countries (LDCs) and several unresolved issues in the trade facilitation agenda ... None of these texts require the developed countries to make binding commitments for the benefit of developing countries. In contrast, developing countries would be required to undertake significant commitments in trade facilitation. If this imbalance in the Bali package is not redressed, the world at large would accuse all of us of collectively making hollow promises and keeping the tank empty on development content.
>
> Historical imbalances in trade rules must be corrected to ensure a rule-based, fair and equitable order.
>
> The Doha Round, with its strong development mandate, unambiguously recognized the centrality of food security, livelihood security, and rural development in trade negotiations. It acknowledged the inherent imbalance and asymmetries in trade rules, and promised to correct historical distortions.
>
> Agriculture sustains millions of subsistence farmers. Their interests must be secured. Food security is essential for over 4 billion people. I recall the words of Mahatma Gandhi 'There are people in the world so hungry that God cannot appear to them except in the form of bread'. Unlike other areas, the 'survival' aspect of agriculture far outweighs any of its 'commercial' aspects.
>
> A trade agreement must be in harmony with our shared commitments of eliminating hunger and ensuring the right to food. These are an integral part of the MDGs.
>
> For India food security is non-negotiable.[35]

Through much of the ministerial conference at Bali, and indeed in the run-up to it, India objected to the inclusion of trade facilitation into the agenda until the problem of food security had been addressed. In particular, at stake were the issues of public stockholding of food reserves and a peace-clause. The G33 had rightly pointed out that the Aggregate Measure of Support (AMS), which used the baseline of 1986–1988 to calculate domestic support, was antiquated and placed unreasonable pressures on developing countries with food security programmes.[36] India backed the G33 stance, and argued that the WTO

---

[35] WTO (2013).
[36] WTO (2012a); analysis of updated non-paper by G33 available at ICTSD (2013). For a helpful overview of the debate, and India's position, see Hoda (2017).

establish flexibilities for developing countries for subsidized food stockholdings. It also insisted on an indefinite peace clause until a permanent solution
had been found, in contrast to the United States, which proposed a four-year
peace clause. Notably, India claimed to speak on behalf of developing countries as it pushed for the provisions on food security and agriculture, and
perhaps went too far in doing so. Even in the summer of 2013, several months
before the conference, some developing countries had expressed reservations
with the G33 proposal.[37] These divisions came to the fore at the ministerial
conference. Reporting on Bali soon after the ministerial conference was over,
the *Wall Street Journal* offered the following account of India:

> At a contentious Dec. 5 press conference, Mr. Sharma told reporters that he
> had come to Bali not 'to make a deal', but 'to secure the interests of the poor,
> as well as food security'. India was no longer a 'beggar nation', he insisted,
> and called all criticisms of his position wrong or misinformed.
>
> That infuriated a journalist from Benin, one of the world's poorest coun-
> tries, who at the conference shouted to Mr. Sharma, 'You don't speak for us'.
> WTO members like Benin recognize they cannot afford to lavish subsidies
> on their poor farmers, Indian style. They did not want Bali to fail.
>
> ...Mr. Sharma offended many peers and undermined his claims to be
> negotiating in good faith by asserting that his demands were 'non-negotiable'.
> Diplomats privately called the Indian position 'arrogant', 'condescending',
> and 'insulting'.[38]

After protracted negotiation that lasted through the night and into the early
hours of the morning, a deal was cobbled together. But it did not last long: in
July 2014, India blocked what should have been a straightforward 'protocol of
amendment' to bring trade facilitation within the WTO's legal framework. It
did this again emphasizing the issue of food security and public stockholding,
and in the name of developing countries and LDCs. The minister explained
this position to the Indian Parliament in the following terms (emphasis
added):

> In contrast to their efforts on Trade Facilitation in the WTO, some developed
> countries have been reluctant to engage on other issues. Seeing the resistance

---

[37] ICTSD (2013), for instance, reports that African countries had expressed 'lukewarm support' for
the revised G33 non-paper, partly because most of them did not have the resources to finance
large-scale subsidized food aid programmes that India and other rising powers could afford, and
partly because they worried that 'subsidized food purchases in major developing country
economies could be exported to world markets – potentially undermining their own poor
producers, and damaging food security'.
[38] Rushford (2013).

to taking forward the other Decisions, *the apprehension of developing countries* was that once the process of bringing the Trade Facilitation Agreement into force was completed, other issues would be ignored, including the important issue of a permanent solution on subsidies on account of public stockholding for food security purposes. India, therefore, took the stand that till there is an assurance of commitment to find a permanent solution on public stockholding and on all other Bali deliverables, *including those for the Least Developed Countries (LDCs)*, it would be difficult to join the consensus on the Protocol of Amendment for the Trade Facilitation Agreement.[39]

As a result, the deadline of 31 July for signing the protocol of amendment was missed. The standoff of July 2014 was finally overcome in November, as a result of intensive bilateral talks directly between President Obama and Prime Minister Modi in September, and also between government officials on both sides. A bilateral agreement was signed between the United States and India, and was touted as a victory for both parties.[40] In fact, however, the damage to the system was considerable, not least because India's readiness to renege on the agreed commitments of Bali showed how fragile the WTO had become.

Doha never quite recovered from these shocks. As discussed in Section 4.4, it went down a slippery slope of delays and deadlocks to a point where negotiators could not even come up with a face-saving joint ministerial text in Buenos Aires (2017). India's use of poverty narratives (in cooperation with other developing countries) had been crucial in giving the global south an advantage in the early stages of the DDA negotiations. But by 'overplaying its hand', India 'damaged its reputation as the champion of the world's poor'.[41] It also contributed to the ideological polarization that came to characterize the DDA in later years, and inadvertently became one of the underwriters for the demise of the development round. As such, the overuse of its specific poverty narrative came at a cost not only to its own reputation, but also the poor worldwide who would have stood to gain from a completed Doha negotiation.

4.2 CAUGHT IN BETWEEN: THE LDCS

Given the explicit focus of the DDA on development, it would have been reasonable to expect that the concerns of the poorest developing countries –

---

[39] Sitharaman (2014) (emphasis added).

[40] For details on the Bali breakthrough and its aftermath, see Narlikar and Tussie (2016).

[41] Rushford (2013) provides this assessment of India's negotiating behaviour at the Bali ministerial conference; in fact, the same description can be applied to India's behaviour pattern through much of the Doha round.

the LDCs – would finally be prioritized. The start was promising, as already outlined in Chapter 3. The Doha Ministerial Declaration promised: 'to help least-developed countries secure beneficial and meaningful integration into the multilateral trading system and the global economy'.[42] Towards this, the declaration had references built in throughout acknowledging the needs of the LDCs via SDT. Even as negotiators clashed over the seemingly intractable issues of agriculture and NAMA, the willingness of multiple parties to make some concessions at least towards the LDCs offered hope.

4.2.1 *Breakthrough for LDCs*

The Hong Kong Ministerial Conference in 2005 resulted in two important achievements for LDCs. Progress on these issues, moreover, was delinked from the Single Undertaking, which meant that the LDCs would not have to wait until the completion of the round to secure the benefits of the measures that were on the table.[43]

The first important result of the Hong Kong ministerial conference was Annex F of the declaration, which was devoted specifically to the question of SDT for the LDCs. Annex F stated:

> developed-country Members shall, and developing-country Members declaring themselves in a position to do so should:

(a) (i) Provide duty-free and quota-free market access on a lasting basis, for all products originating from all LDCs by 2008 or no later than the start of the implementation period in a manner that ensures stability, security and predictability.

(ii) Members facing difficulties at this time to provide market access as set out above shall provide duty-free and quota-free market access for at least 97 per cent of products originating from LDCs, defined at the tariff line level, by 2008 or no later than the start of the implementation period. In addition, these Members shall take steps to progressively achieve compliance with the obligations set out above, taking into account the impact on other developing countries at similar levels of development, and, as appropriate, by incrementally building on the initial list of covered products.

(iii) Developing-country Members shall be permitted to phase in their commitments and shall enjoy appropriate flexibility in coverage.

---

[42] WTO (2001).
[43] WTO (2005).

(b) Ensure that preferential rules of origin applicable to imports from LDCs
    are transparent and simple, and contribute to facilitating market access . . .

The language of 'shall' with reference to developed countries was important,
and made DFQF a legal obligation, rather than just a best-endeavour clause.
Annex F further confirmed that LDCs themselves would be required to take
on new commitments and make concessions only 'to the extent consistent
with their individual development, financial or trade needs, or their adminis-
trative and institutional capacities'.

The second part of the breakthrough at Hong Kong was the establishment of
the Aid for Trade initiative: 'Aid for Trade should aim to help developing
countries, particularly LDCs, to build the supply-side capacity and trade-related
infrastructure that they need to assist them to implement and benefit from
WTO Agreements and more broadly to expand their trade'. This was a significant step for the WTO to take: it marked a move away from the more market-
driven logic that had guided the Uruguay Round negotiation, and a recognition
that aid and trade might sometimes need to complement each other.

Taken against the lacklustre progress that the DDA was making on all other
issues, these were no mean achievements on the part of the LDCs. The Bali
Package of 2013 saw a further strengthening of the system in favour of the
poorest countries, especially via critical specifications of preferential Rules of
Origins that could allow LDCs to make better use of DFQF.[44] If anything, the
successes of the LDCs reveal an interesting twist to the power of the powerless.
Negotiators from both the developed countries and larger developing countries may have realized that they would be judged harshly if they failed to
deliver on the cause of development. This was especially so, given that the
round was explicitly dedicated to development, and also because of the high
levels of civil society mobilization for this cause. Concessions for LDCs in the
form of Annex F and Aid for Trade were – relatively speaking – politically and
economically expedient to make, in contrast to overcoming fundamental
disagreements on agriculture, NAMA, the Singapore issues, services, and
more. The cause of the LDCs thus showed an inverse relationship to overall
progress in the round: the more the round stalled on some major issues, the
more developed and developing countries came under pressure to show some
successes elsewhere.[45] But these gains were not an unadulterated good. And
the exercise of the power of the powerless had a sting in its tail.

---

[44] For a useful summary of DFQF coverage for LDCs, see WTO (2016).
[45] I owe this interesting insight to a senior official of the WTO. It is worth clarifying that this is not
    an argument about a free ride for the LDCs. Several factors – their own activism, better
    BATNAs (such as being able to play off multiple actors against each other on aid), cooperation

4.2.2 *The Limits of LDC Successes*

Although the LDCs had theoretically accrued gains independent of the conclusion of the DDA negotiations as a whole, several problems emerged. These problems go beyond the long-standing debate in economics on the value of SDT in the first place, and the argument that it (usually) creates perverse incentives for its recipients: instead of facilitating their integration into the world economy and thereby allowing them to avail themselves of the opportunities of world trade, it encourages their further marginalization.[46] Similarly, longer periods of implementation and lighter obligations may deter the economic reform process. But, even if we put these concerns aside, and accept the demand for SDT by LDCs at face value, the LDC-specific measures generated three sets of costs.

First, the entry of Aid for Trade into the WTO, while hailed as a major innovation and concession at the time, also took the organization into a trap of controversies. Several critics challenged the expertise of the WTO to take on this new task, especially when there are other organizations (including the World Bank and the OECD) better equipped to deal with development concerns.[47] An additional point of criticism was that the Aid for Trade agenda had served as 'a bonanza for consultants, nothing for development'.[48] Different organizations competed with each other to secure this agenda within their mandates, with each one claiming to act in the interest of the poor but in fact seeking to expand and legitimize their bureaucratic reach.[49] Turf wars over development policy did not help the already overloaded DDA, and contributed to further stasis within the organization. There was also some ambiguity on the gains generated by Aid for Trade for LDCs. For example, according to one study, in the first five years, LDCs occupied second place for Aid for Trade disbursements (at $35.1 billion) whereas the largest recipients were lower-middle income countries (at $49.2 billion).[50] The WTO's credibility came under further stress, having already been dented due to delays and deadlocks.

Second, the special concessions granted to LDC members of the WTO did not translate into easier conditions for LDCs that were seeking entry into the

---

as a coalition, and the support of transnational social movements – all contributed to the pressure on both developed countries and emerging market economies to not hold the interests of the poorest hostage as they fought out their battles.

[46] Bagwell and Staiger (2011); Conconi and Perroni (2015); Roessler (1998).

[47] Finger (2008a); Kim (2013).

[48] Finger (2008b).

[49] Kim (2013).

[50] Basnett et al. (2012). Also Kim (2013).

organization.[51] Accession guidelines for LDCs were established in 2002 by the Sub-Committee on Trade and Development, which aimed to simplify and accelerate the process.[52] These guidelines were updated in 2012.[53] Despite these efforts though, LDC aspirants continued to complain that 'WTO members routinely ask them to take on commitments beyond their capacities during the bidding process. These commitments also tend to exceed those required from LDCs and other developing countries that joined the organization in its early years'.[54] A report of the South Centre argued 'There has been a feeling that no real "restraint" has been exercised, especially by some developed countries in the bilateral accession negotiations'. The report also highlighted examples of onerous 'WTO-plus' obligations that LDC members had had imposed on them, as well as 'WTO-minus' obligations (i.e., where 'LDCs have had to agree to waive their rights to certain WTO provisions ... that are otherwise available to existing LDC Members').[55] Although an explicit link between improved SDT terms for LDCs as part of the DDA and increased demands on new entrants for accession cannot be proven, it is at least possible to see an inverse relationship at work. Especially in the context of the DDA, where there is a culture of little challenge to LDCs, it is not difficult to see why entry into this club has become more prized: knowing that it will be difficult to extract concessions from LDCs once they become members of the WTO, members have tried to exploit concessions through the accession process.[56]

---

[51] Thirty LDCs acceded to the WTO as original members. For almost a decade after the creation of the WTO, no LDCs acceded to the organization. Cambodia and Nepal were the first to do so in 2004, followed by Samoa in 2012 (and graduated out of LDC status in 2014), Vanuatu in 2012, Lao People's Democratic Republic in 2013, and Yemen in 2014. At the timing of completing this manuscript (summer 2019), eight LDCs are in the accession process: Bhutan, Comoros, Ethiopia, Sao Tomé and Principe, Somalia, South Sudan, Sudan, and Timor-Leste. Eritrea, Kiribati, and Tuvalu are the three that remain outside the WTO and are not yet negotiating accession.

[52] WTO (2002).

[53] WTO (2012b).

[54] ICTSD (2012).

[55] South Centre (2012).

[56] Heightened difficulties of accession for new LDC members in fact suggest some similarity with labour relations and unionized bargaining. Workers already employed in firms – the insiders – have incentives to keep wages higher than the equilibrium level. In contrast, the outsiders reap the consequences of these high wages via unemployment. There are ways to correct this, for example via 'he centralization of wage bargaining and the role of government in the bargaining process' that gives more influence to outsiders (Mankiw 2010, p. 172). But in the case of an international organization, especially a member-led one like the WTO that affords rather limited powers to its secretariat, such a model would be difficult to apply.

Third, developed countries have also shown a cynical willingness to play off the LDCs against each other. This is most obvious in the debates over erosion of preference margins. The United States, for example, offers special concessions to some groups of LDCs. Besides the Generalized System of Preferences (which applies to designated developing countries plus LDCs), the United States offers region-specific schemes like the African Growth and Opportunity Act (AGOA) and the Caribbean Basin Trade Partnership Act (CBTPA).[57] These are helpful initiatives for subsets of LDCs, and indeed other lower income countries in the respective regions. But they create a system of *de facto* discrimination against LDCs, which are outside the regions that enjoy preferential access, and also differences within the schemes. For the least developed beneficiary countries under GSP, the United States has provided DFQF access to almost all tariff lines via CBTPA, 97.5 per cent tariff lines via AGOA, and only 82.2 per cent tariff lines.

The case of apparel exports from the LDCs is a case in point. Haiti received special trade benefits for its apparel exports through the Haitian Hemispheric Opportunity through Partnership Encouragement (HOPE) Act of 2006 and HOPE II Act of 2008.[58] A United States Trade Representative (USTR) report attributes Haiti's ability to alleviate poverty and hunger to 'the very large role preference exports' played in Haiti's GDP, exports, and industrial employment, which in turn was facilitated by preferential treatment schemes.[59] Other LDCs within the Caribbean and African schemes have also gained greater market access to the United States. But those excluded from the region-specific preferential schemes found themselves considerably disadvantaged. Writing in 2009, Craig Van Grasstek summarizes the dichotomy that the US policy produced:

> ... As can be appreciated from the data illustrated in Figure 1, the differing treatment extended to distinct LDCs has produced a real irony: LDCs are subject to either the lowest or the highest average tariff rates, depending on the group. Four apparel-dependent LDCs in Asia are denied preferential treatment for their most important exports, and are subject to tariffs that average 15–16%. Those averages have in fact increased since the Uruguay Round results began to take effect in the mid-1990s, even though average tariffs on most other countries have decreased during that period. The decrease has been especially notable for all other LDCs. Those countries

---

[57] The Caribbean Basin Initiative was expanded into the Caribbean Basin Trade Partnership Act (CBTPA) to overcome the negative third-party effects of NAFTA in the region.
[58] WTO (2018c).
[59] USTR (2016).

had faced somewhat higher than average tariffs prior to 2000, when new preferences were enacted, but since then they have dropped to almost nothing.[60]

The political result of the distributive effects of US policies was to sow dissension within the LDC grouping – a coalition that stands the most to gain by maintaining a united front. LDCs which are members of preferential access schemes have expressed their concerns at the prospect of DFQF to other LDCs. The US official line has not alleviated these fears among the LDCs. In fact, it has sometimes even reinforced their fears through a divisive poverty narrative that frames trade liberalization in zero-sum terms.[61] Such a narrative also works all too conveniently for the United States itself, and serves as a counter-argument for it against offering across-the-board DFQF to all LDCs as per the recommendations and obligations envisaged under Annex F.

Finally, the larger developing countries also had their own ideas on the uses of SDT. Most importantly, they were convinced (on various grounds) that these provisions were intended for the broad church of the global south. As per this view, despite the variations in development levels within the global south, all countries that believed themselves to be entitled to use SDT should be allowed to do so.[62] This has created a double jeopardy for the LDCs. First, even though the evidence is not clear on the extent to which the LDCs would compete against each other even with preference margin erosion, what seems

---

[60] Van Grasstek (2009).

[61] E.g., 'U.S. preferences will naturally have the most impact on countries that are both highly reliant on the U.S. market and large users of preference benefits; they will have less effect as use of preference margins and reliance on the U.S. market diminish' (USTR 2016, p. 17). Similarly, Jones et al. (2013) make the following argument in a Congressional Research Service paper: 'As tariffs fall worldwide, the benefit of zero tariffs in preference programs becomes smaller. It is an important point in the Doha Round negotiations from LDC perspectives. Particularly affected are countries participating in preference programs that cover most of their trade. There is a disincentive for LDCs to support multilateral trade liberalization should it result in reducing the benefits of their preference programs' (p. 15). Whether the LDCs are actually competitors against each other is not so obvious. A different view can be found in Van Grasstek (2009, p. 109), who argues: '. . . while it is in the interests of these countries to maintain and seek improvements in the preferential access that they enjoy to the US market, the competitive threat that they face from the Asian LDCs is vastly exaggerated. While it is true that access to the US apparel market tends to be seen in zero-sum terms, and that any benefit extended to one country might come at the expense of others, the actual value of apparel imported from the Asian LDCs is far below that of other countries with which all of the apparel-exporting LDCs must compete. Simply stated, the Asian LDCs comprise an almost negligible share of the threat posed to the other LDCs'. Despite this, as Van Grasstek also argues, the LDCs are a divided group.

[62] For a useful summary of some of these arguments, see Kwa and Lunenborg (2019).

to be quite clear is that cheaper imports from the rising powers have proven to be tough competition. The fact that even rising powers like China and India have the right to self-designate themselves as developing economies means that the special provisions, which were always intended for the genuinely weak, end up getting shared also among the more powerful. Not all the concerns of the rising powers are unfounded as the previous section illustrated with reference to India's use of the poverty narrative in agricultural negotiations. The problem, however, derives from the fairly persistent and indiscriminate use of this narrative, and the accompanying over-exploitation of SDT provisions, by countries that should have shown at least some willingness to embrace graduation. Not only do the LDCs thus find their own exports in competition with those from larger developing countries (Haiti is again a case in point)[63], but they further encounter a second challenge.

The graduation expectations that underpinned SDT were always an issue of contention between the developed and developing countries. But amidst the changing balance of power underway with the rise of the BRICS, as well as the limitations of the existing trade multilateralism to regulate the uses of SDT which have become more grating to the developed countries (especially amidst the changing balance of power underway), they have begun to show increasing disillusionment and disengagement with the system. The United States has gone the furthest in expressing its discontent with the system. These expressions include President Trump's twitter diplomacy and trade wars (discussed in detail in Section 4.4), plus an official paper submission that delivers a particularly scathing attack on SDT in the WTO.[64] Referring to the 'self-declared paralysis at the WTO', the paper takes aim quite pointedly at the 'economic powerhouses' such as China and India – and indeed some of the wealthiest members of the WTO[65] – for self-declaring themselves as developing countries, and thereby making use of the same SDT provisions

---

[63] For example a report by USITC (2008) focuses on the case of Haiti and the textiles and apparel sector. It argues that, with the expiry of the Agreement on Textiles and Clothing in 2005 (and the abolition of quotas), textiles and apparel producers in Haiti found themselves exposed to price-based competition especially from China and Nicaragua, as well as Vietnam, India, and Mexico.

[64] Note that the United States is not alone in demanding a reform of SDT, but it is especially withering in its attack. For instance, even the title of the proposal is indicative: 'An Undifferentiated WTO: Self-declared development status risks institutional irrelevance' (WTO 2019). The content of the proposal also stands out in comparison to the more moderate and compromising language of other reform proposals that are on the table, such as by Canada (WTO 2018d) and the European Union (European Commission 2018).

[65] E.g., Singapore, Hong Kong, Macao, Israel, Kuwait; South Korea, United Arab Emirates, Brunei Darussalam, and Qatar (WTO 2018d).

as members from Sub-Saharan Africa. It summarizes its case in the following
words:

> Simply put, self-declaration has severely damaged the negotiating arm of the
> WTO by making differentiation among Members near impossible. By
> demanding the same flexibilities as much smaller, poorer Members, export
> powerhouses and other relatively advanced Members . . . create asymmetries
> that ensure that ambition levels in WTO negotiations remain far too weak to
> sustain viable outcomes. Members cannot find mutually agreeable trade-offs
> or build coalitions when significant players use self-declared development
> status to avoid making meaningful offers. Self-declaration also dilutes the
> benefit that the LDCs and other Members with specific needs tailored to the
> relevant discipline could enjoy if they were the only ones with the flexibility
> (paragraph 4.5) . . .
> . . . Self-declaration and its first-order consequence – an inability to differ-
> entiate among Members – puts the WTO on a path to failed negotiations. It
> is also a path to institutional irrelevance, whereby the WTO remains
> anchored to the past and unable to negotiate disciplines to address the
> challenges of today or tomorrow, while other international institutions move
> forward. (paragraph 5.2)[66]

An unfortunate aftertaste of bitterness marks the prior successes that the LDCs
had achieved via their poverty narrative: the key mechanisms that had helped
enable the power of the powerless seem to have now turned against the LDCs.
The rapid and continuous rise of emerging markets should have improved the
BATNAs of the poorest countries. In practice, a continued use of the poverty
narrative by the rising powers (within the context of their self-classification in
the category of developing countries, and thus entitlement to SDT provisions),
has created competition for the genuinely poor countries.[67] Coalitions –
another important mechanism that had facilitated the use of the power of
the powerless in previous years – have also had adverse effects in this case.
First, larger developing countries have appealed to a logic of the global south
to argue against reclassification, and insisted that the alliance between
developing countries at large (including LDCs) must hold strong. In doing
so, they have effectively chosen to freeride on the weakest countries in the
group. As a result, what had in the past been quite an effective (if somewhat
large and amorphous) development-oriented grouping of the global south for

---

[66] WTO (2018d).
[67] The United States too has not been averse to point to this conflict of interest between
developing countries and LDCs, as illustrated in the quote on the previous page (WTO 2018d,
paragraph 4.5).

the LDCs is turning out to be a liability on the issue of SDT. Second, the LDCs themselves are divided over the issue of preference erosion, given the differential coverage of specific schemes for countries within the LDC category. The weakening of the LDC coalition potentially undermines the bargaining power of these countries even further. Supportive transnational social movements – facilitated by the use of social media technologies – had helped stoke concern and commitment towards the condition of poorer countries, and have perhaps also contributed to the transformation of SDT from an operational narrative to a higher-level norm. But the LDCs now find themselves squeezed between an adamant and principled insistence by the middle- and higher-income developing countries for their right to designate themselves as eligible for SDT status, and an equally adamant and principled insistence by the developed countries that the lack of differentiation between developing countries on SDT is counter-productive. The seriousness of this type of critique (from the United States and others) must not be underestimated. The United States especially has cited misuses of the system by larger developing countries – particularly China – as a reason for its readiness to hold up and also potentially walk away from the WTO. As a result, the system of multilateral trade rules faces its greatest threat of breakdown. If such a collapse does indeed transpire, the costs will be highest for the weakest members of the system.[68]

4.3 TRUMP'S TRADE WARS

The United States is, by most measures, neither a poor nor a powerless country. Indeed, by some indicators, it is one of the richest: if one takes GDP figures into account, the United States occupies the first position; if one takes a look at GDP per capita (taking into account purchasing power parity), the United States comes up respectably in position 11. Interestingly, however, under President Trump, the United States has appropriated the poverty narrative to its own ends. In this case study, I show how even a rich country like the United States can use the power of the powerless. I provide an overview of the workings of this narrative, and illustrate its translation into US trade policy. I further suggest that this distorted use of the power of the powerless poses considerable risks for the world at large, and especially the poor within the United States and globally.[69]

---

[68] Parts of this argument were made in Narlikar (2015b) and Narlikar (2018).
[69] I conduct my analysis up to summer 2019.

4.3.1 *In the Name of the Poor: A New Narrative for the World's Largest Economy*

Even though the United States is not a poor country in aggregate or per capita terms, President Trump and his team have tapped into a visceral anger on poverty and marginalization that permeates large parts of the country and harnessed it to shape policy. It is important to bear in mind that the roots of this anger predate Trump. Trump is not the first President in recent US history to signal some protectionist leanings to address domestic woes.[70] But the Trump administration has transformed the poverty narrative from being one about the Global South to a story about marginalization and victimhood within the Global North, via three claims:

(a) America's 'forgotten men and women' have been systematically marginalized and impoverished;

(b) a major cause for this condition is external: America's trading partners have taken an unfair advantage of the United States, and the multilateral trading system has allowed this to happen through sins of both omission and commission; and

(c) the time has come to finally put 'America First'; for Trump, this translates into a policy of unilateral protectionist measures and holding the system hostage until American terms are met.

The inaugural addresses of Presidents Obama (first term) and Trump provide interesting points of initial similarity and then stark divergence.[71] Both speeches showed some comparability in expressing concern about the plight

---

[70] For example, Barack Obama, as senator in 2007, was one of the co-sponsors of the Patriot Employer Act, which was not so different from some of Trump's pronouncements towards offering companies better incentives for creating more jobs for American workers, plus maintaining corporate headquarters in the United States. The strong criticism that the proposal received from economists was prescient of the outcry that some of Trump's ideas have generated more recently. Buiter and Sibert (2008) wrote the following: 'The Patriot Employer Act seeks to transfer wealth from the truly downtrodden of the world to a limited number of favoured US workers: mainly those in once dominant manufacturing industries that have lost their global competitive edge ... Sen. Barack Obama's proposal is reactionary, populist, xenophobic and just plain silly. It is time for him to stop pandering and to show the world that hope and reason are not mutually exclusive'. The Obama administration had also imposed a fivefold increase on steel import duties from China in 2016 and also launched a total of sixteen challenges against China in the DSM. Claims of job losses in the steel industry due to unfair competition from China provided the political background for some of these actions (BBC 2016).

[71] Obama (2009); Trump (2017a).

Box 4.1 Identifying the Challenges: Economic Deprivation within the United States

Obama (2009)	Trump (2017)
'Our economy is badly weakened, a consequence of greed and irresponsibility on the part of some, but also our collective failure to make hard choices and prepare the nation for a new age. Homes have been lost, jobs shed, businesses shuttered. Our health care is too costly, our schools fail too many – and each day brings further evidence that the ways we use energy strengthen our adversaries and threaten our planet.	'Americans want great schools for their children, safe neighborhoods for their families, and good jobs for themselves. These are the just and reasonable demands of a righteous public. But for too many of our citizens, a different reality exists: Mothers and children trapped in poverty in our inner cities; rusted-out factories scattered like tombstones across the landscape of our nation; an education system, flush with cash, but which leaves our young and beautiful students deprived of knowledge; and the crime and gangs and drugs that have stolen too many lives and robbed our country of so much unrealized potential.
These are the indicators of crisis, subject to data and statistics. Less measurable, but no less profound, is a sapping of confidence across our land; a nagging fear that America's decline is inevitable, that the next generation must lower its sights …'.	This American carnage stops right here and stops right now'.

of the economically disadvantaged within their country, even though Trump's language was more dramatic and polarizing, as highlighted in Box 4.1.[72]

Preliminary similarities aside, the narratives of the two presidents showed significant divergence when they identified the sources of the problem. Obama allocated responsibility, not blame, and suggested that there may have been areas where government might not have worked, and markets may have been poorly regulated. Trump, in contrast, laid the blame first on the country's political elite, but squarely and ultimately on external actors, as highlighted in Box 4.2.

Policy prescriptions that resulted from these contrasting causal narratives were also fundamentally different. For Obama, the solutions lay in greater

---

[72] There is some irony even in terms of this small difference, not least because President Obama had taken office in a tougher economic context (directly amidst the after-shocks of the global financial crisis of 2008).

Box 4.2 Putative Causes for Economic Difficulties

Obama (2009)	Trump (2017)
'The question we ask today is not whether our government is too big or too small, but whether it works – whether it helps families find jobs at a decent wage, care they can afford, a retirement that is dignified. Where the answer is yes, we intend to move forward. Where the answer is no, programs will end. And those of us who manage the public's dollars will be held to account, to spend wisely, reform bad habits, and do our business in the light of day, because only then can we restore the vital trust between a people and their government. Nor is the question before us whether the market is a force for good or ill. Its power to generate wealth and expand freedom is unmatched. But this crisis has reminded us that without a watchful eye, the market can spin out of control. The nation cannot prosper long when it favors only the prosperous . . .'.	'For many decades, we've enriched foreign industry at the expense of American industry; Subsidized the armies of other countries while allowing for the very sad depletion of our military; We've defended other nation's borders while refusing to defend our own; And spent trillions of dollars overseas while America's infrastructure has fallen into disrepair and decay. We've made other countries rich while the wealth, strength, and confidence of our country has disappeared over the horizon. One by one, the factories shuttered and left our shores, with not even a thought about the millions upon millions of American workers left behind. The wealth of our middle class has been ripped from their homes and then redistributed across the entire world'.

accountability of government, better regulation of the market (as implied in the quote in Box 4.2), improved welfare mechanisms, as well as some transfer of wealth to the Global South. In stark contrast for Trump, reform involved protectionism, as highlighted in Box 4.3.

While Obama had called for the remaking of America, this call was still premised on a bottom line that recognized America's power and riches: 'We remain the most prosperous, powerful nation on Earth'. In contrast, Trump presented the United States as the injured party, and promised the American people, 'You will never be ignored again'. Americans, according to Trump, had been taken advantage of for far too long, but now 'America will start winning again, winning like never before'.

Trump's story of America's victimization has continued to run through different parts of government. When complaining about the misuses of

---

Box 4.3 Programmes for Reform

Obama (2009)	Trump (2017)
'... The success of our economy has always depended not just on the size of our gross domestic product, but on the reach of our prosperity, on the ability to extend opportunity to every willing heart – not out of charity, but because it is the surest route to our common good ... ... To the people of poor nations, we pledge to work alongside you to make your farms flourish and let clean waters flow; to nourish starved bodies and feed hungry minds. And to those nations like ours that enjoy relative plenty, we say we can no longer afford indifference to the suffering outside our borders, nor can we consume the world's resources without regard to effect'.	'From this moment on, it's going to be America First. Every decision on trade, on taxes, on immigration, on foreign affairs, will be made to benefit American workers and American families. We must protect our borders from the ravages of other countries making our products, stealing our companies, and destroying our jobs. Protection will lead to great prosperity and strength ... ... We will bring back our jobs. We will bring back our borders. We will bring back our wealth. And we will bring back our dreams. We will build new roads, and highways, and bridges, and airports, and tunnels, and railways all across our wonderful nation. We will get our people off of welfare and back to work – rebuilding our country with American hands and American labor. We will follow two simple rules: Buy American and Hire American'.

---

economic statecraft by competitors, the USTR justified its actions by appealing to the victimization of the American people: 'The goal is to address unfair Chinese economic practices and create a level playing field that will give all Americans a better chance to succeed'.[73] When attacking the WTO's DSM, Trump again argued that the United States had been short changed, for example,

> We rarely won a lawsuit except for the last year. You know, in the last year, we're starting to win a lot. You know why? Because they know if we don't, I'm out of there. I'll take them out. We're starting to win lawsuits that we

---

[73] USTR (2018b).

never – you know that. We never won lawsuits because the courts are stacked. You know they – it's sad. We have a minority on the courts. So, the WTO was a horrible deal.[74]

At its 14th Trade Policy Review in 2018, the US government's report adhered to the narrative that the country and its people had been ill-served by the WTO – for example, 'For too long, the rules of global trade have been tilted against US workers and businesses. The United States has demonstrated that it will alter – or terminate – old trade deals that are not in the US national interest'.[75]

4.3.2 *How the Powerful Have Harnessed the Power of the Powerless: Mechanisms of Change*

When the world's supposedly most powerful nation takes on the role of the victim, this is a remarkable redirection in the use of the power of the powerless towards new goals. Amongst the mechanisms that contributed to this transformation, particularly interesting and surprising may have been the rich repertoire of recent research on issues of inequality and relative poverty.[76] Trump himself does not cite this enlightened scholarship in his tweets or his other forms of proclamation. Nor can one establish a causal claim between scholarship on inequality and relative poverty on the one hand, and Trump's use of the poverty narrative on the other. But one can surmise that impactful scholarship on these issues – especially when the scholars themselves are prominent public intellectuals – can provide a vital contextual backdrop against which it is seen as legitimate and responsible to address issues of domestic poverty in rich countries (rather than 'just' absolute poverty globally). At the very least, recent writings and public debates on inequality created a heightened social awareness. This may have served as a convenient backdrop against which Trump and others developed their new poverty-powerlessness narrative, and then made a bigger jump that goes beyond anything that the authors of these ideas likely ever intended.[77]

While scholarly ideas provided a useful background, altered boundaries and coalitions were key to implementing the narrative that Trump and his advisers developed. Some of these realignments were domestic. Researchers are

---

[74] Trump, Interview (2018a).
[75] WTO (2018b).
[76] E.g., Milanovic (2016); Piketty (2014); Stiglitz (2015). For a different point of view on poverty versus inequality, see Dutt and Tsetlin (2015, 2016).
[77] Reeves (2016).

divided on the ways in which boundaries were redrawn in the Trump campaign. One set of interpretations primarily emphasizes economic interests (especially of the working class) and links this up with race and ethnicity. For example, in their content analysis of his electoral campaign speeches, Lamont et al. argue that Trump's 'political rhetoric, which led to his presidential victory, addressed the white working class's concern with their declining position in the national pecking order'.[78] The campaign drew boundaries between the white working class and several 'others': the so-called elite, ethno-religious, and racial minorities, as well as women and sexual minorities. They write:

> Many of these workers think of themselves as society's invisible and under-recognized 'backbone', who keep the American economy going, yet experience a recognition gap (Lamont 2017). They believe they 'deserve better' and ache to see the country recognize their value and contributions. During the 2016 presidential election, many of these workers rose in protest and anger to follow a man who promised them what they believed was their due after too many years of enduring abuse in silence.[79]

In contrast, Diana Mutz offers a different picture.[80] She argues that Trump's electoral victory was a result of support from not the actually downtrodden, but a product of efforts by 'members of already dominant groups to assure their continued dominance and by those in an already powerful and wealthy country to assure its continued dominance'. Increasing racial diversity domestically and a relative decline in America's economic dominance internationally led white Americans to believe they were under siege. Mutz writes, 'Those who felt that the hierarchy was being upended – with whites discriminated against more than blacks, Christians discriminated against more than Muslims, and men discriminated against more than women – were most likely to support Trump'. Trump's electoral success was a product of the anxiety of dominant groups concerned about their future status, rather than a reaction against having been left behind in the past.[81] Citing a post-election survey conducted by *The Atlantic Magazine* and the Public Religion Institute,[82] David Graham similarly argues, 'The truly poor voted for the Democrat. The people who voted for Trump are not those with no economic

---

[78] Lamont et al. (2017).
[79] Lamont et al. (2017), p. S154.
[80] Mutz (2018).
[81] Mutz (2018).
[82] Green (2017).

status – it is those who are worried they could lose the status they already hold'.[83]

If the second claim is right, then we have an interesting demonstration of a reversal of the powerlessness narrative: Trump's victory represents the hopes and aspirations of the still powerful, but who nevertheless see their relative decline as the basis of their claims of powerlessness and victimhood. But the more nuanced version of the argument,[84] which recognizes both economic grievance and status threat as equally important drivers that led the American electorate to vote Trump to power, also shows us a fundamental change in the narrative of poverty and powerlessness. Trump was able to harness and fan the economic disappointments of a white working class; he further pitted these against the interests of various other marginalized social groups domestically as well as the poor internationally, that is the very same groups that had traditionally claimed domestic and international redress on account of their marginalization and poverty, respectively.[85]

The coalitions that backed Trump were moreover not limited to the domestic arena. Trump's political narrative of standing up for a newly defined powerless had resonance across different parts of the world. It tapped into and further fed what Cas Mudde had, writing in 2004, termed the 'Populist Zeitgeist'.[86] The populist zeitgeist in recent times – both in terms of the Left and the Right – may have spread through convincing demonstration effects of success, but John Slocum also gives examples of how populism is being 'intentionally exported'.[87] In other words, not entirely unlike the transnational coalitions that had come together to fight global poverty (as analysed in Chapter 3), new transnational networks emerged.

Especially for variants of populism that plead the cause of nationalism (in Trump's case, 'America First'), the use of transnationalism may at first sight appear to be paradoxical. Historically too, though, we have seen such alliances emerge. Harold James, for instance, writes:

> While intensely nationalist movements such as Mussolini's fascists and Adolf Hitler's Nazis did compete with one another over who was more genuinely fascist, they ultimately united to oppose the liberal order. Similarly, today's

---

[83] Graham (2018).

[84] E.g., Morgan (2018).

[85] Interestingly, despite his newfound poverty and powerlessness narrative, Trump created a 'curious coalition' of the white working class and the 'nation's ownership class' (see Reich 2018).

[86] Mudde (2004).

[87] Slocum (2017).

political revolt may be following an unstoppable logic, whereby every country must close itself off to trade, migration, and capital flows, or risk losing out in a zero-sum game.[88]

The existence of a right-wing 'Populist International' appears to be at least an amorphous facilitating background factor that contributed to the welcome that Trump's newfound use of the poverty narrative received. Although the Mueller Report, for example, admits that 'the investigation did not establish that members of the Trump campaign conspired or coordinated with the Russia government in its election interference activities', it is unambiguous in its finding that '... the Russian government perceived it would benefit from a Trump presidency and worked to secure that outcome, and that the Campaign expected it would benefit electorally from information stolen and released through Russian efforts'.[89] Narratives of marginalization created new transnational sympathies and networks between the United States that brought Trump to power and those in the United Kingdom who sought to 'take back control' by voting Brexit in the referendum in 2016.[90] Even after Trump was ensconced in power, these trends have continued. Strongmen leaders who have expressed support for Trump's politics and policies include Jair Bolsonaro, Shinzo Abe, Victor Orban, Narendra Modi, Benjamin Netanyahu, and others.[91] These affinities have not been limited to the leaders' level; Steve Bannon's expansion to Europe, via *The Movement* in Brussels[92] and the creation of an academy in Italy,[93] is a case in point.

In furthering his version of the poverty narrative, Trump made effective use of social media, especially Twitter. Trump himself showed awareness of the importance of social media in his campaign, stating in an interview, '... the fact that I have such power in terms of numbers with Facebook, Twitter, Instagram,

---

[88] James (2016).

[89] US Justice Department (2019), Vol. 1., p. 13.

[90] Mayer (2018).

[91] Luce (2019).

[92] Horowitz (2018).

[93] The Dignitatis Humanae Institute has been set up under Steve Bannon's initiative in the Trisulti Abbey in Collepardo, Italy. The mission statement of the academy states that the 'DHI is a direct response to a growing secularist intolerance to Christians of all confessions that has led to a myriad of attacks on human dignity. Just as many secularist groups have mobilized to create effective advocacy groups across the world, so the Institute plans on doing the same, pushing back the tide of radical secularism which is threatening the dignity of increasing numbers of people, especially the vulnerable and the weak'. For an overview of this initiative, see Zerofsky (2019). Bannon's cultural populist narrative – as exemplified in the DHI – is, I would argue, perfectly in keeping with the powerlessness narrative reversed.

et cetera, I think it helped me win all of these races . . .'.[94] Academic analyses corroborate this. Trump's tweets taking up 'controversial positions' during the election campaign attracted 'disproportionate attention' from television news-casts and newspaper headlines.[95] In as early as March 2016, using data provided by mediaQuant, the *New York Times* had reported that Trump had clocked up almost US$2 billion worth of free media attention;[96] by the time that the election was done, it is estimated that this figure had risen to $5 billion (double the amount that Clinton had been able to earn).[97]

In large measure, these coalitions and networks – magnified in their voice through the use of social media – represent a reaction to the empowerment of the poor and the powerless (measured in absolute terms) in the global South over the last fifteen or so years. We now see a capture of the same agenda by the (relatively) poor and powerless in the global North and powerful polit-icians who claim to represent these interests. That these networks are using the same language of an empowerment narrative, even while fundamentally transforming the uses to which it is being put, is an important illustration of how narratives adapt and change.[98]

---

[94] Trump (2016).

[95] Schroeder (2018).

[96] Confessore and Yourish (2016).

[97] Gibson and Smith (2016).

[98] It is worth mentioning at this point that the emergence of this version of the narrative – the powerlessness narrative reversed – was facilitated by the failure of liberal thinkers and practitioners to convincingly adapt the original narrative to meet the challenges of relative poverty within the west. Neither the Democrats nor those who had campaigned for Remain in the Brexit referendum, for instance, gave much indication that they took seriously the concerns of the many who felt increasingly disenfranchised in their own societies. They did little to construct coalitions within their societies around an updated narrative, nor did they do anything to build transnational networks and movements along the lines that right-wing populists did. They also offered few policy solutions that would appeal to groups that now saw themselves as excluded. At most, they denounced the opposition, sometimes in vitriolic terms, as Jeffrey Sachs (2018):

'Trump's so-called policies are not really policies. Trade wars are on, off, on hold, on again, within the span of days. . . Global agreements and rules are ripped to shreds. Trump's garbled syntax and disorganized thoughts are impossible to follow.

The US has probably never before had a delusional President, one who speaks gibberish, insults those around him including his closest associates, and baffles the world'.

Such critique, however, may have had the unintended effect of reinforcing support for Trump and hardening the backlash against what the self-identified marginalized in the west see as the 'global elite'. Trump's team is aware of the advantages of being targeted by such critique. The Chairman of the GOP, Sarasota, Florida, John Gruters, is quoted in the FT (Weaver 2018) as follows: 'The more the president gets attacked by outside groups and outside factors, the more people are digging the hole alongside him and [are] willing to follow him across the galaxy to do whatever needs to be done to be successful'.

4.3.3 *Resulting Policies and Impact of Trump's New Use of the Poverty Narrative*

Trump's success in reversing the former powerlessness-poverty narrative has translated into a series of changes in its negotiation behaviour. Some changes are moderate enough: an increased use of the DSM by the United States, and also the push for an agenda for reform. At the distributive end of the negotiating strategy spectrum are Trump's trade wars against various trading partners via unilaterally imposed tariffs, the blocking of the appointment/re-appointment of members to the Appellate Body of the WTO, and ferocious invective against WTO. Both sets of changes derive directly from Trump's peculiar appropriation and application of the poverty narrative. They present the multilateral trading system as having swung too far in the interests of the global poor and seek redress in favour of America and its workers.[99] I provide an overview of both sets of measures, before discussing the overall impact of these changes.

The first set of changes involves a proactive use of the DSM and pressing an agenda for reform. As respondent on nineteen cases brought against it in 2018, the United States faced an especially high number of legal challenges in the DSM.[100] This high number of cases was perhaps to be expected, given the aggressive protectionism that the United States had pursued against multiple trading partners.[101] Interestingly though, the United States also acted as complainant on eight cases (two were against China; respondents on the remaining six were India, European Union, Canada, Mexico, Turkey, and Russia). This was still a relatively high number in comparison to most other years. Additionally, the United States also sought a reform of the multilateral trading system on a range of areas.[102] In 2017, the Trump administration put forth a proposal for improving transparency in the WTO, particularly via more

---

[99] In the case of tariffs, the administration has sometimes referred specifically to Section 232 of the Trade Expansion of 1962 (see US Bureau of Industry and Security 2007). Concerns about economic statecraft in a world of power transition have provided the broad framework for this line of argumentation (for agenda-setting work in this area, see Farrell and Newman 2019, and Drezner 2019). Interestingly though, this may also be seen as a further variant of the victimization narrative that Trump has developed, as per which the United States has suffered not only in economic terms but has also jeopardized its security interests – all because unscrupulous foreigners have taken advantage of it and international rules have allowed them to do so.

[100] In most other years since the creation of the WTO, this had been a single-digit figure; only in 2002 did we see a matching number of nineteen cases that were brought against the United States.

[101] Nine of these cases in the DSM, for instance, deal specifically with steel and aluminium.

[102] Congressional Research Service (2019).

stringent notification requirements.[103] Having launched this debate, the
United States then worked with other countries to revise and update this
proposal.[104] Another illustration of the United States taking the lead on the
issue of reform is on Special and Differential Treatment (SDT). Divisions
over the question of 'graduation' from SDT provisions go back to the days of
the GATT, but this is an area in which the current administration has
sharpened focus and critique. For example, in a submission to the WTO,
the United States argued, 'Whether the WTO's status quo approach to
development status was sensible at its dawn, it makes no sense today in light
of the vast changes in development and increasing heterogeneity among
Members . . .'.[105] So far so good. But in parallel with these steps that suggest
that the United States is willing to play by the rules of the game and seeks to
reform the system from within, the Trump administration has also adopted
some highly distributive negotiation moves.

The most dramatic distributive move resulting from Trump's appropriation
of the poverty narrative has been the imposition of tariffs. After much sabre-
rattling during the election campaign and in the first year of the presidency,
the first actual salvo in this direction came in January 2018 with the imposition
of global tariffs on certain types of washing machines and solar panels.[106] Soon
after this, while speaking with representatives from the US steel and aluminium industry on 1 March, the US President declared his intention to impose
25 per cent tariffs on steel and 10 per cent tariffs on aluminium imports for an
indefinite period of time.[107] The next day, Trump announced on Twitter:
'Trade wars are good and easy to win'. The tariffs that followed came in several
waves, and had multiple targets.[108] They allowed exemptions for some countries in different periods, and the administration also showed different degrees
of openness to selectively negotiate bilateral deals with target countries as well
as companies from affected countries.[109] As already mentioned earlier, Trump
is not the first US President to use protectionist sticks against rivals and
competitors.[110] But the range of targets and the scope of the tariffs was

[103] WTO (2017), Communication from the United States.
[104] WTO (2018a), Communication from Argentina, Costa Rica, the European Union, Japan, and
the United States.
[105] WTO (2019), Communication from the United States, paragraph 4.3.
[106] USTR (2018a).
[107] Trump (2018b).
[108] For a step-by-step account of Trump's trade wars, Bown and Kolb (2019) offer a particularly
useful starting point; further useful sources are available at www.ustr.gov, including fact sheets,
relevant reports, and press releases.
[109] E.g., Beattie (2018); Cassello (2018); Crooks and Fei (2018).
[110] Also see Goldberg (2016).

unprecedented, and marked a difference of not just degree but of kind. Amiti et al. group the tariff actions by the United States into six waves thus far, and estimate that in the course of 2018, the United States imposed tariffs on approximately $283 billion worth of US imports, and also found itself subject to tariffs of $121 billion on US exports via retaliation from trading partners.[111] Fajgelbaum et al. report that tariffs increased from an average of 2.6 per cent to 17 per cent on 12,007 products covering 12.6 per cent (i.e., $303 billion) of 2017 annual US imports. Retaliatory measures by US trade partners resulted in an increase in average tariffs from 6.6 per cent to 23 per cent on 2,931 products, covering 6.2 per cent (i.e. $96 billion) of 2017 annual US exports.[112] Importantly, even though dispute actions via the WTO are now underway, the unilateral imposition of tariffs by the United States in the first place as well as subsequent bilateral attempts to manage their consequences by way of exemptions and quotas were all actions that *de facto* sidelined the WTO.

Also within the umbrella of distributive moves, the United States increased its pressure on the WTO by blocking the appointment/re-appointment of members of the WTO's Appellate Body. Again, the Trump administration is not the first to do this. Rather, encroachments on the independence of the WTO's judiciary go back to the second Bush administration.[113] They became even more overt under the Obama administration, which blocked the reappointment of Jennifer Hillman (the American 'representative'[114] on the Appellate Body).[115] Nor did it stop there: rather, the United States in 2016, under President Obama, blocked the reappointment of the South Korean national, Seung Wha Chang.[116] But under Trump, the willingness of the United States to disrupt the dispute settlement process seems to have undergone a qualitative change. Not only has this administration persisted in blocking reappointments, but it has also blocked new appointments for vacancies created through retirement. By March 2019, only three of the seven seats of the Appellate Body were occupied (by nationals from the United States, China, and India).[117] This reduction in numbers makes it difficult for the

---

[111] Amiti et al. (2019).
[112] Fajgelbaum et al. (2019).
[113] Bacchus (2018).
[114] The members of the Appellate Body are in fact supposed to be independent, and do not 'represent' any country. They are appointed for four-year terms, and can be re-appointed; any country can put forward nominations. But by 'unwritten tradition' (Hufbauer 2011) the United States, the European Union, and Japan have always had their own nationals on the seven-member body.
[115] Hufbauer (2011).
[116] Bacchus (2018).
[117] www.wto.org/english/tratop_e/dispu_e/ab_members_descrp_e.htm

Appellate Body to carry out its duties (especially at a time when the number of disputes being filed in the WTO is very high) because three members are necessary to form a division that adjudicates an appeals' process. Were the United States to persist in its strategy of blocking new appointments, the Appellate Body risks being paralyzed by the end of 2019. This, in turn, would jeopardize the entire dispute settlement process.

Besides its onslaught against the WTO's negotiating arm as well as its dispute-settlement arm, the Trump administration has unleashed severe critique and invective against the organization. In the race for the US presidency, Trump had been unambiguous in expressing his disdain of the WTO. For example, in an interview in 2016, when questioned whether his plans to impose taxes on US companies that had moved production to Mexico could be in violation of WTO rules, he had stated, 'It doesn't matter. Then we're going to renegotiate or we're going to pull out. These trade deals are a disaster, the World Trade Organization is a disaster'.[118] This line of argumentation persisted after Trump assumed power. In an interview with Bloomberg he stated, 'I would say the WTO was the single worst trade deal ever made. And if they don't shape up, I would withdraw from the WTO'.[119] This invective matters, especially when it comes from the economy that had served as the driving force behind the founding of the multilateral trading system. At a minimum, these types of pronouncements create uncertainty in the system, and further undermine the credibility of a waning WTO that has been beleaguered by crisis and deadlock for more than a decade.

The Trump administration's mix of rhetoric and action has adversely impacted on the global economy. Forecasts suggest further disruption.[120] Chinese economic growth in the third quarter of 2018 sank to its lowest ever since 2009.[121] Further, in keeping with economic theory, recent models confirm that trading partners taking retaliatory action against the United States would also be adversely affected.[122] A few studies suggest that a handful of third countries may capture some of the market created by trade diversion, but the overall effect is not clear: the positive effects could be offset by the disruption caused in global value chains.[123] Plus the slowdown in global economic growth is likely to affect many countries not directly involved in the crossfire. But, at least from the Trump administration's perspective, a global downturn

[118] Dyer (2016).
[119] Trump, Interview (2018a).
[120] Berthou et al. (2018); International Monetary Fund (2019); World Bank (2019).
[121] Worland (2019).
[122] Amiti et al. (2019).
[123] Coke-Hamilton (2019).

and an impoverishment of the global poor may be unfortunate but acceptable costs, if the original goal of these policies were achieved. The president may also point to the costs to geoeconomic rivals, such as China, as evidence of success. But the crux of the matter lies in the impact of these policies on the United States itself, and the people in whose name they were put into effect in the first place: are these policies really putting America first and uplifting America's forgotten men and women? Several studies highlight the negative consequences of Trump's tariffs. Amiti et al. summarize their results as follows:

> While the long-run effects are still to be seen, over the course of 2018, the US experienced substantial increases in the prices of intermediates and final goods, large changes to its supply chain network, reductions in availability of imported varieties, and complete passthrough of the tariffs into domestic prices of imported goods. Therefore, although in principle the effect of higher tariffs on domestic prices could be offset by foreign exporters lowering the pre-tariff prices that they charge for these goods, we find little evidence of such an improvement in the terms of trade up to now, which implies that the full incidence of the tariff has fallen on domestic consumers so far. Our results imply that the tariff revenue the US is now collecting is insufficient to compensate the losses being born by the consumers of imports.[124]

Fajgelbaum et al. also estimate significant costs to US consumers: annual losses of $68.8 billion from the increased costs of imports alone.[125] On factoring in the costs of retaliation against the United States by trading partners, the paper further shows that the greatest losses are borne by farmers and blue collar workers in strongly Republican counties. This effect derives partly from the fact that the United States raised the input costs for agriculture via its own tariffs on imports, and partly because trading partners have targeted agricultural exports from the United States in retaliation. In other words, the impact of Trump's policies appears to be adverse for the United States in aggregate, and generates the highest costs for those very groups that Trump had appealed to most explicitly in his powerlessness narrative reversed.[126]

Trump's trade wars provide us with an alarming illustration of how narratives are appropriated and altered. In this case, the changes work to the advantage of neither the original beneficiaries (the global poor) nor the

---

[124] Amiti et al. (2019).

[125] Fajgelbaum et al. (2019).

[126] Note that both Amiti et al. (2019) and Fajgelbaum et al. (2019) focus on the short-term effects of Trump's actions, and not the additional longer-term costs, for instance the adverse effects of trade policy uncertainty on investment.

potential beneficiaries in whose name the re-applied poverty narrative was developed (the poor within the United States).

4.4 DELAY, DEADLOCK, AND THE DEATH OF DOHA: NOT BUSINESS-AS-USUAL IN THE WTO[127]

While the previous case shows ways in which interested actors appropriate and change the nature of narratives, this section illustrates an unintended and costly systemic consequence of the powerlessness narrative – an almost constant logjam in decision-making in the WTO's decision-making processes from 2003 onwards.

The Doha Development Round, as discussed in Chapter 3, had been launched with great aplomb and optimism in 2001 as the first trade round dedicated to the cause of development. It was hailed as a major achievement for developing countries – and rightly so, given the many hurdles that poor countries had faced in agenda-setting in the GATT and in the early years of the WTO. Negotiators decided to set themselves an ambitious mandate: the Ministerial Declaration of 2001 stated that the negotiations would be concluded no later than January 2005. What actually transpired was recurrent deadlock and delay.

The Cancun Ministerial of 2003 was the first significant point in the Doha negotiations, when negotiators ended up in deadlock. The July Package was agreed on in 2004, but only after arduous negotiation and a significant reduction in the original mandate (three of the four Singapore Issues were taken off the agenda). The Hong Kong Ministerial of 2005 brought some small but important successes. In July 2006, after another round of failed attempts to achieve a breakthrough, and agriculture proving to be a major sticking point, negotiations had to be indefinitely suspended. Although the negotiations were renewed a few months later, the credibility of the organization began to suffer. July 2008 offered a potential breakthrough moment via a deal on agriculture (one of the most difficult issues in the round), but this opportunity was also lost. A good gauge of the low morale in the organization was the ministerial process. Even though the Agreement establishing the WTO decrees that ministerial conferences will be held every two years, a four-year gap emerged between the Hong Kong Ministerial of 2005 and the Geneva Ministerial of 2009. The 2009 Ministerial Conference focused almost entirely on systemic issues, rather than being geared towards completing DDA negotiations. The

---

[127] Parts of this section draw on Narlikar (2010, 2013b).

ministerial conference of 2011 – again held in Geneva – also failed to close a deal on the DDA after a weak, lacklustre, and lethargic show of effort by members. The Bali Ministerial in 2013 finally gave some signs of progress, for example, with a deal being agreed to on Trade Facilitation. But even this narrow success was threatened in the post-Bali implementation phase due to the fundamental disagreement that re-emerged between the United States and India on food security (as discussed in Section 4.1). The year 2015 – marking the twentieth anniversary of the founding of the WTO – was in fact one that delivered another major blow to the DDA: at the Nairobi Ministerial Conference, members finally – and publicly and officially – recognized the fundamental divisions among themselves.[128] The Buenos Aires Ministerial in December 2017 marked an unprecedented new low for the WTO: for the first time, a ministerial conference of the organization had failed to come up with an overarching ministerial declaration.[129] The DDA seems to have painfully whimpered its way to an unmarked grave.

In the early years of stalemate, negotiators would joke about the 'curse of Geneva': given the history of previous rounds, it was only to be expected that the DDA would take longer to complete than the preceding round. The Kennedy Round had taken three years (1964–1967) to complete, the Tokyo Round had lasted for six years (1973–1979), while the Uruguay Round had needed eight years (1986–1994) of hard diplomatic graft. Deadlocks were not alien to these long rounds. But business-as-usual explanations, which rely on steadily increasing issue-complexity to explain the curse of Geneva, do not suffice for the DDA's fifteen years of deadlocks (which have been multiple and relentless) and the *de facto* (even if not officially declared) failure of the round. Rather, the explanation lies in the evolution of the poverty narrative. The same narrative that had served so well in bringing the causes of

---

[128] For example, Paragraph 30 of the Nairobi ministerial declaration stated, 'We recognize that many Members reaffirm the Doha Development Agenda, and the Declarations and Decisions adopted at Doha and at the Ministerial Conferences held since then, and reaffirm their full commitment to conclude the DDA on that basis. Other Members do not reaffirm the Doha mandates, as they believe new approaches are necessary to achieve meaningful outcomes in multilateral negotiations. Members have different views on how to address the negotiations. We acknowledge the strong legal structure of this Organization'. Paragraph 32 further noted, '... Many Members want to carry out the work on the basis of the Doha structure, while some want to explore new architectures' (see WTO 2015a).

[129] Instead of an umbrella ministerial declaration covering a range of issues (e.g., to address the Doha mandate or new directions for the WTO) as is usually the case, what resulted from Buenos Aires was an issue-specific ministerial declaration on fisheries subsidies, another on a narrow aspect of TRIPs and complaints, and two work programmes on e-commerce and small economies.

development and poverty to the heart of the WTO, and had ensured dramat-ically enhanced voice for developing countries, alas subsequently played out to the detriment of all parties.

On paper, decision-making processes in the WTO remained unchanged. In practice, as a result of the effective use of the poverty narrative (as described in Chapter 3), the high table of decision-making in the organization underwent a fundamental transformation in the early Doha years. The old Quad (United States, European Union, Canada, Japan) of the 'Rich Man's Club' was replaced by a 'New Quad' (United States, European Union, China, India). In allowing – even enabling – this transformation, the WTO proved itself to be a pioneer in global governance: unlike the UN Security Council, or indeed the IMF or the World Bank, this is the one organization that had adapted its governance structures to match critical external changes in the balance of power in a timely manner. And insofar as China, and especially India, worked in coalitions with other developing countries, including them at the high table also gave indirect voice and representation to a bigger group in the Global South. These improvements in inclusiveness and pluralism should have increased the sustainability of the WTO's decisions with greater ownership among all its stakeholders – all the more so given that the reformed processes were targeted towards achieving a shared and noble goal of development. In fact, however, they produced new inefficiencies, heightened the proclivity of the organization to deadlock, and exacerbated disengagement and disillusion-ment among all players. This happened via three mechanisms.

4.4.1 *Inadequacy of Consensus-Based Diplomacy*

The transformation of the WTO from the 'Rich Man's Club' into an inclusive body was a product of the remarkable exercise of the power narrative by developing countries, as argued in Chapter 3. But an unintended conse-quence of this development was the trade-off that followed between the gains of legitimacy and efficiency.

The Doha negotiations saw a more diverse group of countries in the driving seat. The old Quad had displayed far greater homogeneity of interests than its newer incarnations have ever done, whether they took the shape of the smaller G4 or the bigger G7. Even China and India – admittedly among the more advanced developing countries – saw themselves at very different stages of development from the European Union, United States, Canada, Japan, and others. Additionally, as became increasingly apparent, centralized China was driven by geoeconomic imperatives that were quite different from the old Quad's, while India's political economy too showed different constraints (hence, for instance, although agriculture has been a difficult area for most parties to make concessions on, the constraints that India faces in terms of its poor farmers are fundamentally different from those faced by the European Union and the United States). They also brought very different ideas of negotiating cultures and ideas of fairness and distributive justice to the negotiating table.[130] Add to this the factor of multipolarity. The distribution of power within the WTO was now considerably more even, in contrast to the days of the GATT or the duopoly that emerged with Europe's post-war recovery. In this more diverse and more equal setting, it became considerably harder to reach agreement using the old instrument of consensus.

Enabling a voice for China and India (sometimes along with developing countries such as Brazil and South Africa) further complicated the bargaining game because these countries worked in coalitions. These coalitions – often with other developing countries (such as NAMA-11 and G20) – had allowed them to apply the poverty narrative even more effectively, and thereby also gain a place in the key consensus-building forums. As discussed in Chapter 3, they were also 'strong coalitions' – in contrast to their predecessors, they had successfully resisted the divide-and-rule strategies of negotiating counterparts. But once at the negotiating table, these coalitions found it very difficult to make concessions. This is because a concession made in any one issue area, or a subissue, risked antagonizing one or more members of the coalition, thereby triggering defection. Bernard Hoekman has also noted this problem: 'The move towards the creation of negotiating coalitions of groups of countries may reduce the number of "principals" but possibly at the cost of greater inflexibility and at a higher risk of breakdown, especially in a setting where there is little room to consult'.[131] The case of the G20 coalition in 2008, which was discussed in Section 4.1, illustrated a problem that afflicts most strong coalitions, especially when comprising countries from the Global South (which have lower resistance points, and face greater pressures of both carrots and sticks): a willingness to compromise by some players over particular issues may be seen as a sign of potential defection by allies and a sign of weakness of the coalition by the outside party. The alternative, of standing firm (as the G20 ended up eventually doing), heightens the systemic problem of deadlock.

---

[130] Narlikar (2013a). Specifically for the case of India, Narlikar and Narlikar (2014). On the importance and impact of differences in negotiating culture, see Cohen (2002). The polarized attitudes of different countries also drew the attention of newspaper reports at the time, see for instance Elliott et al. (2003).

[131] Hoekman and Newfarmer (2003). Also see Rolland (2007) for a legal analysis of coalitions.

Both the initial gains and subsequent costs of coalition diplomacy were apparent in the Doha negotiations.[132]

4.4.2 *From Narratives to Norms*

For some time, use of the poverty narrative worked to the great advantage of the developing world. But it also gradually produced disengagement from developed countries. This disengagement paradoxically increased even as the poverty narrative acquired greater use – possibly even greater acceptability – in wider circles, and began to influence international norms.

As highlighted in Chapter 1, narratives differ from norms. In comparison to norms, narratives are a lower order of framing; norms represent higher order principles (or 'principled beliefs'[133]). Narratives, when effectively used, can shape norm formation. But an embrace and internalization of a narrative to the level of a norm does not necessarily guarantee its success or longevity, even though the process of transition itself is usually proof of a successful narrative at work. Depending especially on how contested the norm is, the transition process can jeopardize both norm and narrative. Players may end up believing that the particular narrative represents an end in itself, rather than a means towards achieving a goal. They may end up digging their heels in and refusing agreement until *all* their demands are met because they are convinced that their own viewpoint is *morally* right.

This is indeed partly what seems to have transpired with the DDA negotiations. Key developing countries – often backed by NGOs – ended up taking hard-line positions over issues like agriculture and SDT, probably because they believed that they were now negotiating over fundamental values over which no compromise could be made.[134] India, for instance, when defending its refusal to open its agricultural markets, had appealed to not just the livelihoods but the actual lives of millions of its farmers. A pragmatic climbdown from this moral high ground would have been very difficult, if not impossible. And while emotive narratives had been used in varied ways in the past as well, the evocative narrative of poverty and powerlessness – interestingly even as it got amplified through multiple networks, and found greater acceptance among a growing number of actors – may have triggered passion and polarization in unprecedented ways.[135]

[132] Narlikar (2012).
[133] Goldstein and Keohane (1993).
[134] Andrew Gamble (2010) draws a distinction between first-order and second-order questions.
[135] In contrast, for instance, to the relatively dry tariff reductions of the early GATT rounds.

4.4.3 *Disengagement of the Developed Countries*

Only a few short years after its high-minded, well-intentioned launch, the DDA became a source of growing dissatisfaction and resentment on the part of the developed world. As already indicated in Section 4.3, the disillusionment of the United States with the DDA preceded Trump's arrival on the scene, and neither the United States nor the European Union were in a particularly cooperative mood. Jagdish Bhagwati, writing in 2011, argued, 'In place of what the economist Charles Kindleberger once called an "altruistic hegemon", the America that the world now faces is what I call a "selfish hegemon". Thus, the United States has virtually pulled out of the Doha Round of multilateral trade negotiations, with Obama acquiescing to greedy business lobbies that will not settle unless more of their demands are met'.[136] Just how the hope and good will from the developed world were transformed into grievance and disengagement lies in the evolution of the poverty narrative and how it was perceived by the global north.

First, the emphasis on the development content of Doha may have given rise to the misimpression that the round was less about reciprocity and more about charity. Such a round had little intuitive value for business interests in the North. Add to this the narrowing agenda of the DDA. Initially, when the DDA was launched, it had offered at least some attractions to governments and businesses in the United States, the European Union, and other OECD via the basket of Singapore Issues. By 2004, as a result of the July Package negotiations, three of the four Singapore Issues were taken off the negotiating table as a result of the resistance to them by developing countries. The perceived gains of the DDA diminished in value for the developed world, while regional and bilateral arrangements offered quicker fixes.

Second, the commitment of the DDA to the principle of LTFR, while initially an apparent win for developing countries, in fact turned out to be a mixed blessing. The WTO still allowed countries the prerogative to self-identify themselves as developing countries rather than set clear demarcations between LDCs and middle-income countries. This had always been controversial – hence also the long-standing polarization between the North and South on the question of 'graduation' – but came to rankle the developed world more than ever in the Doha years, amidst the changes in the relative balance of power. In 2011, Susan Schwab, former United States Trade

---

[136] Bhagwati (2011).

Representative (2006–2009), was clear in expressing the disappointment of the United States on this issue:

> From almost the start of the negotiations, the rapidly evolving nature of the global economy had rendered Doha's dichotomy between developed and developing countries outdated and its negotiating structure obsolete. And even as it became obvious over the decade that emerging economies had become a dominant force in global economic growth and trade, those nations' perceptions of their consequent needs and responsibilities had failed to keep pace . . .
>
> . . . Multilateral trade talks have traditionally called for the United States and fellow developed countries to take the lead in offering concessions to jump-start flagging negotiations – the idea being that a significant unilateral initiative by a large economy will encourage others to reciprocate, thus paying dividends to all. Yet during the Doha Round, such efforts by the United States – even those explicitly conditioned on a meaningful response – have not been met in kind. And as time has passed, US and EU compromises have effectively been pocketed, forming the base line for the next set of demands'.[137]

Developing countries, by pointing to their own poverty and powerlessness, had effectively achieved some promising wins with the launch of the DDA. But decision-making also became much more complicated amidst diversity and multipolarity. And the lessons of victimhood did not go unlearnt on the part of other actors, including developed countries. The last sentence in the above quote is an illustration that the narrative of grievance and victimhood was not restricted to the Global South, even in the pre-Trump era.

4.5 NARRATIVE REVERSAL BEYOND TRADE POLITICS

As this chapter has illustrated, the poverty narrative has taken a new shape in recent years with different effects. Deliberate misuse by the rich plus the proclivity to overuse a successful strategy by the poor together risk blunting the weapon of powerlessness. Additionally, we also see well-intentioned attempts to improve power and wealth balances, but which in fact produce the opposite results. While such moves leave no one better off, they also often impact most severely and negatively on the very same people and states that they had hoped to help. And the problems that the poverty narrative has run into within the context of the WTO translate unfortunately all too well into other areas of politics, as well as our everyday lives.

---

[137] Schwab (2011).

4.5.1 *Climate Change*

Climate change politics is a powerful example of the misuse of the powerlessness narrative by the rich. Chapter 3 illustrated ways in which developing countries – especially the rising powers of China and India – successfully managed to shape the Paris Agreement by appealing to the cause of their per capita poverty levels. But these successes also offered some important takeaways for the rich countries, which Trump put to use. On 1 June 2017, he announced that he would withdraw the United States from the Paris Agreement. He justified this decision by claiming that the Paris Agreement was unfair because it was depriving hard-working Americans of jobs, depriving America of key industries, and 'while imposing no meaningful obligations on the world's leading polluters':

> The Paris Climate Accord is simply the latest example of Washington entering into an agreement that disadvantages the United States to the exclusive benefit of other countries, leaving American workers – who I love – and taxpayers to absorb the cost in terms of lost jobs, lower wages, shuttered factories, and vastly diminished economic production . . .
>   . . . the bottom line is that the Paris Accord is very unfair, at the highest level, to the United States . . .
>   . . . the agreement doesn't eliminate coal jobs, it just transfers those jobs out of America and the United States, and ships them to foreign countries. This agreement is less about the climate and more about other countries gaining a financial advantage over the United States . . .
>   . . . No responsible leader can put the workers – and the people – of their country at this debilitating and tremendous disadvantage.
>   At what point does America get demeaned? At what point do they start laughing at us as a country? We want fair treatment for its citizens, and we want fair treatment for our taxpayers. We don't want other leaders and other countries laughing at us anymore. And they won't be. They won't be.
>   I was elected to represent the citizens of Pittsburgh, not Paris. . . .'[138]

President Trump appropriated the same power of the powerless that developing countries had formerly used in securing the Paris deal, and was now using similar arguments to withdraw from the agreement.

4.5.2 *Immigration Policies and Refugees*

An even more vivid illustration of the adverse consequences of acting in the name of the poor – sometimes possibly even with the best intentions – can be

---

[138] Trump (2017b).

found in the example of Germany's refugee policy in 2015–2016. The year 2015 saw a swell in the number of refugees fleeing to Europe. Some 48 per cent of the arrivals were from war-torn Syria and 21 per cent from Afghanistan (which had seen a resurgence of Taliban control in the aftermath of the withdrawal of foreign troops).[139] Unfazed by the numbers (2015 saw a total of 1 million refugees enter Germany), Chancellor Angela Merkel declared in August 2015, 'Wir schaffen das!'[140] At the time, her approach received the backing of not only the mainstream political parties, but also business groups and civil society. Merkel's team built a narrative in which any discussion of 'Obergrenze' (upper limit) for immigrants was equated with 'Fremdenfeindlichkeit' (literally animosity towards foreigners, i.e., xenophobia).[141] Humanitarian grounds as well as economic pragmatism (German firms needed workers amidst demographic decline) provided the rationalization for a heady liberal narrative that was captured by the term *Willkommenskultur*. The plethora of photos and footage on social media and traditional media of German citizens greeting exhausted refugees with welcome packages made for many feel-good, indeed inspiring, stories. The 'friendly face' of Merkel won her much international approbation.[142] But the warm glow of this welcome culture proved to be short-lived.

Thomas Bagger summarizes the after-effects of the German 'welcoming, even cosmopolitan' response to the refugee crisis of 2015 as follows:

> Whatever the merits of the initial reaction, Germany's response not only encountered stiff rejection in parts of Central Europe but also contributed to a renewed polarization of German society and politics unseen since the days of the Cold War. Center-left social democrats are losing public support just as center-right conservatives are. The political fringes grow stronger. The radical, right-wing AfD (Alternative for Germany) is for the first time represented in the federal and all 16 regional parliaments.[143]

---

[139] Benček and Strasheim (2016); Deutsche Welle (2017).

[140] Merkel's exact words were 'Ich sage ganz einfach: Deutschland ist ein starkes Land, und das Motiv, in dem wir an diese Dinge herangehen, muss sein: Wir haben so vieles geschafft, wir schaffen das! Wir schaffen das, und wo uns etwas im Wege steht, muss es überwunden werden, muss daran gearbeitet werden' (Merkel 2015). This translates as: 'I say very simply: Germany is a strong country, and our approach to these things must be: we have accomplished so much, we can manage this! We will manage this, and when something stands in our way, it must be overcome, it must be worked on'.

[141] Streek (2016a).

[142] E.g., Merkel was named the person of the year for *Time Magazine* in 2015, http://time.com/time-person-of-the-year-2015-angela-merkel/.

[143] Bagger (2019). Also see Otto and Steinhardt (2017). An increase in violence against refugees within Germany was another unsavoury after-effect, e.g., Benček and Strasheim (2016); Deutsche Welle (2015).

The blowback moreover was not limited to Germany, but extended across Europe. Even as Germany – rather belatedly – tried to build a consensus that could somehow accommodate the influx of refugees, Europe became increasingly polarized.[144] A variety of explanations is likely for this souring of mood. Despite Germany's admirable moral stance on the matter, its consultations with European partners had been inadequate in the crucial first phase, and came across as rather imperious and judgemental in the latter phases. Domestically too, amidst the euphoria of 'doing good', the consensus-building process was fast-tracked in a variety of ways, often without an adequate consideration of the follow-through.[145] Some blame must also go to the inadequacy of European institutions, which were not equipped to provide a timely collective response to the humanitarian disasters they were facing. Further failures on the part of the European Union included fundamental divisions over national interests and the absence of a shared worldview on the question of deep integration. But uniting these different types of explanations is a larger one, which relates to the unintended adverse consequences of overusing the power of powerlessness.

Germany had acted to help those in desperate need.[146] But it had acted unilaterally, and without reserve or restraint.[147] Building in some flexibilities and updates to the existing immigration rules, with due consideration towards the demands that were being placed on European citizens, might have worked had Germany coordinated its normative preferences and policies with other European Union members and had ensured domestic engagement. In contrast, unilateral – and blanket, across-the-board, no-questions-asked – opening of borders to asylum seekers and economic migrants alike was going to be unsustainable at all levels (local, regional, national, and European). That the AfD would pick up on, and then twist, the powerlessness narrative on immigration by claiming to defend Germany's poor against its liberal migrant-loving elite was perhaps unsurprising[148] – as indeed the false but highly

---

[144] Wolfgang Streek (2016b) includes the British referendum decision in favour of Brexit as one of the results of Germany's refugee policy in the year before: 'The prospect of having to comply with the way Germany, with its particular political, demographic and labour market situation, had chosen to interpret international law, subject to reinterpretation whenever required by changing German economic and political interests, was without doubt a major force behind the historical blow to European integration, as we know it, that was Brexit'.

[145] E.g., Streek (2016a, 2016b).

[146] Angela Merkel defended her decision in an interview in 2017: 'It was an extraordinary situation and I made my decision based on what I thought was right from a political and humanitarian standpoint' (quoted in de la Baume 2017).

[147] Blume et al. (2016).

[148] Vehrkamp and Wratil (2017).

emotive claims by President Trump on the ill-effects of immigration by citing Germany as an example.[149]

4.5.3 *The Power of Powerlessness in the Everyday*[150]

The negative effects of the power of the powerless are not limited to high politics. More and more people – and not just states – have realized that powerlessness and victimhood sell. The temptation to misuse this knowledge is high. Lower thresholds for complaints (themselves a product of the power of powerlessness), and the absence of strong safeguards against misuse, increase the likelihood of abuse. Depending on how far the misuse and abuse go, and also depending on relative power discrepancies, we can see (sometimes disproportionately severe and misguided) backlash.

'Voluntourism' – the act of travelling the world and doing good – is an example of how well-meaning attempts by ordinary people have also resulted in the trivialization of poverty.[151] In some aspects of this case – for instance the representation of voluntourism in photographs on social media platforms – there is some evidence also of a positive counter-reaction that serves as a self-regulatory device to the problems that these attempts generates.[152] But there are other cases where such self-correction and self-regulation results in even more negative consequences. 'Orphanage tourism' is one example, where the ill-effects include commodification and new forms of exploitation of children, and minimum revenue transfers to the orphanages. As awareness of the harmful consequences of such interventions has grown, organizations are withdrawing their support for these initiatives. While this wariness may stop some of the corruption and misuse of the poverty-powerlessness narrative, it also risks stifling the positive efforts of local groups and or organizations. Caught between these interventions and counter-initiatives, the most vulnerable – the children themselves – find themselves between a rock and a hard place.[153]

---

[149] Trump tweeted: 'The people of Germany are turning against their leadership as migration is rocking the already tenuous Berlin coalition. Crime in Germany is way up. Big mistake made all over Europe in allowing millions of people in who have so strongly and violently changed their culture!' (18 June 2018).
   https://twitter.com/realdonaldtrump/status/1008696508697513985?lang=en

[150] An early version of this argument was presented in Narlikar (2015a).

[151] Conran (2011); Crossley (2012).

[152] Sin and He (2018), for instance, suggest that the emergence of the satirical Instagram account of 'Barbie Saviour' and other such online forms of critique may result in self-regulation of voluntourism.

[153] Daley (2013).

'Ethical consumerism' too, for all the euphoria, also poses some serious challenges. Ben White cites the example of child workers in Bangladesh, and cites a petition that some 100 child workers had issued in 1994 asking their employers not to dismiss them, in response to a wave of mass dismissals that manufacturers were taking on. These dismissals, in turn, were a product of pressure from the Bangladesh Garment Manufacturers and Exporters Association, 'which feared an international boycott of their products'. White writes, 'The fact (although an uncomfortable one for many people) is that working in the export garment industry is not the worst thing that can happen to a Bangladeshi child ...'.[154] *New York Times* columnist, Nicolas Kristof, had similarly written a piece titled 'Where sweatshops are a dream', and argued, '... sweatshops are only a symptom of poverty, not a cause, and banning them closes off one route out of poverty'.[155] The FairTrade movement has also come under scrutiny. The criticisms have ranged from the small proportion of gains that actually accrue to the producer, to the perverse logic of trying to overcome the distortions of a highly protected market through more distortions.[156] Anand Giridharadas has questioned both the motivations and effects of philanthropy.[157] Even crowd-funding, which seemed to be doubly empowering – both for the giver and the receiver – raises a multiplicity of issues, ranging from the sudden withdrawal of investors that may turn out to be highly disruptive for dependent communities, to the lack of ethical checks on either side. One can also raise questions about the extent to which crowd-funding results in a diversion of resources away from desperately needy causes, and exacerbates inequalities even further (e.g., the successful GoFundMe campaign that was launched to transform Kylie Jenner from a multi-millionaire to a billionaire!).

Domestic politics and society have also been affected by the power of the powerless, and not only in developing countries. The 'Plebgate' scandal in the United Kingdom, which ran through 2012–2014, is an example of the misuse of the narrative. The accusations of the 'small' policemen against the rich and powerful politician were given immediate credence, whereas Andrew Mitchell's own vehement denials were viewed with suspicion. Mitchell was subsequently able to clear his name and the allegations were found to be false, but not without a long-drawn investigation and also his own resignation from the post of the Chief Whip of the Conservative party.[158] Even something as

---

[154] White (1996), pp. 833–834.
[155] Kristof (2009). Also see Bhagwati and Narlikar (2013).
[156] Narlikar and Kim (2013).
[157] Giridharadas (2019).
[158] *The Guardian* (2014).

apparently straightforward as a law to curb dowry deaths in India has produced unscrupulous misuse. In 2014, judges of India's Supreme Court ruled in a court order, 'The fact that Section 498A is a cognisable and non-bailable offence has lent it a dubious place of pride amongst the provisions that are used as weapons rather than shield by disgruntled wives . . .'.[159] But with such a ruling, there is now a risk that women facing dowry-related threats to their lives may be boxed into the 'disgruntled wives category', and horrific crimes against women end up getting encouraged.

Hitherto vulnerable school pupils are now able to bring just cause against abusive teachers, and rightly so. But they can also go several steps further and hold the fortunes of innocent teachers to hostage by playing the victim. The statistics reveal the double-edged nature of this sword that pupils wield: one study by the Department of Education reveals that almost 50 per cent of such allegations are 'unsubstantiated, malicious or unfounded'.[160] Teachers' unions further point out that such allegations severely damage the reputations of teachers, who 'often find it hard to go back to work, even though they've been completely exonerated'.[161] Student empowerment is a valuable and note-worthy achievement in favour of the weak in an asymmetric power relation-ship. But it generates considerable costs when misused, not only for the wrongly accused individual but also the cause of student empowerment. It further generates a price for society as a whole when qualified, committed, and experienced educators are pushed out of their profession for fear of false accusations.[162]

The costs do not stop with a crowding-out effect. They create much polarization within society, and potentially also trigger a backlash. This in turn risks taking the powerlessness debate several steps backwards (by denying credibility to even genuine complaints and grievances). In politics, this has taken the shape of populism, and indeed contributed to a legitimization of white supremacist movements. As cases of misuse of India's dowry laws come up and laws are amended to protect the accused, there is a credible risk that not only do the actual abusers feel exonerated, but the real victims find themselves under false suspicion and intimidated against speaking up (despite the terrible atrocities that they endure). Women's empowerment created by #MeToo is also prompting a negative reaction and also active backlash.

[159] BBC (2014); also see BBC (2017).
[160] *Telegraph* (2011). www.telegraph.co.uk/education/educationnews/8828589/Teachers-lives-ruined-by-false-allegations-warns-minister.html.
[161] BBC (2012). www.bbc.co.uk/news/uk-wales-16927479.
[162] *The Guardian* (2015). www.theguardian.com/education/2015/mar/30/one-in-five-school-staff-victims-of-false-claims-survey-shows.

A Gallup poll presents an example of this reaction: 'Seventeen months after the #Metoo movement exploded, US men are less convinced than they were at the start of the movement that sexual harassment in the workplace is a major problem. They are also more likely to believe that people in the workplace are too sensitive to the problem of sexual harassment'.[163] Going beyond simply (what many would judge as a regressive) reaction, we also see examples of backlash rising. A Bloomberg report, for example, shows that Wall Street is adapting to the #MeToo era by isolating women, and 'Wall Street risks becoming more of a boy's club, rather than less of one'.[164] Feminists, even as they toil to carve out much-needed space for equal opportunity along multiple fronts, also find themselves under attack. A leading candidate for the Conservative Party leadership in the United Kingdom, Dominic Raab, in June 2019, tried to defend his claim (made in 2011) that: 'From the cradle to the grave, men are getting a raw deal. Feminists are now amongst the most obnoxious bigots'.[165] That a serious Tory politician could make such a claim in the first place is surprising enough; even more so is the fact that he attempted to defend it eight years later, and that in the age of #MeToo; and perhaps the most interesting from our point of view is that his defence was underpinned by a reclamation of victimhood for men.

4.6 CONCLUSION

While Chapter 3 had illustrated the overturning of past power discrepancies by putting poverty narratives to effective use, this chapter has shown that it is not only the genuinely powerless and the deserving poor (however one defines them) who are aware of the effectiveness of this instrument. The rich can and do use the same power of the powerless to re-frame their demands and enrich themselves further, while others who technically fall within the 'powerless' bracket also sometimes use the narrative to unscrupulously or vindictively abuse the powerful. When trade unions in the developed world demand the

---

[163] Brenan (2019). The poll does not offer detailed explanations for this behavioural change. It does suggest though, as plausible explanations, that either men have been put on the defensive (as a result of the 'torrent of sexual misconduct allegations' and media coverage on these, in the wake of the #MeToo movement) or have become 'somewhat desensitized' on the issue with the passage of time.

[164] Tan and Porzecanski (2018) write: 'In this charged environment, the question is how the response to #MeToo might actually end up hurting women's progress. Given the male dominance in Wall Street's top jobs, one of the most pressing consequences for women is the loss of male mentors who can help them climb the ladder'.

[165] *The Guardian* (2019).

imposition of stringent labour standards on the South, it is not always clear that they are not making these demands to undermine the one source of comparative advantage of the poor countries, that is cheap labour. In the WTO too, we have seen that it is all too easy for rich countries to refuse to make concessions even to the world's poorest countries, the LDCs, and to defend this position in the name of a sub-set of poor countries and the possible erosion of preference margins. Ironically therefore, by claiming to act in the name of a sub-set of the poor, the rich countries have conveniently managed to avoid making concessions, and have also been able to hold the welfare of the global poor to ransom. Even worse, we have recently witnessed the launch of trade wars, where one of the most powerful countries in the world has hijacked the poverty narrative: especially under President Trump, we see the United States claiming victimhood for some of its own citizens and demanding recompense from the global poor. That these strategies are detrimental to all parties – including the poor in the United States – makes this misuse of the poverty narrative all the more counter-productive.

It is not only deliberate misuse and conscious overuse of the power of powerlessness that produces adverse consequences. The WTO's Doha negotiations – and the processes underpinning them that I discussed in this chapter – are a case in point. The poverty narrative has facilitated the transformation of the 'Rich Man's Club' into one of the most equitable international organizations, which includes Brazil, India, and China at the high table of consensus-building and also accords considerable voice to the LDCs. But in place of consensus has emerged a cacophony of voices, and the newfound willingness of the developing world to exercise its veto has resulted in a permanently deadlocked WTO. The response of the developed countries – the United States most vociferously, the European Union more quietly – has been to move the negotiations to alternative bilateral deals or regional forums, in which developing countries enjoy neither the support of their allies that they do in the WTO nor the recourse to a strong Dispute Settlement Mechanism. The poverty narrative has given procedural power to the hitherto powerless, but the resulting outcomes have not left the poor countries better off.

These adverse consequences can reinforce each other. At a human level, the overuse, misuse, and abuse of the powerlessness/poverty narrative create a climate of distrust and litigiousness. The narrative may have acted as a great enabler for a short period of time, but now risks creating more polarized politics where the divisions between the self-identified powerless and the 'othering' of the powerful becomes even more entrenched. Against #Me Too and minority empowerment, we are already witnessing unsavoury and alarming backlashes. And amidst the game-playing between the overusers, misusers, and abusers of this narrative, the weakest and most vulnerable members of society may end up even more disempowered. Has the power of the powerless already come a full circle?

BIBLIOGRAPHY

Agarwal, Bina. 2014. 'Food sovereignty, food security, and democratic choice: Critical contradictions, difficult conciliations.' *Journal of Peasant Studies*. 41: 6. Pp. 1247–1268.

Amiti, Mary, Stephen J. Redding, and David E. Weinstein. 2019. 'The impact of the 2018 trade war on US prices and welfare.' CEPR Discussion Paper, DP13564 (Centre for Economic Policy Research, International Trade and Economics Programme). 1 March. www.princeton.edu/~reddings/papers/CEPR-DP13564.pdf.

Bacchus, James. 2018. 'Might unmakes right: The American assault on the rule of law in World Trade.' *CIGI Papers*. 173. May. www.cigionline.org/sites/default/files/documents/Paper%20no.173.pdf.

Bagger, Thomas. 2019. 'The world according to Germany: Reassessing 1989.' *Third World Quarterly*. 41: 4. Pp. 53–63.

Bagwell, Kyle and Robert Staiger. 2011. 'Can the Doha round be a development round? Setting a place at the table.' NBER Working Paper. No. 17650. December. www.nber.org/papers/w17650.pdf.

Basnett, Yurendra, Jakob Engel, Jane Kennan, Christian Kingombe, Isabella Massa, and Dirk Willem te Velde. 2012. 'Increasing the effectiveness of Aid for Trade: The circumstances under which it works best.' *ODI Working Paper*. No. 353. August. www.odi.org/sites/odi.org.uk/files/odi-assets/publications-opinion-files/7793.pdf.

BBC. 2006. 'India "to pursue own trade deals".' 25 July. http://news.bbc.co.uk/2/hi/south_asia/5212932.stm.

2014. 'India Court says women "misusing" dowry law.' 3 July. www.bbc.com/news/world-asia-india-28140205.

2016. 'US slaps China steel imports with fivefold tax increase.' 18 May. www.bbc.com/news/business-36319141.

2017. 'India top court orders changes in anti-dowry law to stop misuse.' 28 July. www.bbc.com/news/world-asia-india-40749636.

Beattie, Alan. 2008a. 'Expectations low as Doha talks begin.' *The Financial Times*. 21 July.

2008b. 'Q&A trade negotiations: What's at stake for rich, poor, and emerging markets.' *The Financial Times*. 30 July.

2018. 'Trump global trade shake-up leaves rivals trailing.' *The Financial Times*. 1 October.

Benček, David and Julia Strasheim. 2016. 'Refugees welcome? A data-set on anti-refugee violence in Germany.' *Research and Politics*. October–December. Pp. 1–11. https://journals.sagepub.com/doi/pdf/10.1177/2053168016679590 .

Berthou, Antoine, Caroline Jardet, Daniele Siena, and Urszula Szczerbowicz. 2018. 'Costs and consequences of a trade war: A structural analysis.' Rue de la Banque. No. 72. Paris: Banque de France. December. https://publications.banque-france .fr/sites/default/files/medias/documents/818459_rdb72_en_v5.pdf.

Bhagwati, Jagdish. 2011. 'Deadlock in Durban: Will COP-17 produce substance?' *Economic Times*. 11 December.

Bhagwati, Jagdish and Amrita Narlikar. 2013. 'Don't blame the brands.' *Prospect Magazine*. 2 April. www.prospectmagazine.co.uk/magazine/bangladesh-pakistan-factory-fire-jagdish-bhagwati-amrita-narlikar.

Blume, Georg, Marc Brost, Tina Hildebrandt, Alexej Hock, Sybille Klormann, Angela Köckritz, Matthias Krupa, Mariam Lau, Gero von Randow, Merlind Theile, Michael Thumann, and Heinrich Wefing. 2016. 'The night Germany lost control.' *Die Zeit*. 30 August. Nr. 36/2016. www.zeit.de/gesellschaft/2016-08/ refugees-open-border-policy-september-2015-angela-merkel/komplettansicht.

Blustein, Paul. 2009. *The Misadventures of the Most-Favoured Nations*. New York: Public Affairs.

Bown, Chad and Melina Kolb. 2019. Trump's Trade War Timeline: An Up-to-Date Guide. https://piie.com/blogs/trade-investment-policy-watch/trump-trade-war-china-date-guide. Originally published on 19 April 2018; regularly updated.

Brenan, Megan. 2019. 'US Men less concerned than in 2017 about sexual harassment.' *Gallup News*. 18 March. https://news.gallup.com/poll/247823/men-less-concerned-2017-sexual-harassment.aspx. Details of question and trends available at https:// news.gallup.com/poll/247901/americans-views-sexual-harassment-workplace-vic timization-trends.aspx?g_source=link_newsv9&g_campaign=item_247823&g_ medium=copy.

Buiter, Willem and Anne Sibert. 2008. The Dangerous Protectionism of Barack Obama. 26 February. https://voxeu.org/article/dangerous-protectionism-barack-obama.

Cassello, Megan. 2018. 'Trump trade adviser: All countries exempted from steel tariffs will face quotas.' 2 May. www.politico.eu/article/trump-trade-adviser-all-countries-exempted-from-steel-tariffs-will-face-quotas-peter-navarro/.

Chatterjee, Bipul and Sophia Murphy. 2013. 'Trade and food security.' In *Agriculture, Trade and Food Security Challenges: Proposals and Analysis*. E15 Expert Group Compilation Report. December. Geneva: ICTSD and World Economic Forum.

Clapp, Jennifer. 2015a. 'Food security and food sovereignty: Getting past the binary.' *Dialogues in Human Geography*. 4: 2. Pp. 206–211.

   2015b. 'Food security and contested agricultural trade norms.' *Journal of International Law and International Relations*. 11: 2. Pp. 104–115.

Cohen, Raymond. 2002. *Negotiating across Cultures*. Washington D.C.: United States Peace Institute.

Coke-Hamilton, Pamela. 2019. How Trade Wars Pose a Threat to the Global Economy. 8 February. https://unctad.org/en/pages/newsdetails.aspx?OriginalVersio nID=1992.

Conconi, Paola and Carlo Perroni. 2015. 'Special and differential treatment of developing countries in the WTO.' *World Trade Review*. 14: 1. Pp. 67–86.

Confessore, Nicholas and Karen Yourish. 2016. '$2 Billion worth of free media for Donald Trump.' *New York Times*. 15 March.

Congressional Research Service. 2019. *World Trade Organization: Overview and Future Direction*. Washington D.C. https://crsreports.congress.gov/product/pdf/R/R45417/3. Updated 15 February.

Conran, M. 2011. 'They really love me!: Intimacy in volunteer tourism.' *Annals of Tourism Research*. 38: 4. Pp. 1454–1473.

Crooks, Ed and Fan Fei. 2018. 'Which countries are winning exemptions from US Steel Tariffs?' *The Financial Times*. 1 October.

Crossley, E. 2012. 'Poor but happy: Volunteer tourists' encounters with poverty.' *Tourism Geographies*. 14. Pp. 235–253.

Daley, Patricia. 2013. 'Rescuing African bodies: Celebrities, consumerism and neoliberal humanitarianism.' *Review of African Political Economy*. 40. 375–393.

Davis, Christina. 2003. *Food Fights over Free Trade: How International Institutions Promote Agricultural Trade Liberalization*. Princeton, NJ: Princeton University Press.

de la Baume, Maia. 2017. 'Angela Merkel defends open border migration policy.' 27 August. www.politico.eu/article/angela-merkel-defends-open-border-migration-refugee-policy-germany/.

Deutsche Welle. 2015. 'Anti-refugee attacks rise four-fold in Germany.' 9 December. www.dw.com/en/anti-refugeeattacks-rise-four-fold-in-germany/a-18907776.

2017. 'Two years since Germany opened its borders: What happened next?' 4 September. www.dw.com/cda/en/two-years-since-germany-opened-its-borders-to-refugees-a-chronology/a-40327634.

Drezner, Daniel. 2019. 'Economic statecraft in an age of Trump.' *The Washington Quarterly*. 42: 3. Pp. 7–24.

Dutt, Pushan and Ilia Tsetlin. 2015. 'Beyond Gini: Distribution and economic development.' INSEAD Working Paper. 2015/99/EPS/DSC. December.

2016. What Really Matters Is Poverty, Not Income Inequality. 29 November. https://knowledge.insead.edu/economics/what-really-matters-is-poverty-not-income-inequality-5056.

Dyer, Geoff. 2016. 'Trump threatens to pull US out of WTO.' *Financial Times*. 24 July.

Elliott, Larry, Charlotte Denny, and David Munk. 2003. 'Blow to world economy as trade talks collapse.' *The Guardian*. 15 September. www.theguardian.com/world/2003/sep/15/business.politics.

European Commission. 2018. EU Concept Paper on WTO Modernisation. 18 September. http://europa.eu/rapid/press-release_IP-18-5786_en.htm.

Fajgelbaum, Pablo, Pinelopi Goldberg, Patrick Kennedy, and Amit Khandelwal. 2019. The Return to Protectionism. 10 March (first draft 28 September 2018). www.econ.ucla.edu/pfajgelbaum/RTP.pdf.

Farrell, Henry and Abraham Newman. 2019. 'Weaponized interdependence: How global economic networks shape state coercion.' *International Security*. 44: 1. Pp. 42–79.

Financial Times. 2008. 'Multilateralism not dead as a Doha.' Editorial. 31 July.

Finger, Michael J. 2008a. 'Aid for Trade: How we got here, and where we might go.' In Dominique Njinkeu and Hugo Cameron (eds). *Aid for Trade and Development*. Cambridge: Cambridge University Press.

2008b. 'Aid for trade: Bonanza for consultants, nothing for development. Interview with Centre for Trade and Development.' *Reality Check: The Reality of Aid*. April. www.realityofaid.org/reality_check/aid-for-trade/. Accessed 3 August 2013.

Friends of the Earth International. 2003. 'Trade and people's food sovereignty.' Position Paper. April. www.foei.org/wp-content/uploads/2014/12/newfinallowres.pdf.

Gamble, Andrew (2010). 'The politics of deadlocks.' In Amrita Narlikar (ed.), *Deadlocks in Multilateral Negotiations: Causes and Solutions*. Cambridge: Cambridge University Press.

Gibson, Ginger and Grant Smith. 2016. 'At under $5 each, Trump's votes came cheap.' 9 November. www.reuters.com/article/us-usa-election-spending-idUSKBN1341JR.

Giridharadas, Anand. 2019. *Winner Takes All: The Elite Charade of Changing the World*. New York: Allen Lane.

Goldberg, Joshua. 2016. 'The Obama doctrine.' *The Atlantic*. April.

Goldstein, Judith and Robert O. Keohane. 1993. *Ideas and Foreign Policy*. Ithaca: Cornell University Press.

Graham, David. 2018. 'The paradox of Trump's populism'. *The Atlantic*. June.

Green, Emma. 2017. 'It was cultural anxiety that drove white working-class voters to Trump.' *The Atlantic*. May.

The Guardian. 2014. 'Plebgate: The report's key points.' 1 September. www.theguardian .com/politics/2014/sep/01/plebgate-report-key-points-andrew-mitchell-met-police.

    2019. 'Dominic Raab defends calling feminists bigots: the potential future PM says he does not want "double standards" in equality debate.' 26 May. www .theguardian.com/politics/2019/may/26/dominic-raab-defends-calling-feminists-obnoxious-bigots?CMP=Share_AndroidApp_Tweet.

Hoda, Anwarul. 2017. 'Public stockholdings issue in the WTO: The way forward for India.' ICRIER. No. 17. November. https://icrier.org/pdf/Policy_Series_17.pdf.

Hoekman, Bernard and Richard Newfarmer. 2003. 'After Cancun: Continuation or collapse?' Trade Note 13: World Bank. 17 December. http://documents.worldbank.org/ curated/en/543871468139499387/text/320990TradeNote13.txt. Accessed 6 May 2019.

Horowitz, Jason. 2018. 'Steve Bannon's 'movement' enlists Italy's most powerful politician.' *New York Times*. 7 September.

Hufbauer, Gary. 2011. 'WTO judicial appointments: A bad omen for the trading system.' Realtime Economic Issues Watch. Peterson Institute for International Economics. 13 June.

ICTSD. 2012. 'An analysis of the WTO guidelines for least developed countries.' Information Note. November. www.ictsd.org/sites/default/files/downloads/2012/11/ an-analysis-of-the-wto-accession-guidelines-for-least-developed-countries.pdf.

    2013. 'WTO: Ag talks chair seeks to reconcile conflicting visions for Bali.' *Bridges*. 17: 15. 2 May. www.ictsd.org/bridges-news/bridges/news/wto-ag-talks-chair-seeks-to-rec oncile-conflicting-visions-for-bali.

International Monetary Fund. 2019. Global Economic Outlook. April. www.imf.org/ en/Publications/WEO/Issues/2019/03/28/world-economic-outlook-april-2019.

Ismail, Faizel. 2009. 'Reflections on the July 2008 collapse.' In Amrita Narlikar and Brendan Vickers (eds). *Leadership and Change in the Multilateral Trading System*. Leiden: Martinus Nijhoff.

James, Harold. 2016. 'Containing the populist contagion.' Project Syndicate, 24 November; also accessible on www.socialeurope.eu/containing-populist-contagion.

Jones, Vivian C., J. F. Hornbeck and M. Angeles Villarreal. 2013. Trade Preferences: Economic Issues and Policy Options. Congressional Research Service. 10 January. https://fas.org/sgp/crs/misc/R41429.pdf.

Khor, Martin. 2008. 'Behind the July failure of the WTO talks on Doha.' *Economic and Political Weekly.* 16 August. www.twn.my/title2/wto.info/twninfo20080901/12560.pdf.

Kim, Dan Dong-Jin. 2013. *The Political Economy of Trade and Development in the Multilateral Trading System: The World Trade Organization's Aid for Trade Agenda.* PhD Thesis. University of Cambridge.

Kristof, Nicholas. 2009. 'Where sweatshops are a dream.' *New York Times.* 14 January.

Kwa, Aileen and Peter Lunenborg. 2019. *Why the US Proposals on Development will Affect all Developing Countries and Undermine WTO.* South Centre Policy Brief. No. 58. March.

Laborde, David and Will Martin. 2012. "Agricultural trade: What matters in the Doha round.' *World Bank Policy Research Working Paper.* No. 6261. Washington D.C.: World Bank, Development Research Group, Rural Development Team. November.

Lamont, Michele, Bo Yun Park, and Elena Ayala-Hurtado. 2017. 'Trump's electoral speeches and his appeal to the American white working class.' *British Journal of Sociology.* 68: S1, Pp. S153–S180.

Luce, Edward. 2019. 'Donald Trump is building a populist global club.' *Financial Times.* 11 April.

Mankiw, Gregory. 2010. *International Economics.* 7th ed. New York: Worth Palgrave.

Martin, Will and Kym Anderson. 2012. 'Export restrictions and price insulation during commodity price boom.' *American Journal of Agricultural Economics.* 94: 2. Pp. 422–427.

Matthews, Alan. 2014. 'Trade rules, food security and the multilateral trade negotiations.' *European Review of Agricultural Economics.* 41: 3. Pp. 511–535.

Mayer, Jane. 2018. 'New evidence emerges of Steve Bannon and Cambridge Analytica's role in Brexit.' *The New Yorker.* 17 November.

Merkel, Angela. 2015. Summer Press Conference. 31 August. www.bundesregierung.de/breg-de/aktuelles/pressekonferenzen/sommerpressekonferenz-von-bundeskanzlerin-merkel-848300.

Milanovic, Branko. 2016. *Global Inequality: A New Approach for the Age of Globalization.* Cambridge, MA: Harvard University Press.

Morgan, Steve. 2018. 'Status threat, material interests, and the 2016 presidential vote.' *Socius: Sociological Research for a Dynamic World.* 4. July. https://journals.sagepub.com/doi/10.1177/2378023118788217.

Mudde, Cas. 2004. 'The Populist Zeitgeist.' *Government and Opposition.* 39: 4. Pp. 541–563.

Mutz, Diana. 2018. 'Status threat, not economic hardship, explains the 2016 presidential vote.' *Proceedings of the National Academy of Sciences.* April. www.pnas.org/content/115/19/E4330.

Narlikar, Amrita. 2010. 'New powers in the club: The challenges of global trade governance.' *International Affairs.* 86: 3. Pp. 717–728.

2012. 'Coalition diplomacy.' In Amrita Narlikar, Martin Daunton, and Robert Stern (eds). *Oxford Handbook on the WTO.* Oxford: Oxford University Press.

Narlikar, Amrita (ed.). 2013a. 'Negotiating the rise of new powers.' Special Issue: *International Affairs.* 89: 3.

2013b. 'The Doha development agenda.' In Andrew Cooper, Jorge Heine, and Ramesh Thakur (eds). *Oxford Handbook for Modern Diplomacy*. Oxford: Oxford University Press.

2015a. 'The power paradox.' *Current History*. 114: 768. Pp. 29–33.

2015b. 'The power of the powerless: The politics of poverty in the Doha round.' *Foreign Affairs*. 12 March.

2018. 'A trade war on the poor: How a collapse of the WTO would hurt the worst off.' *Foreign Affairs*. 5 March.

Narlikar, Amrita and Aruna Narlikar. 2014. *Bargaining with a Rising India: Lessons from the Mahabharata*. Oxford: Oxford University Press.

Narlikar, Amrita and Dan Kim. 2013. 'Unfair trade: The fair-trade movement does more harm than good.' *Foreign Affairs*. 4 April. www.foreignaffairs.com/articles/africa/2013-04-04/unfair-trade.

Narlikar, Amrita and Diana Tussie. 2016. 'Breakthrough at Bali? Explanations, aftermath, implications.' *International Negotiation*. 21: 2. Pp 209–232.

Narlikar, Amrita and Pieter van Houten. 2010. 'Know the enemy: Uncertainty and deadlock in the WTO.' In Amrita Narlikar (ed.). *Deadlocks in Multilateral Negotiations: Causes and Solutions*. Cambridge: Cambridge University Press.

Obama, Barack. 2009. Presidential Inaugural Address. 21 January. https://obamawhitehouse.archives.gov/blog/2009/01/21/president-barack-obamas-inaugural-address.

Office of the High Commissioner for Human Rights. 2000. *The Right to Food*. Commission on Human Rights Resolution 2000/10. 52nd Meeting. 17 April.

Otto, Alkis Henri and Max Friedrich Steinhardt. 2017. 'The relationship between immigration and the success of far-right political parties in Germany.' IFO DICE Report 4/2017. December. Volume 15. www.cesifo-group.de/DocDL/dice-report-2017-4-otto-steinhardt-december.pdf.

Piketty, Thomas. 2014. *Capital in the Twenty-First Century*. Cambridge, MA: Belknap.

Reeves, Richard. 2016. 'Inequality built the Trump coalition, even if he won't solve it.' *Las Vegas Sun*. 26 September. www.brookings.edu/blog/fixgov/2016/09/26/inequality-built-the-trump-coalition-even-if-he-wont-solve-it/.

Reich, Robert. 2018. 'Trump's curious coalition.' *The American Prospect*. 22 May. https://prospect.org/article/trumps-curious-coalition.

Roessler, Frieder. 1998. 'Domestic policy objectives and the multilateral trade order: Lessons from the past.' In A. O. Krueger (ed.). *The WTO as an International Organization*. Chicago, IL: University of Chicago Press.

Rolland, Sonia. 2007. 'Developing country coalitions at the WTO: In search of legal support.' *Harvard International Law Journal*. 48: 2. Pp. 483–551.

Rushford, Greg. 2013. 'India's Bali debacle: Delhi holds free trade hostage to score political points at home.' *Wall Street Journal*. 9 December. www.wsj.com/articles/india8217s-bali-debacle-1386607833.

Sachs, Jeffrey. 2018. Trump's Insane Trade War. CNN Op-Ed. 1 June. https://edition.cnn.com/2018/06/01/opinions/trumps-insane-trade-war-sachs/index.html.

Schwab, Susan. 2011. 'After Doha: Why the negotiations are doomed and what we should do about it.' *Foreign Affairs*. 90: 3. www.foreignaffairs.com/articles/2011-04-09/after-doha?cid=rss-essays-after_doha-000000.

Schroeder, Ralph. 2018. *Social Theory after the Internet: Media, Technology, and Globalization*. London: University College London Press.

Sin, Harng Luh and Shirleen He. 2018. 'Voluntouring on Facebook and Instagram: Photography and social media in constructing the 'Third World' experience.' *Tourist Studies.* 19: 2. Pp. 1–23.

Sitharaman, Nirmala. 2014. *Statement in Lok Sabha regarding India's Stance in the WTO.* 5 August 2014. Press Information Bureau, Government of India, Ministry of Commerce and Industry. http://pib.nic.in/newsite/PrintRelease.aspx?relid=107999.

Slocum, John. 2017. The Transnational Diffusion of Populism. CIDOB Report. January. Barcelona Centre for International Affairs. April. www.cidob.org/en/articulos/cidob_report/n1_1/the_transnational_diffusion_of_populism.

South Centre. 2012. Operationalising the 2002 LDC Accession Guidelines: An Analysis. Analytical Note. SC/TDP/AN. July. www.southcentre.int/wp-content/uploads/2013/08/AN_Operationalising-the-2002-LDC-Accession-Guidelines_EN.pdf.

Stiglitz, Joseph E. 2015. *The Great Divide: Unequal Societies and What We Can Do about Them.* New York: WW Norton.

Streek, Wolfgang. 2016a. 'Scenario for a wonderful tomorrow.' *London Review of Books.* 38: 7. Pp. 7–10.

2016b. 'Exploding Europe: Germany, the refugees, and the British vote to leave.' SPERI Paper. No. 31. Sheffield Political Economy Research Institute. September. http://speri.dept.shef.ac.uk/wp-content/uploads/2018/11/SPERI-Paper-31-Wolfgang-Streeck-Exploding-Europe.pdf.

Tan, Gillian and Katia Porzecanski (2018). 'Wall street rule for the #MeToo era: Avoid women at all costs.' *Bloomberg.* 3 December. www.bloomberg.com/news/articles/2018-12-03/a-wall-street-rule-for-the-metoo-era-avoid-women-at-all-cost.

Trump, Donald J. 2016. President-elect Trump speaks to a divided country: Interview with Lesley Stahl. 13 November. www.cbsnews.com/news/60-minutes-donald-trump-family-melania-ivanka-lesley-stahl/.

2017a. Presidential Inaugural Address. 20 January. www.whitehouse.gov/briefings-statements/the-inaugural-address/.

2017b. Statement by President Trump on the Paris Climate Accord. 1 June. www.whitehouse.gov/briefings-statements/statement-president-trump-paris-climate-accord/.

2018a. Interview transcript. Bloomberg News Agency. 31 August. www.bloomberg.com/news/articles/2018-08-31/president-donald-trump-interviewed-by-bloomberg-news-transcript.

2018b. Remarks by President Trump in Listening Session with Representatives from the Steel and Aluminum Industry. 1 March. www.whitehouse.gov/briefings-statements/remarks-president-trump-listening-session-representatives-steel-aluminum-industry/.

US Bureau of Industry and Security. 2007. Section 232 Investigations Program Guide: The Effect of Imports on National Security. www.bis.doc.gov/index.php/documents/section-232-investigations/86-section-232-booklet/file. For an updated list of investigations, see www.bis.doc.gov/index.php/other-areas/office-of-technology-evaluation-ote/section-232-investigations.

US Justice Department. 2019. *Report on the Investigation into Russian Interference in the 2016 Presidential Election: Special Counsel Robert S. Mueller III.* March. Washington D.C. www.justice.gov/storage/report.pdf.

USITC. 2008. *Textiles and Apparel: Effects of Special Rules for Haiti on Trade Markets and Industries.* Investigation No. TR-5003-1. Publication 4016. Washington D.C. June.

USTR. 2006. Press conference with Susan Schwab and Mike Johanns, 24 June. www.kommers.se/upload/Analysarkiv/Arbetsomr%C3%A5den/WTO/DDA%20-%20Schwab.pdf.

2016. U.S. Trade Preference Programs: Reducing Poverty and Hunger in Developing Nations Through Economic Growth. Report by Ambassador Michael Froman. https://ustr.gov/sites/default/files/TPEA-Preferences-Report.pdf.

2018a. Section 201 Cases: Imported Large Residential Washing Machines and Imported Solar Cells and Modules. January. https://ustr.gov/sites/default/files/files/Press/fs/201%20FactSheet.pdf.

2018b. Section 301 Factsheet. 22 March. https://ustr.gov/about-us/policy-offices/press-office/fact-sheets/2018/march/section-301-fact-sheet.

Van Grasstek, Craig. 2009. 'US trade policy towards the least developed countries: Are these countries' interests congruent or in conflict?' In Simon Evenett (ed.). *Africa Resists the Protectionist Temptation.* The 5th GTA Report. London: Centre for Economic Policy Research. http://www.washingtontradereport.com/GTA5_vangrasstek.pdf

Vehrkamp, Robert and Christian Wratil. 2017. A populist moment? Populist attitudes of voters and non-voters before the German Federal Election 2017. Bertelsmann Foundation. www.bertelsmann-stiftung.de/fileadmin/files/BSt/Publikationen/GrauePublikationen/ZD_Studie_Populismus_EN.pdf.

Weaver, Courtney. 2018. 'How a Florida mid-term exposes the fault-lines in Trump's America.' *Financial Times.* 18 October.

White, Ben. 1996. 'Globalisation and the child labour problem.' *Journal of International Development.* 8: 6. Pp. 829–839.

World Bank. 2019. Global Economic Prospects: Darkening Skies. Washington D.C. January. www.worldbank.org/en/publication/global-economic-prospects.

WTO. 2001. Doha Ministerial Declaration. WT/MIN(01)/DEC/1. Adopted on 14 November.

2002. Accession of Least-Developed Countries: Decision of 10 December. WT/L/508. 20 January 2003.

2005. Hong Kong Ministerial Declaration. WT/MIN(05)/DEC. Adopted on 18 December.

2008. Kamal Nath, TNC Statement on July 23rd, 2008: Statement of Shri Kamal Nath, Minister of Commerce and Industry, India. 30 May 2013. www.wto.org/english/tratop_e/dda_e/meet08_stat_ind_21jul_e.doc.

2009a. Trade Liberalization and the Right to Food: Debate between Olivier de Schutter and Pascal Lamy. 11 May. www.wto.org/english/forums_e/debates_e/debate14_e.htm.

2009b. UN Rapporteur and WTO Delegates debate the Right to Food. WTO News Item. 2 July. www.wto.org/english/news_e/news09_e/ag_02jul09_e.htm.

2010. Refocusing Discussions on the Special Safeguard Mechanism (SSM): Outstanding issues and concerns on its design and structure submission by the G33. Committee on Agriculture, Special Session. TN/AG/GEN/30. 28 January.

2012a. G33 Proposal on Some Elements of TN/AG/W/4/REV.4 for Early Agreement to Address Food Security Issues. Committee on Agriculture, Special Session. JOB/AG/22. 13 November.

2012b. Communication to the General Council: Recommendations by the Sub-Committee on LDCs to the General Council to Further Strengthen, Streamline and Operationalise the 2002 LDC Accession Guidelines. WT/COMTD/LDC/W/55/Rev.2. 29 June.

2013. Address by Shri Anand Sharma, Union Minister of Commerce and Industry, India, at the Plenary Session of the 9th Ministerial Conference of the WTO. Bali Ministerial Conference. 4 December. www.wto.org/english/thewto_e/minist_e/mc9_e/stat_e/ind.pdf.

2015a. Nairobi Ministerial Declaration. WT/MIN(15)/DEC. Adopted on 19 December.

2015b. India: Trade Policy Review, Report by the Secretariat. WT/TPR/S/313. 25 April. www.wto.org/english/tratop_e/tpr_e/s313_e.pdf.

2016. Duty-Free and Quota-Free (DFQF) Market Access for LDCs: Report by the Secretariat. Committee on Trade and Development. WT/COMTD/W/222. 22 November.

2017. Communication from the United States. *Procedures to Enhance Transparency and Strengthen Notification Requirements under WTO Agreements.* JOB/GC/148; JOB/CTG/10. General Council; Council for Trade in Goods. 20 October.

2018a. Communication from Argentina, Costa Rica, the European Union, Japan, and the United States. *Procedures to Enhance Transparency and Strengthen Notification Requirements under WTO Agreements.* JOB/GC/204; JOB/CTG/14. General Council; Council for Trade in Goods. 1 November.

2018b. Trade Policy Review: Report of the United States. Trade Policy Review Body. WT/TPR/G/382. 12 November.

2018c. Market Access for Products and Services of Export Interest to Least Developed Countries: Note by the Secretariat. Sub-Committee on Least Developed Countries. WT/COMTD/LDC/W/66. 2 October.

2018d. Strengthening and Modernizing the WTO: Discussion Paper, Communication from Canada. JOB/GC/201. 21 September.

2019. Communication from the United States. 2019. An Undifferentiated WTO: Self-Declared Development Status Risks Institutional Irrelevance. WT/GC/W/757/Rev.1. General Council. 14 February.

Worland. Justin. 2019. 'The China trade war comes home.' *Time Magazine.* January. http://time.com/5498915/china-trade-war-affect/10.

Young, Alasdair. 2010. 'Transatlantic intransigence in the Doha round: Domestic politics and the difficulty of compromise.' In Amrita Narlikar (ed.). *Deadlocks in Multilateral Negotiations: Causes and Solutions.* Cambridge: Cambridge University Press.

Zerofsky, Elisabeth. 2019. 'Steve Bannon's roman holiday.' *The New Yorker.* 11 April.

5

Conclusion

How to Sustain the Power of the Powerless and Build Winning Narratives

The central argument of this book is that narratives about poverty and powerlessness have played a critical role in shaping multilateral trade negotiations. Such narratives have exercised an important influence on processes and outcomes of trade negotiations, via their background rumblings in the GATT, their increasing dominance in the Doha years of the WTO, and the progressively perverse uses to which they have been put in recent times. The empirical cases of trade negotiations are interesting in their own right because of the controversies that have surrounded them, as well as the potential impact that trade policy and trade negotiations can have on the lives of millions of people. But as I have outlined in this book through numerous examples, the use of poverty and powerlessness narratives has not been limited to trade. This corpus of empirical material is useful for developing a theoretical understanding of narratives more generally: where do narratives come from, what makes winning narratives, how do they change in the hands of different actors, and how do they dissipate? Given the agency that winning narratives entail, this project has always had a policy orientation. Drawing on the empirical detail presented in the previous chapters, I now bring together the theoretical and policy implications of this study.

In Section 5.1, I offer a brief summary of my research findings, and then develop some generalizations on the lifecycles of narratives. I offer some guidelines in Section 5.2, which may assist practitioners in building effective narratives as vital instruments of public policy and diplomacy.

5.1 LIFECYCLES OF NARRATIVES

The previous chapters have traced a fundamental transformation that has been taking place in international trade negotiations, and politics at large. Through the effective use of narratives, developing countries and apparently powerless people have managed to convert their intrinsic weaknesses into a bargaining strength. Chapters 2 and 3 have illustrated the transformative effect of poverty narratives: through the use of this instrument, the global south was able to move from the margins of the 'Rich Man's Club' to the heart of a new organization that came to prioritize their concerns. In other words, narratives can be formidable instruments of positive change. This is an important takeaway from this book, and represents a departure from recent writings in economics that seek to explain economic *failure* via culture, identity, and narratives.[1]

I argued in Chapter 1 that the adaptability of narratives to re-interpretation and negotiation makes them a flexible and ready policy instrument, in contrast to norms, identities, and cultures. But this also makes them vulnerable to manipulation. Two consequences follow. First, the successes or failures of particular narratives are intricately bound up with the agency wielded by key players. Narratives do not emerge nor evolve in a vacuum; they are created and disseminated by actors. Narratives can trigger change, but they too can undergo changes as they pass through different hands. And second, the susceptibility of narratives to manipulation leads winning narratives to act like asset bubbles. As an increasingly large number of actors becomes aware of the uses of dominant narratives, the temptation to overuse and misuse them also increases. Chapter 4 provided an analysis of this pattern in trade negotiations as well as in other aspects of social and political life. This raises some worrying policy implications, which need to be addressed. In the remainder of this section, I focus on the agency that underpins narratives, and also the risks inherent in the lifecycle of narratives.

5.1.1 *How Narratives Develop, Dominate, Disseminate, and Dissipate*

As I set out in Chapter 1, narratives are stories of causality, which help us make sense of the world. But at what point does a story – a causal explanation deriving from several sources including individual experience, 'stylized facts', and 'folk causal theories'[2] – become a 'narrative'? What makes a winning narrative? And finally, what are the threats that winning narratives face? I offer a brief recap here.

---

[1] E.g., Collier (2015). In a recent article for the *New York Times*, Shiller (2019) highlights the links between narratives and the occurrence of economic depressions: 'If enough people begin to act fearfully, their anxiety can become self-fulfilling, and a recession, sometimes a big one, may follow'.

[2] Hirschman (2016).

A narrative begins as a story of causation, and has to be consciously developed – and at least for the kinds of questions this book has been addressing, with a strategic purpose. It needs to be backed by some scientific findings, or at least 'stylized facts', especially for legitimation. Narratives do not exist in a vacuum: they require agency. Originators of the story can be statesmen, academics, pundits, 'influencers', or concerned citizens. The origin does not matter per se as much as the dissemination process: even if coming from a highly legitimate source and even if backed by scientific fact, a narrative must get picked up widely across society as well as by policymakers. This is why the mechanisms of agency and dissemination deserve special attention.

As highlighted in Chapter 1, and further developed in the subsequent chapters, three types of actors can be vital in influencing the take-up that a narrative comes to enjoy: coalitions of states, transnational social movements, plus networks of multiple actors that can include states, NGOs, lobby groups, businesses, and individuals. In Chapter 2 we saw that the weaknesses of their coalitions and the inability of developing countries to exploit synergies with NGOs together compounded the challenges that the global south faced in establishing winning narratives in the GATT years. In contrast and as discussed in Chapters 3 and 4, both use and indeed misuse of poverty narratives – when successful – involved a reliance on coalitions, social movements, and networks. Ease of connectivity via the internet increased the opportunities for building such platforms; hashtag activism via social media platforms can amplify the reach of some narratives especially dramatically.

Whether narratives win or lose depends not only on the effectiveness of agents that facilitate their spread and legitimacy, but also on the available BATNAs that actors harness, and the framing strategies that they use.

Actors may try to advance certain narratives, but in the absence of a strong BATNA, they will probably not get heard; a narrative, no matter how convincing, is unlikely to thrive under such conditions. Recall, for instance, from Chapter 2, how the poverty narrative advanced by developing countries allowed for only limited gains, in good measure due to the lack of a BATNA. Developing countries tried to generate their own BATNAs by creating new forums – such as the UNCTAD (and indeed a variety of schemes for regional integration, which lie beyond the scope of this study) – but these did not provide a strong enough alternative to allow them to walk away from GATT negotiations. As their BATNA worsened with the end of the Cold War and the growing acceptance of the Washington Consensus, the southern narrative that poverty in the developing world was mainly a result of external conditions that needed redress (rather than structural reform within developing countries) suffered a further decline. In contrast, as Chapter 3 highlighted, the rise of the BRICS opened up new options for them in terms of aid and also alternative development models, plus strengthened their coalitions (and thereby an important route for dissemination of the narrative).

The value of the BATNA in creating winning narratives of powerlessness can also be observed in the politics of the everyday. The powerless today have many courts of appeal that go beyond the formal institutional channels, and also resources to better access the official channels. When a South Korean farmer committed suicide to protest against the WTO's talks at Cancun in 2003, his death did not generate a reaction anywhere near the level that a much smaller act of protest will generate via Facebook and Twitter today. The presence of social media platforms has created a much wider community, which can act even as a *de facto* social court of justice, if people believe the formal pathways to justice have failed or are inaccessible to them. Individuals who see themselves as victims can generate not only moral support online, but also trigger a snowballing effect with the emergence of new complaints against a usually 'powerful' target. Recourse to crowdfunding, also via social media platforms, can in fact allow 'powerless' individuals to raise funds and thereby take an online battle into a courtroom litigation. The internet – via the moral support it can bring in, the public outrage it can generate, and the material resources that it can raise via crowdfunding – provides valuable alternatives to negotiated outcomes, and has become a great equalizer.[3]

How a narrative is framed can be crucial in terms of determining its success. The previous chapters have highlighted two interesting ways in which framing can make a difference.

(1) Appeal to the individual and group level, and existential causes:
   In the previous chapters, we have seen that narratives framed in terms of their impact on individual lives mattered more, and all the more so when they made reference to existential threats. For example, as analysed in Chapter 3, developing countries injected new vim into their poverty narrative, and made it dramatically more potent and influential, when they framed the TRIPS agreement as a cause for the killing of sick people. Posited against commercial gain for pharmaceutical companies, the frame of dying individuals was rightly more evocative, and it produced the intended result via the TRIPs and Public Declaration (2001).[4] And again,

---

[3] I made this argument in Narlikar (2015).
[4] This finding is in line with the work of Keck and Sikkink (1998), who argue that norms about protecting vulnerable and innocent individuals from bodily harm will find it easier to reach a critical mass and tipping point. Also see Odell and Sell (2006).

as discussed in Chapter 4, President Trump perversely – and rather effectively – mobilized a poverty narrative in his own favour by attributing individual job losses in the United States to the workings of the international trading system, and promising to put 'America fiist'. In doing so, he appealed to a group identity of American workers and a broader nationalist identity of American people, all framed in clear us-versus-them language (e.g., 'At what point do they start laughing at us as a country?' in the context of the Paris climate agreement). Counter-narratives on the gains of trade (or indeed the critical importance of abiding by the commitments of Paris on climate) – even if factually correct – offered scarce solace and unconvincing alternative focal points for those who bought into Trump's version. We have seen the effectiveness of narratives that use emotive appeal, and tap into individual experiences and/or group identities, in other walks of political life too. The #MeToo campaign exemplified these dynamics. Here was a narrative that tapped into painful individual stories of victimhood and transformed them into a collective story of a reclamation of power. Social activists, NGOs, and also individuals worked together to build and disseminate the narrative: individual cases resonated across large groups of women worldwide. These transnational networks harnessed social media to mobilize further support and build momentum. A long-standing issue, involving gender and the misuses of power, finally began to get the attention that it deserved.

(2) Narratives and norms:

The relationship between framing and norms is mediated through narratives, and is a complicated one. On the one hand, less challenging, regime-conforming narratives seem to have an easier ride. As Odell and Sell argue, when negotiation demands are framed in a way that is antithetical to the mandate of an organization, they are less likely to be successful. By implication, narratives that do not fundamentally challenge the core beliefs or norms of a system should encounter less resistance.[5] This logic is reinforced by the fact that deadlocks are more likely when the parties attempt to negotiate over first-order issues;[6] fights over dearly held values are more bitter than over functional gains and losses. Narratives that challenge first-order assumptions are thus likely to find it harder to gain dominance. This renders narratives and norms out of sync with each

---

[5]   Odell and Sell (2006).
[6]   Gamble (2010).

other: if actors push narratives that are framed as a challenge to existing norms, it is likely that the narratives will encounter more resistance.

This book partly confirms these arguments. Chapter 3, for example, showed us that the successes that developing countries secured in the WTO were premised on the underlying acceptance by the global south of the main principles and processes underpinning trade multilateralism, including the virtues of trade liberalization. The demands that they raised – and in good measure achieved – focused on securing the means to use the system more effectively, rather than a fundamental challenge to the system itself. A movement like #MeToo owes its successes to the strategies that its supporters have used, but also to the fact that it calls out derogations from a norm that is already established and legitimized, namely the equality of men and women. Chapter 2, in contrast, showed that more radical demands, for example the creation of an alternative system via the UNCTAD or the NIEO resulted in few concrete gains;[7] more modest demands within the GATT framework delivered better results.

This is a slightly depressing find for those who seek real change. It suggests that if one wishes to use narratives effectively, one has to at least go through the pretence of framing them as somehow conforming to existing norms. Luckily though, this book has also found some evidence to the contrary: we have seen cases where actors have launched a fundamental challenge to existing norms, and created winning narratives in surprising ways.

Recall from Chapter 4 Trump's appropriation of the poverty narrative, which attributes domestic poverty to external causes and 'unfair' international institutions. Trump's challenge to trade multilateralism is fundamental, both in terms of principle and practice. On a matter of principle, Trump and his team have taken the WTO to task, challenging the special and differential treatment it grants to the rising powers, and also the deliberate exemptions and inadvertent loopholes in its rules that allow China (in particular) to get away with much misuse of the system. In practice too, the Trump administration has clearly signalled its willingness to walk away from an organization that it regards as unfair via its tariff wars as well as attacks on the Dispute Settlement Mechanism. Within the United States, this has turned out to be a winning narrative; outside, it remains contested, but is seen as credible enough to require addressing by

---

[7] Also see Krasner (1985).

other players. The reason why this narrative is taken seriously, even though it goes against fundamental features of the multilateral trade regime, is only partly because it comes from such a powerful player, that is the United States, which had served as the *de facto* guarantor of the system in the post-war years. But additionally, the scepticism that the United States expresses towards the regime does not come out of the blue: for some time now, the credibility and functioning of the WTO have been under threat, as illustrated by the recurrence of the Doha deadlocks since over fifteen years as well as the turn to regionalism and bilateralism by major and minor players. Within the United States, a further reason why this narrative has enjoyed support from those who elected Trump to power is because of its emotive appeal, especially to stakeholders at the individual and group level. We can find a similar pattern in the Brexit campaign, and the attractiveness of a promise to 'take back control' that seemed to play into group identities and individual interests.

Narratives that go against the grain and against the established norm, can then still emerge as dominant ones. The success of such narratives becomes more likely if the existing regime – and the norms underpinning it – is already under external and internal challenge, and if the bearers of the narrative make use of the vectors of dissemination and employ frames with emotive appeal that play on individual and group identities. Feed-back loops and reflexivity also mean that certain narratives can in turn undermine the credibility of existing regimes and norms, and new narratives in turn can emerge from these changes.[8]

A successful narrative faces at least two threats, and both can be potentially damaging to its effectiveness:

(1) The first threat is a complacency trap: actors who have developed winning narratives may be reluctant to update them in keeping with changing ground realities. We have seen this threat play out repeatedly in the case of liberal narratives regarding the gains of globalization and multilateralism. For large parts of the technocratic and academic worlds, the benefits of having international institutions – like the WTO and the EU – have been so obvious that they do not need spelling out. But by failing to remind different stakeholders of the gains of globalization and multilateralism, and by failing to include disillusioned parties in a serious debate on

---

[8] For example, just as we seen the Trump administration adapt the poverty narrative in its own favour and transform its original purpose (of the empowerment of the global poor), one can also expect alternative narratives to emerge to replace the one that Trump has been using.

how these institutions might be reformed, the institutions themselves as well as policy and intellectual 'elites' have attracted a populist backlash.

(2) The second threat is rooted in the fact that winning narratives resemble asset bubbles: as others see the successes that a winning narrative generates, the temptation to overuse and misuse them increases. Chapter 4 focused on these problems. Successes in the recent past of using the narrative of powerlessness and victimhood have led countries and other actors to rely increasingly on the same narrative, even when the case in favour of their use is less justified. Even the rich and the powerful have learnt that appealing to weakness and victimhood can be a winning strategy. We have thus seen rich countries and other powerful actors appropriate and adapt these strategies to their own advantage in recent years. Both overuse and misuse generate costs for the system as a whole, and undermine the credibility of the narrative.[9]

Take the asset bubble analogy to its logical conclusion, and the bubble of the empowering poverty narrative actually 'bursts' with overuse and misuse, we would end up with a highly suboptimal scenario. In this scenario, we would see the creation of a new disenfranchised and disengaged political class of the hitherto rich and powerful, and former patterns of national and international cooperation break down. Even higher levels of societal and political polarization would follow, and would produce results akin to what we see in Charles Dickens' novel, *Bleak House*, with all parties embroiled in high levels of wasteful litigation. As learning takes place, those most adept at misusing the system would further crowd out the legitimate demands of the genuinely powerless and desperately poor. Chapter 4 has given several examples of how this scenario may already be transpiring.

The question then arises, can the empowerment gains of the poverty/powerlessness narrative somehow be preserved, and misuses of the narrative curtailed? Three solutions seem possible. And, although none of them is perfect on its own, a combination of the three could help address some of the problems that I have raised in this book. I outline these below.

(1) The simplest solution would be better designed institutions. Such indeed had been my hope when I started working on the project. And institutional reform and re-design might still go some way towards a possible solution:

---

[9] Note that my explanation for the dissipation of a winning narrative is the bursting of the asset-bubble: the demonstrable successes of winning narratives make them prone to overuse and misuse, and then declining credibility and failure. For a different type of explanation that sees the 'expiry' of issues in terms of structural path-dependency, see Morin (2011).

one can imagine an improved decision-making system in the WTO that overcomes the problems of consensus-based diplomacy and perpetual deadlock (for instance via critical-mass decision-making systems). There may also be ways in which misuses of the rules can be reduced, and loopholes closed, for instance by coming up with clearer conditions on the use of legitimate trade defence instruments, and clearly demarcating the mandate of the Appellate Body of the Dispute Settlement Mechanism. But as I worked through this project, I observed the diversity of cases that go beyond trade governance, and yet show a similar pattern of overuse and misuse of poverty/powerlessness narratives. If different types of governance institutions (with considerably different structures and processes) neverthe-less yield a similar behaviour pattern and adverse outcomes, and that too among different types of actors, then the problem seems to be more fundamental. Institutional tinkering may mitigate the problem somewhat, but is unlikely to solve such a widespread problem on its own.

(2) A second solution would involve putting tighter measures and higher thresholds in place on the uses of the power of powerlessness/poverty, for instance via burden of proof requirements for complainants. This in turn, however, would require a rethinking of the newfound presumptions of powerlessness and victimhood. Possible penalties may have to be put in place for those found to be misusing the system. But solutions along such lines would have to be implemented with great care. For example, in response to abuses of anti-dowry legislation in India, the Supreme Court of India ordered the police not to automatically arrest the accused, but satisfy themselves beforehand whether an arrest was necessary by going through a nine-point check-list.[10] This move by the Supreme Court, however, was greeted with great concern by women's rights groups in India. Between laws that oscillate between overprotecting self-declared victims, and sub-sequently the wrongly accused,[11] there is a very grave danger that the genuinely vulnerable end up getting penalized. A balancing act will be necessary between these two extremes if, amidst a practice of overuse and misuse, the smallest and weakest are to retain their agency. Political leaders and judiciaries would have to keep a close eye on the results they produce, and laws and rules would have to be regularly updated to prevent

---

[10] BBC (2014).

[11] Internationally, this would, for instance, be equivalent to rising powers claiming SDT in equal measure, the developed countries reacting in the way that the current US administration has done, and the LDCs and poor people across the global north and south taking the biggest hit from a breakdown of the system (as discussed in Chapter 4).

new forms of misuse. And given how slow the law-making process usually is (with good reason) across most democracies, this solution will not be easy to implement.

(3) The third solution may be the most important one. I have shown in this book that narratives are dynamic entities, malleable and responsive to agency, and potent instruments of policy. This also means that actors may be able to adapt and update their own successful narratives, avoiding the complacency trap and the asset bubble trap. This would require relevant actors to stay ahead of the curve, and innovate in advance of imitation and misuse by other groups. It could mean building specialized narratives that are harder for others to imitate (e.g., by building on a shared set of values and identities). Self-moderation in the use of successful narratives could guard against the overuse that contributes to the blunting of this weapon. Even an awareness of how narratives work could be a significant advantage, both in terms of improving one's own narratives and in being prepared for competing narratives and counter-narratives.

5.2 HOW TO BUILD WINNING NARRATIVES

In this concluding section, drawing on the insights of this study, I offer a set of guidelines on how practitioners might be able to build winning narratives.

(1) *A winning narrative has to be negotiated.*
It cannot be imposed by the diktat of politicians, nor the scribblings of intellectuals, though both political commitment and intellectual backing can contribute usefully to the making of an influential narrative. All the examples of successful narratives in this book show the importance of mobilizing diverse actors – states, NGOs, transnational social movements, networks – in support. This multi-level, multi-actor involvement is especially crucial in the dissemination stage. But inputs from different stakeholders in the development stage may also help enhance the legitimacy of the narrative.

(2) *A winning narrative usually appeals to a core interest, or even identity, of individuals or groups.*
This means that narratives that focus on the universal – and just on the universal – are unlikely to win, especially in times of economic distress or social upheaval. On the other hand, if the narrative maintains a commitment to the universal or global or multilateral, and also explains how it benefits individuals and their families, it has a high chance of emerging as a dominant narrative.

Recall, for example, Trump's narrative of 'America First', which I discussed in Chapter 4, and how he has claimed that his desire to 'Make America great again' (via tariffs and other measures) will directly benefit the ordinary working men and women of his country. In contrast, Macron's narrative of 'let's make our planet great again', may be a global and uplifting message that warms the hearts of many liberals, but it offers little hope to individuals within France who would be left economically worse off by climate change mitigation policies. Affected individuals would, moreover, pay for these policies and endure adversity in their own lifetimes, in return for a promise of justice for future generations (and that too conditional on other countries taking similar action). Seen in this light, the protests of the Yellow Vests were not so surprising. One way in which a message such as this could have generated better results is if it had made clear why mitigation measures would benefit not only the planet, but also the French people in their own lifetimes.

(3) *A winning narrative will usually have explanatory value as well as emotive appeal.*

While the previous point highlighted the importance of attending to the core interests, it is important to note that this does not translate into a simplistic appeal to economic interests. This means that high levels of abstraction, and tomes of statistical evidence in support, will not suffice to build a winning narrative, even though it would be helpful to have these as solid grounding and back-up.

We saw this dynamic play out in the Brexit referendum: while there was a sound economic case to 'remain' in the European Union (EU), the 'exit' narrative won given its atavistic appeal of 'taking back control'. One could make a similar argument about the crisis that multilateralism faces today. Despite the economic gains that multilateralism has facilitated worldwide, efforts to revive it are yet to take off. If politicians, practitioners, and academics – harnessing coalitions, social movements, and networks – were to together develop a narrative that included attention to the *values* that a new multilateralism would uphold, the project would stand a better chance. If these creators and disseminators of such a narrative were to also include considerations of how a new multilateralism could work to the advantage of individuals and groups, a winning narrative would likely be in the offing.

(4) *A winning narrative tends to be polarizing and divisive.*

Populist and nationalist movements show this most dramatically. This could be partly related to the previous point about emotive appeal. It could also involve political economy reasons: groups fight most strongly against targeted losses, rather than diffused gains. This, along with the last two points, makes the task of winning considerably harder for liberal narratives, which are – by definition – open and inclusive.[12]

(5) *A winning narrative cannot be built in a technocratic bubble.*
There has been a tendency of different versions of the liberal institutionalist narrative to assume that all creases and faultlines, which they have developed over time, can be smoothed out in a technocratic bubble. This is probably true of the narratives of most international organizations (such as the IMF, the World Bank, the WTO, the European Union, and others). Technocratic fixes are of course necessary and long overdue in many international organizations. But if liberal narratives have any chance of winning, they will have to break out of their technocratic comfort zones. Besides having emotive appeal and relevance for the core interests/identities of individuals/groups, they would need to be effectively communicated to relevant stakeholders. Here, the use of hashtag diplomacy to build networks of support could be quite valuable.

Ultimately, not even the perfect technical solution – advanced by the most sincere political leader, which creates win–win scenarios for all parties, and is backed by rich data – can win hearts and minds. But a good narrative can.

BIBLIOGRAPHY

BBC. 2014. 'India Court says women "misusing" dowry law.' 3 July. www.bbc.com/news/world-asia-india-28140205.

Collier, Paul. 2015. 'The cultural foundations of economic failure: A conceptual toolkit.' *Journal of Economic Behavior and Organization*. 126: B. Pp. 5–24.

Gamble, Andrew. 2010. The politics of deadlocks. In Amrita Narlikar (ed.). *Deadlocks in Multilateral Negotiations: Causes and Solutions*. Cambridge: Cambridge University Press.

Hirschman, Daniel. 2016. 'Stylized facts in the social sciences.' *Sociological Science*. 3. Pp. 604–626.

Keck, Margaret and Kathryn Sikkink. 1998. *Activists beyond Borders: Advocacy Networks in International Politics*. Ithaca, NY: Cornell University Press.

Krasner, Stephen D. 1985. *Structural Conflict: The Third World against Global Liberalism*. Berkley, CA: University of California Press.

Morin, Jean-Frederic. 2011. 'The life-cycle of transnational issues: Lessons from the access to medicines controversy.' *Global Society*. 25: 2. Pp. 227–247.

---

[12] Note that this observation does not imply a normative case in favour of building polarizing and divisive narratives. Rather, it seeks to alert the reader to the uphill task that policymakers seeking inclusive narratives face. Recognizing the difficulties is a necessary step to overcome them, as is an awareness of a menu of alternative strategies that ambitious practitioners could turn to.

Narlikar, Amrita. 2015. 'The power paradox.' *Current History*. Global Trends Special Issue. 114: 768. Pp. 29–33.

Odell, John and Susan Sell. 2006. Reframing the issue: the WTO coalition on intellectual property and public health, 2001. In John Odell (ed.). *Negotiating Trade: Developing Countries in the WTO and NAFTA*. Cambridge: Cambridge University Press.

Shiller, Robert. 2019. 'What people say about the economy can set off a recession.' *New York Times*. 12 September.

Index

African Growth and Opportunity Act (AGOA),
    145
agriculture
    Agreement on Agriculture (AoA), 128,
        see also WTO – agriculture
    Cairns Group, 128, see also coalitions
    defensive agenda, 127–128, 133–134, 136
    dependency on, 130, 132
    Doha negotiations, 97, 127, see also WTO –
        Doha Development Agenda, Doha
        Ministerial
    export opportunities, 127
    liberalization of, 125, 127, 132
    linkage of land use and culture, 126
    offensive agenda, 127–128, 133–134
    opening of agricultural markets in the EU
        and the US, 101
    price volatility, 128
    protectionism, 127, see also protectionism
    special interests, 126
    subsidies, 101, 128
    subsistence, 132, 136
aid, 3, 11
    Aid for Trade, 142, see also WTO – Hong
        Kong Ministerial
    as one-way street, 65
    sources of, 14
AIDS, 91, 93
    compulsory licencing for access to
        medicines, 95, see also WTO – Public
        Health Declaration, TRIPS
Akerlof, George, 6, 8, 10
Allison, Graham, 6
Alternative für Deutschland (AfD), 173
Anglo-American relations, 40, 44
Azevedo, Roberto, 105

Bagger, Thomas, 172
bargaining, 1, 13–15, 92, 189, see also coalitions
Barshefsky, Charlene, 73, 83–84
beliefs, 7–8, 14
    three types of, 8, see also Collier, Paul
Best Alternative to Negotiated Agreement
    (BATNA), 14, 16, 22–23, 57, 99, 190–191
best endeavour, 3, 49
Bhagwati, Jagdish, 169
Blair, Tony, 108, 110
Blustein, Paul, 134
Brazil, 14, 22, 104, 133, 167
    as ally of India, 134
    growth, 17
    in the GATT, 52, see also GATT
    in the ITO, 39, see also ITO
Bretton Woods, 59
    conference, 32, 35, 41
    institutions, 39
    narrative, 66
    negotiations, 35, 40
Brexit, 157, 194, 198
BRICS, 14, 17, 22, 104, 110, 191
    in the WTO, 105
    rise of, 14, 117
    Special Differential Treatment (SDT).
        see also GATT – SDT
Brown, Gordon, 108

campaigns, 5, 11
    #MeToo, 23, 114, 176, 192–193
    #WomenAlsoKnow, 115
    FairTrade, 11, 175
    Fridays for Future, 23, 115
    global justice movement, 76
    Jubilee 2000, 11, 108

Group of Seven (G7), 23, 64, 104
Group of Twenty (G20), 18
  2008 financial crisis, 23
  as crisis committee, 111
  emergence of, 23
  guest countries, 23
  as improvement of the G7, 111, *see also* G7
  mobilization of, 110
  negotiations, 18
  outreach processes, 111

Haberler Report, 47
Haitian Hemispheric Opportunity through
    Partnership Encouragement (HOPE),
    145
Hulme, David, 85

identities, 7–9
India, 14, 20, 22, 24, 39, 105, 126, 167
  in the G33, 132, 138, *see also coalitions*
  in the GATT, 51, *see also GATT*
  in the ITO, 38–39, *see also ITO*
  agriculture, 24, 135, *see also agriculture*
  anti-dowry legislation, 114, 176, 196
  as developing economy, 147
  corruption, 24
  deadlock responsibility, 136
  in the Doha negotiations, 24, *see also WTO*
  emissions, 112
  growth, 17
  influence on Brazil, 137
  representing developing countries, 139
  responsibility for deadlocks, 139
  as rising power, 24, *see also BRICS*
  use of poverty narrative, 25, 140, *see also*
      narratives
inequality, 26, 109, 154
International Labour Organization (ILO), 81
International Monetary Fund (IMF), 4, 13, 59
  stabilization measures, 66
International Trade Organization (ITO), 19–20
  in comparison to Bretton Woods, 37, *see also*
      Bretton Woods
  decision-making processes, 39
  Economic Development and
      Reconstruction, 39
  employment, 38
  Executive Board, 39
  failure of, 19, 33, 35, 62
  Havana Charter, 35–36, 44, 46, 66
  Havana Conference, 35

negotiations, 34, 41
role of Britain and US, 42
role of Latin American countries, 36
US withdrawal, 43
wins of developing countries, 36

James, Harold, 156

Kahneman, Daniel, 6, 15
Keohane, Robert O., 9
Keynes, John Maynard, 6
  animal spirits, 6
Khor, Martin, 95
Kindleberger, Charles, 169
Krasner, Stephen, 64

Lamy, Pascal, 100, 105, 131, 134
Latin America, 39, 83
  in the ITO, 41, *see also ITO*
  in the WTO, 83, *see also WTO*
Least Developed Countries (LDCs), 12, 14, 17,
    22, 25
  achievements, 141
  capacity constraints, 57, 61, 112, 144
  competing with each other, 147
  concessions for, 25, 125
  Special and Differential Treatment (SDT),
      see also GATT – SDT
  special needs of, 50
  special treatment by the US, 145
legitimacy, 9, 14, 23, 26, 57, 110, 166, 190
liberalization
  of agriculture, 126, *see also agriculture*
  of trade, 119, 146
liberalism, 27, 59, 64, 66, 85, 116

Macintyre, Alasdair, 5
Macron, Emmanuel, 198
Maran, Murasoli, 80
marginalization, 3, 11
  in decision-making processes, 3, 16
  of developing countries within the GATT,
      20, *see also GATT*
  of developing countries within the WTO,
      102, *see also WTO*
  of the Global North, 150
  perceptions in the US, 150
Marshall Plan, 37
Meade, James, 34
media reports, 172
Merkel, Angela, 26, 172

Index